The MORMON CONSPIRACY

A REVIEW OF PRESENT-DAY AND HISTORICAL CONSPIRACIES TO MORMONIZE AMERICA AND THE WORLD

CHARLES L. WOOD LLC

Black Forest Press
San Diego, California
March 2004
Second Edition
Second Printing

The MORMON CONSPIRACY

A REVIEW OF PRESENT-DAY AND HISTORICAL CONSPIRACIES TO MORMONIZE AMERICA AND THE WORLD

CHARLES L. WOOD LLC

PUBLISHED IN THE UNITED STATES OF AMERICA
BY
BLACK FOREST PRESS
P.O. Box 6342
Chula Vista, CA 91909-6342

The Mormon Conspiracy
by
Charles L. Wood, Ph.D.
**A Review of Present Day and Historical Conspiracies
to Mormonize America and the World**
email: wood1@mormonconspiracy.com

Order and read preface and excerpts on our website:
www.mormonconspiracy.com
Our address: P.O. Box 3234, Mesquite NV 89024

Cover Design: Dale and Penni Neely

DISCLAIMER

Printed in the United States of America
Library of Congress
Cataloging-in-Publication

ISBN: 1-58275-036-X

CONTENTS

ACKNOWLEDGMENTS

This book has been written with the assistance and counsel of many others, including numerous library personnel, authors and publishers of books and those who helped with editing.

Special thanks are given to my wife, Dr. Lenora M. Wood, who spent many hours reviewing the manuscript, checking English usage and grammar and making suggestions concerning all aspects of the book. I also thank my daughter, Sandra L. Wood, a librarian, who gathered materials to use in researching this writing.

I am indebted to Rauni Higley who edited the manuscript for accuracy, credibility and readability, and to Dennis Higley who brought compatibility between two different computer systems.

Preface

The author first became interested in researching the Mormon Church when he was given a copy of the *Book of Mormon* and was told that it had been translated from some golden plates that God had given to twenty-one year old Joseph Smith in the early 1800s in New York. According to the story, Smith had translated this book by using a seer stone that God had provided him along with the golden plates. The book that Smith had "translated" was a story about Nephi, an Israelite, who with his father and mother and other family members from a lost tribe of Israel, traveled to America about 600 B. C. After they arrived in America, this tribe built cities and developed an advanced civilization.

After several years, according to Smith's account, the lost tribe was split into two groups, one called the Nephites and the other called the Lamanites. The Nephites were the God-favored group and endeavored to please God through their worship and clean living. The Lamanites, on the other hand, were enemies of the Nephites and often lived in primitive dwellings and huts in the mountains and forests. The Nephites and Lamanites were constantly at war and suffered many deaths and casualties. At times the Nephites were victorious in these wars, and at other times the Lamanites were the victors. Finally a great battle between these two opposing groups took place, and the Nephites were defeated and annihilated with the exception of one survivor called Moroni.

Moroni, the son of one of the great leaders of the Nephites, was given the task of protecting the historical records of the Nephites. He did this with help from God by burying these records on golden plates on a hill near Palmyra, New York. Joseph Smith when a boy of fourteen was told of these records by the angel Moroni and finally at the age of twenty-one was led to the golden plates which contained the seer stone needed to translate them.

The author could not accept the concept that a church claiming a membership of eleven million members and having a corporate worth estimated to be more than fifty billion dollars is using as its basis the highly improbable story of Smith's *Book of Mormon*. Because the author believed that the story was unlikely, he decided to investigate the *Book of Mormon* and the Mormon religion. This book relates the findings of this investigation that resulted in the author's conclusion that Smith's book is fraudulent, and the Mormon religion which claims Smith's book as its basis is also untrue. The church has distributed millions of copies of the *Book of Mormon* in many languages to all corners of the earth. And millions of copies of the book are kept in storage for future distribution by missionaries, by members and by direct mail from central church warehouses. Various types of public media are used in advertising to encourage the public world-wide to request a free copy of this book.

Much of the evidence that discredits the authenticity of Smith's *Book of Mormon* is discussed in the first chapter of this book and reinforced in later chapters. One piece of evidence that disproves Smith's contention that the American Indian descended from immigrants of ancient Israel is the DNA (genetic code of cells that have lived) study that compares American Indians' DNA with that of people from Israel and from the Asiatic countries of Mongolia and China. A DNA study of over 2,000 Indians in the past decade shows that their lineages were closely related to those of people from Southern Siberia near Mongolia in Asia. A study at Brigham Young University of 3,000 Indians from Peru also concluded that virtually all these Indians' ancestors came from Asia. Those that did not relate to Asian ancestry, related to European ancestry, most likely Spain.[1]

Smith's *Book of Mormon* story contains much information about "the ancient Israeli immigration" which has been proven false by DNA studies. Since this story and others found to be false by the author are still maintained to be true by Mormon Church teachings, and the church has great financial resources and an extensive missionary network to promote and expand this religion that may threaten free and independent lifestyles and our democracy, American citizens have a duty and responsibility to monitor this religion as well as to research its honesty and truthfulness. The author feels that we cannot sit idly by while these great resources are being utilized through a vast television and human resources network, that is constantly at work with slick public relations and carefully planned missionary programs to expand its membership.

---

[1] *Recovery From Mormonism*, Website DNA Genealogies of the American Indian and the *Book of Mormon*.

The Mormon Church is using all available means to increase its membership by obtaining converts and encouraging large families for the purpose of increasing its power and influence in the world.

Authority, power and influence are key factors of the Mormon movement. Joseph Smith's reign as President and Prophet of the church from 1830 to 1844 created the basis for the authority, power and influence of the church leadership. This was strengthened and expanded by Brigham Young in his thirty year reign from 1847 to 1877. In their forty-four year leadership of the membership of the church Smith and Young held iron-fisted control of their congregations, not just over religious activities, but over their lives outside the church as well. In all possible ways, Smith and Young used dictatorial methods to control the church. Their dictatorial power was accomplished by maintaining that their authority came directly from God.

Several books have been researched, and quotes from them have been used to reinforce and document the conclusions reached in this book. Especially notable among these excellent books are Janice Hutchinson's *The Mormon Missionaries,* Fawn Brodie's *No Man Knows my History,* Sonia Johnson's *From Housewife to Heretic,* Deborah Laake's *Secret Ceremonies,* Latayne Colvett Scott's *The Mormon Mirage* and D. Michael Quinn's *The Mormon Hierarchy, Extensions of Power.* Thanks to the charity of the authors of these books and their publishers, this author was able to employ some of their thoughts into this manuscript. Both Sonia Johnson and Fawn Brodie have special book collections at the University of Utah Library. To underscore the respect that scholars have for the classic work of Brodie's *No Man Knows my History,* that was first published in 1945, a symposium was held in Salt Lake City in 1995 to commemorate the fiftieth anniversary of this great work.[2]

In spite of the numerous attempts by Mormon Church writers to belittle, condemn and discredit Brodie's book, it has withstood all criticisms and remains not only a classic, but the most credible biography of Joseph Smith, not only when it was published in 1945, but to this present day.[3] Laake's book of which more than 500,000

---

[2]Newell G. Bringhurst, Editor, *Reconsidering No Man Knows my History. Fawn M. Brodie and Joseph Smith in Retrospect.* (Logan, Utah: Utah State University Press) 1996, 2

[3]Ibid., 127 (Lavina Fields Anderson, *Literary Style in No Man Knows my History, An Analysis*)

copies were printed in 1993, rose to number eight on the best seller list and remained there for fifteen weeks.[4]

Many of the authors of references used in this book have completed their works at great risk to their employment, as well as being able to remain in the good graces and retain general respect within their Mormon communities. (The Mormon community is a closed society since those who are not members of the church are not generally involved in social and community activities sponsored by the church. Prospective non-Mormon converts are temporarily embraced by the Mormon community, but when they do not join the church, they are excluded from the closed society.) In spite of these risks, these authors have striven to present their conclusions and research findings concerning the Mormon Church honestly and without restraint. Some of these authors have left the Mormon Church and in so doing were forced to leave their families behind since church teachings to other family members have so indoctrinated them that they refuse to accept any findings, though true, that conflict with church instruction. There are numerous instances of ex-Mormons who decided that the church was wrong in its teachings, had their names removed from church rolls and found later that their businesses were boycotted and they were socially discriminated against by the Mormon community. Some of these ex-Mormon stories are summarized in this book. Practices and beliefs of the church historically and today are related in the following pages that the author believes reveal the fraudulent nature of the Mormon Church's teachings. The following chapters include an examination of the close control that the Mormon Church has upon the social, economic, psychological and political life of church members.

The author was dismayed at what he was learning about the church and felt an obligation to put down in writing these concerns, especially since they contrasted sharply with his understanding of freedom of thought, individualism, democracy and independence. Intensive reading and research brought about the discovery by the author that the history of the church was fraught with deception, authoritarian rule and leadership and was conspiratorial in its development. Numerous deceptions and conspiracies were discovered that took place in the fourteen-year reign of Joseph Smith and the thirty-year reign of Brigham Young. The author discovered that these

---

[4] *Phoenix New Times,* February 10, 2000

deceptions and conspiracies have continued to the present day as has been exemplified by a review of the Hofmann forgeries cover-up in the 1970s and 1980s and the continued propagandizing by the current Mormon Church hierarchy of other matters. The author believes that the Mormon Church hierarchy is well aware of the value of its propagandizing program to enhance its image and to expand its influence. Recent efforts have been made by the church to purchase additional radio stations (in the Chicago area) and newspapers. The most controversial attempt to expand its media control was the negotiations to control *The Salt Lake Tribune*. *The Salt Lake Tribune,* established in the 1870s has been independent of church control and has been a competitor of the church-controlled Utah newspaper, *Deseret News.* The *Tribune* in the year 2000, carried a series of embarrassing articles about the Mormon Church's involvement in the 1857 Mountain Meadows Massacre of 120 innocent members of the Fancher wagon train, and many see this as an attempt by the church to throttle the *Tribune* by buying it.

It is not necessary for this author to review the commendable aspects of the Mormon religion since great resources of the church are used to extol the virtues and desirable practices of the church. However, in the opinion of the author, the commendable aspects of the Mormon religion are outweighed by the undesirable aspects as outlined in this book. Numerous spot advertisements appear on television promoting the family and encouraging viewers to obtain a free copy of a video tape and to request a free copy of the *Book of Mormon.* If you want to learn more about the church, they will happily trot over two young "missionaries," usually nineteen to twenty years old, who will "explain" what the church is all about. Billions of dollars are spent every year to propagandize the church not only to their own members, but to prospective members as well. Therefore, the author feels obligated to present the documentation that he feels reveals the fraud and dishonesty that the church's vast propaganda machine dispenses, as well as its real threat to democracy and freedom in America and throughout the world.

"Mormonism must stand or fall on the story of Joseph Smith. He was either a prophet of God, divinely called, properly appointed and commissioned or he was one of the biggest frauds this world has ever seen. There is no middle ground. If Joseph was a deceiver, who willfully attempted to mislead people, then he should be exposed, his claims should be refuted and his doctrines shown to be false."[1]

"It is not necessary for me to suggest that maintenance of the truth of the *Book of Mormon* is absolutely essential to the integrity of the whole Mormon movement, for it is inconceivable that the *Book of Mormon* should be untrue in its origin or character and the Church of Jesus Christ of Latter-day Saints be a true church."[2]

Chapter One
Overview of Mormonism

Introduction

In the following chapters the reader will find a history of the Mormon Church also known as the Church of Jesus Christ of Latter-Day Saints or LDS. In addition, there are discussions about the doctrine of the church, a presentation of the church's organization and finances and ways in which the church restricts individual freedoms, individual thought, independence and democracy. Likewise, the author will present documentation and evidence showing that he believes the Mormon Church is conspiring to control the United States government, and eventually the world, by establishing its "kingdom of God" on earth. The words "kingdom of God" are in quotes, because in reality the author believes that it is not a kingdom of God that the Mormon Church wishes to establish, but a kingdom of the Mormon Church, led by fifteen men, the Presidency (three men) and the Quorum of Twelve apostles of the church. Investigation by the author shows that the Mormon Church is an authoritarian organization much like the monarchy that prevailed in such European countries as France and England before the French Revolution and before a democracy was established in England.

Documentation is presented in the following chapters showing that the Mormon Church requires religious obedience from members and teaches them that individuals need not think for themselves concerning church doctrine as taught by the Church Authorities. Even in areas of non-church affairs, such as politics and economics, investigation by the author reveals that the church hierarchy expects members to follow its directions. This is shown in the author's discussion of the church's involvement in defeating the Equal Rights Amendment in 1982 as well as in numerous other church-led political activities. In addition, data will be presented in the following chapters that show the church has disproportionate influence in such governmental departments as the FBI, the CIA and the FCC (Federal Communications Commission).

Information is also given demonstrating that the Mormon Church is gaining influence in Congress with the election of greater numbers of Mormon members. Church influence is obvious in the lobbying of congressional members to support Mormon programs and to vote for laws that further their goals. Church hierarchy involvement is apparent in all aspects of government, including the Supreme Court, as shown by the church's filing of a legal brief with the court, opposing a New Jersey Supreme Court ruling that would prevent the National Boy Scout organization from excluding gays from Boy Scout groups. (St. George Spectrum, April 27, 2000)

Subsequent chapters will present information about the authoritarian nature of the church from its inception in 1830 and continuing to the present day.

Mormons regard the President (or Prophet) of the church to be infallible, and they believe that he has direct communication with God; therefore, he can do no wrong or make a mistake. Members believe that Church Authorities (fourteen apostles in addition to the President of the church) are also infallible. Therefore, these fifteen Authorities have control of the Mormon Church. There is no democracy in the decision-making of the church since all appointments from the highest to the lowest offices in the church are made under the umbrella of the church President. If the Mormon Church were to gain control of the United States, the author believes that there would be no secret ballot election of congressional representatives, no secret ballot election of state legislators, nor for local governmental officials. All of these officials would be appointed by the President of the Mormon Church, with assistance from other church officials.

It is ironic that the Mormon Church which the author believes is conspiring to control the United States and world governments is based upon false premises. This book will review the documentation that the author believes proves the fraudulent nature of the church, and begins with an analysis of Joseph Smith's *Book of Mormon.* This book is claimed by the church to be the only true gospel, and although the church uses the King James version of the Bible, it is asserted by them to have been altered by man over the centuries. The Mormon Church began its history with a conspiracy by Joseph Smith to fool the local people with his book. This conspiracy has continued to the present day with the church hierarchy's continuing to hide non-faith promoting documents and teaching members not to read such materials.

Pursuant chapters describe the church's worldwide media network (radio, television, etc.), the corporate empire, the organization of its proselytizing efforts (with its 60,000-strong missionary system) and the total involvement of all members in the social, religious and economic life in Mormon communities. The organizational and functional aspects of the conspiracy to control the United States are already in place in many Mormon communities. Doctors, dentists and lawyers in these communities are overwhelmingly members of the Mormon Church. They have been indoctrinated from birth in the tenets and beliefs of the Mormon Church, and many attended Brigham Young University where further indoctrination occurred. Many of these professionals are assuming leadership positions in the church and are ready to take on additional responsibilities if "called" by the church hierarchy.

In Chapter 1, information is presented that sets the stage for the author's contention that the Mormon Church plans to assume control of the United States and eventually all world governments. The stories of Joseph Smith's *Book of Mormon,* the building of the church, polygamy, Danites and apostates (those who leave the church) are among the topics that are reviewed in this chapter. This information is summarized in order to provide a background for the reader's understanding of what the author believes to be a Mormon conspiracy.

Book of Mormon

Many books have been written on the subject of Mormonism, often beginning with the history of the founder of the Mormon Church, Joseph Smith. Smith was born into poverty to a family eking out a living in the New England area of the United States. Many books on Mormonism raise numerous questions about this "religion" that claims the *Book of Mormon* as its basis. Upon reading this book, however, one finds little evidence on which to base the official doctrine of the church. The book describes the migration of the Lost Tribe of Israel coming by boat to America in 600 B.C. (Another migration from Israel occurring about 2000 B.C. is also described in this book, this being accomplished in submarine-like wooden boats.) The story continues describing the attempts of the tribe's leaders (who split into two major groups, the Nephites and Lamanites) to follow the directions of God in order that the Israelites might prosper and attain everlasting life. The book has little continuity and direction for the reader, its sections are disconnected, and it probably would never have been published except that Joseph Smith pressured a farmer, Martin Harris, to sell his farm to pay for the publication costs. He told Harris that he (Joseph Smith) had received a revelation from God threatening death to Harris if he did not publish this book.[3]

Reinforcing the dullness and uninspiring reading of the *Book of Mormon,* Brodie writes: "...But the prose style was unfortunate. Joseph's sentences were loose-jointed, like an earthworm hacked into segments that crawl away alive and whole." Innumerable repetitions bogging down the narrative were chiefly responsible for Mark Twain's pronouncement that the book was 'chloroform in print.'[4] Much of the material in the book is copied directly from the Bible: for example the phrase "on the third day, he (Jesus) arose from the dead."

The *Book of Mormon,* conceived by Joseph Smith and aided and abetted by his several scribes, is a story that arose from American evangelism, which had ignited "the vast camp meetings at the turn of the nineteenth century, which burned eastward from Kentucky. From the soil thus burned over had sprung both the thousands of believers who could accept a prophet and the psychotic boy who took his puberty walking in the woods and there talked with God, various patriarchs, angels and demons. The cheap story of the golden plates and the colonization of the American continent by emigrants from Jerusalem, the mumbo-jumbo of illiterate, semi-Biblical, degraded Masonic rituals and the apocalyptic nonsense of the Mormon meta-physics -such things themselves enough to cause trouble on a frontier enthusiastically Methodist and Presbyterian."[5]

The *Book of Mormon,* written by Joseph Smith, claimed that the angel Moroni led him to the golden plates on Hill Cumorah near Palmyra, New York. These plates supposedly were written in a reformed Egyptian language that Smith claimed he was able to translate by seer stones. Smith's claim that he translated the *Book of Mormon* from these golden plates was apparently an afterthought, for when the book was first published, he identified himself as the author and proprietor. The fact that the book has also been altered several times from its original printing shows that it was not sacred or translated from golden plates by Joseph Smith with the power of God. If it were sacred or translated, as claimed, by God's giving Joseph Smith exact words, why would it have been changed in later editions? Even the title has been changed in recent years by the church hierarchy from simply The *Book of Mormon* to the *Book of Mormon, Another Testament of Jesus Christ.*

Prior to his "discovery of the golden plates," Joseph Smith had led several treasure digging operations in the area of the Hill Cumorah, claiming that he could find treasures by looking through a stone. For this service he charged a fee. According to Scott, Smith was a "money digger" and the most damaging evidence that Smith was involved in such activities was his being found guilty on March 20, 1826, of being disorderly and being an impostor. He "was accused of having used his peepstone for three years to try (unsuccessfully) to find such things as hidden treasure, lost property, money, gold, a salt spring, and a buried trunk."[6]

At first, Joseph's wife Emma served as his scribe for the *Book of Mormon,* supposedly writing as he dictated to her from the other side of a blanket which divided the room where they worked. In his dictations to Emma, Joseph's references most likely not only included the Bible, but other contemporary books such as the *View of the Hebrews.* Many have characterized Joseph as lacking the ability to write the *Book of Mormon,* and therefore, it must have been accomplished with divine help. The fact was that Joseph *did* have great intelligence with an **unusual** imagination and probably knew the Bible in great detail. Brodie underscores his ability by writing:

"There is no doubt, however, that Joseph had developed a remarkable facility for dictation. The speed was not 'far beyond his natural ability'; it was evidence of his ability. To belittle his creative talent is to do him as great an injustice as to say that he had no learning- a favorite Mormon thesis designed to prove the authenticity of the book."[7]

When Emma was unable to perform the writing of the book because of a difficult pregnancy, Martin Harris became Smith's scribe. Harris was followed by Oliver Cowdery, a scribe of much greater skill than Harris, and the writing of the manuscript progressed at a much faster pace. Smith's story was no doubt enhanced by Cowdery's contribution of his knowledge of Ethan Smith's *View of the Hebrews*. The *Book of Mormon* contains many of the ideas presented in this book (1823-second printing 1825), especially the idea that the Lost Tribes of Israel immigrated to the Americas from Israel before the birth of Christ.[8] The 275,000 word manuscript was completed on April 7, 1829, and of this, 27,000 words were quoted directly from the Bible. An additional 10,000 words were added by the numerous inclusions of the phrase: "And it came to pass."[9]

The first 116 pages of the manuscript were lost when Smith finally consented to Harris' request that he be allowed to show these pages to his wife. Mrs. Harris was greatly opposed to Smith's pressuring of her husband to finance the publication of this book. Harris felt that by showing the manuscript to his wife he would convince her to support the project. Instead, Harris' wife caused the manuscript to disappear, and it never appeared again.

Obviously, this loss was a great embarrassment, not only to Harris, but to Smith as well. If the golden plates were still in his possession, as Smith claimed they were, why couldn't they be translated again? In reality, there were no plates, and if Smith attempted to rewrite those missing 116 pages, the writing would be quite different from the original pages. And what if these mysteriously disappeared pages showed up after the "divine" *Book of Mormon* was published, thus disproving Smith's hoax about translating the golden plates by divine revelation. Smith knew that he could not take such a chance, so he announced that he had received a revelation from God saying that the plates need not be retranslated, but that vital information contained in these missing pages would be in other plates, called plates of Nephi. (It seemed that when Smith needed a revelation from God, he was always able to receive one, like when he was secretly practicing polygamy and wanted to avoid his wife's wrath, or when he wanted Harris to finance the *Book of Mormon,* or when he wanted his mansion-hotel built in Nauvoo.)

According to Brodie, Smith languished for several weeks before deciding how to handle the loss of the first 116 pages of the manuscript. "But for weeks, Joseph writhed in self-reproach for his folly. To admit that the whole story of the golden plates was a mere figment of his dreaming would be to destroy Emma's faith in him forever. It would mean the end of Harris' patronage and the undying contempt of his father-in law, upon whom he would probably have to depend for livelihood. His father's family was counting on sales of the *Book of Mormon* to prevent foreclosure on their farm since they had no money for the final payment. A retreat from the fantasy that he had created was impossible."[10]

Joseph Smith's book contains many commands from God that the "Israelite" leaders were to follow, as well as threats of death if such commands were not obeyed. There are also many references to the devil (Satan) who was always trying to thwart God's commands. For the most part, the book describes the history and development of this "lost Israel tribe" during the 600 years prior to the birth of Christ. For example, in this book is the prediction that Christ would walk the earth (several centuries before it happened), and it includes a prediction that the author, Joseph Smith (more than 2400 years before he was born) would be given the golden plates and become the "prophet" of the church of the Latter-Day Saints, a name taken to describe a group of people who would prepare for the coming of Christ for the One Thousand Year Kingdom of God on earth.

According to Smith's book the first group to migrate, called the Jaredites, made the journey from the Tower of Babel to the Promised Land (America) about 2000 B. C. They sailed in wooden submarine-like boats driven by constant strong winds on a journey that lasted 344 days. It also states that for the journey God provided the ships with stones that gave light at all times and equipped them so they were able to travel for many days deep in the depths of the ocean. These boats also carried many types of animals, food and provisions for the Jaredites to use during the journey and after they reached the Promised Land.

The *Book of Mormon,* considered sacred by believers, reveals that a second group led by Lehi and his wife Sarah, along with their

sons left Jerusalem in 600 B. C. In the following years a ship was
built by their son Nephi using directions given by God. The boat,
described by Smith of superior construction in every way, took Lehi
and Sarah, their sons and their wives from Israel to the Promised
Land (America). They were a small group of people that the *Book of
Mormon* claims multiplied (faster than seems possible) and split into
two groups, the Nephites and the Lamanites. The split happened
very quickly, within about 20 years. (See the B o M 2 Nephi 5.) The
righteous and God-fearing of them were called Nephites, and the
others, who were described as non-believers of God, and whose skin
was turned black by God because of the loathsome and filthy way of
living, were called Lamanites. They lived in tents, ate meat of wild
beasts and were generally uncivilized. There were several wars
between the Nephites and the Lamanites and periods of peace, and
finally the Lamanites were driven into the wilderness while the
Nephites were able to build their cities and live in relative prosperity.

During the peaceful periods, the Nephites would gradually
change from God-fearing and God-worshipping to drift into dis-
gusting behaviors, thus losing their support from God. Because of
the lack of His support, God's favored people (the Nephites) would
be defeated by the Lamanites, who had become militarily stronger.
The many changes of the Nephites from worship of God and righteous behavior, to whoredom and loathsome behaviors, is the main
theme of the *Book of Mormon*.

Eventually, according to the story, the Nephites were destroyed
by the Lamanites at Hill Cumorah, near Palmyra, New York, in a
tremendous battle during which hundreds of thousands were slain
with the sword. (B o M Mormon 6:11, 12, 13) No artifacts or any

evidence that such a battle took place at this location has ever been
found. This is one of the fantasies written in the *Book of Mormon,*
which the Church Authorities teach as true and authentic history.
Smith also portrays the victors to be the ancestors of the American
Indians even though there is no archeological or historical evidence
that this is true. All scientific information shows the migration of the
original American Indians as following a path by way of Siberia,
crossing a land bridge which at that time connected to Alaska. The
migration occurred not by sea, or from Israel, as claimed by Smith,
but from Siberia by way of Alaska down the Pacific coast, filtering
toward the east and south on the North American continent and
finally through the Isthmus of Panama to South America. The

Mormon Church is still searching for the "White Indians," descendants of God's chosen people from Israel, but this search has failed.

Actually, archaeological studies of the Indians in the Americas have been numerous and fruitful since Smith's time. Diggings and studies reveal the steady migration of the ancestors of the American Indians coming from China through Siberia over the land bridge into Alaska, and eventual settling throughout North and South America. Fagen estimates that *Homo sapiens* moved into Siberia [setting the stage for entry into the North American continent] about 35,000-40,000 years ago and were supported by a diversity of game animals, including rhinoceros, musk ox, steppe bison, reindeer and the wild horse. Studies of sites in Siberia confirm Fagen's findings.[11]

That the American Indian is a descendant of the Chinese (as opposed to Joseph Smith's claim in his *Book of Mormon* that the Indian Lamanites were descendants of the lost Israelite tribes) is based upon extensive studies of dental morphology of Chinese and Indian burial sites, which show a clear ancestral relationship between the two groups. Further, Fagen shows that geological studies reveal the existence of a "land bridge" between Siberia and Alaska which lasted until about 14,000 years ago. This area and lower coastal areas were obviously settled for many centuries before 14,000 B. C. but are impossible to study today as the area is now covered with sea water.[12]

The flooding of the Siberian-Alaska land bridge, which occurred between 13,000 and 15,000 years ago, forced the migration to higher ground. This is evidenced by the studies of sites in Alaska and the Yukon. After this time, humans spread gradually through the Arctic into Greenland, through Alaska, the Yukon and along the Pacific coast to California and eventually throughout North and South America. Indians hunted bison on the plains of North America for nearly 12,000 years, during which time their customs and hunting techniques changed very little. And they would be doing the same today if the Europeans had not arrived in the 15th and 16th centuries A.D. An article in *Discovery* magazine (June 1998) reported that the earliest evidence of human presence in the New World was found in a 12,500-year-old site in Chile called Monte Verde. Due to the length of time it would take for the migration of Siberian hunters to move across the Siberian-Alaskan land bridge to Chile, it was estimated that the Chilean ancestors may have begun their migration into North America at least 22,000 years ago. This is far earlier than Smith's story shows.

Unfortunately for Joseph Smith and his "assistant" writers, they did not have these data available. Had they had these data they could have prevented the error in the *Book of Mormon*. Smith's "lost tribes of Israel" didn't arrive as he had written. Any attempt by the Mormon Church to hold that Smith's book is the truth is clearly exposed by the archaeological evidence gathered concerning the North and South American Indian.

The Mormon Church has spent large sums of money and expended tremendous efforts to prove the archeological truth of the *Book of Mormon*. But not one shred of evidence has been found to verify this claim. Thomas Stuart Ferguson, a former defender of the faith, who used large monetary grants in an attempt to prove the truth of Joseph Smith's hoax, became disillusioned in his efforts. Tanner and Tanner write: "... that he (Ferguson) had come to the conclusion that Joseph Smith was not a prophet and that Mormonism was not true. He told us that he had spent 25 years trying to prove Mormonism [through archeological research] but had finally come to the conclusion that his work in this regard had been in vain. He said that his training in law had taught him how to weigh evidence and that the case against Joseph Smith was absolutely devastating and could not be explained away."[13]

Even the current Mormon Church President, Gordon B. Hinckley, may have misgivings about some of Joseph Smith's teachings. In a recent newspaper interview concerning Joseph Smith's revelations and visions, Hinckley said, **"Revelation no longer comes by vision, but in the 'still, small voice,' like that heard by Elijah.** Let me say first that we have a great body of revelation, the vast majority of which came from the prophet Joseph Smith. We don't need much revelation. ... Now, if a problem should arise on which we don't have an answer, we pray about it, we may fast about it, and it comes. Quietly. **Usually no voice of any kind, but just a perception in the mind."** (Interview with President Gordon B. Hinckley, as published on the website of the San *Francisco Chronicle,* April 13, 1997.) Are Mormon leaders beginning to doubt the authenticity of Joseph Smith's writings? Smith had written many revelations and visions that he said he received from God. These revelations and visions include Smith's being led to the golden plates as well as boldly announcing many revelations which he received from God, including approval for himself and others to practice polygamy, organizational procedures for the LDS church, tithing and the ordering of Martin Harris to pay for the publication of the *Book of Mormon*. Were Joseph Smith's writings not really divine in nature as President Hinckley said in his descriptions of visions and revelations: **"Usually no voice of any kind, but just a perception in the mind"?**

The Mormons are taught by the Church Authorities to believe that the *Book of Mormon* is incontrovertible, not to be proven by review of scientific or historical facts, but by asking God if the book is true. He will tell you by "divine" means that it is the truth. However, any measurement of its truth by historical and scientific means, provides no evidence of its truthfulness. The heart provides a person with the means to inform one of the truth of the book. In other words, if one **wants to believe** it is true this provides the means to do so. (The author remembers his first encounter in an attempt to convert him to the Mormon Church. The Mormon missionaries and others present were trying to convince him that the *Book of Mormon* was true. He thought at the time that their continually saying— "yes it is true, yes it is true," was showing him that there was doubt in their minds that it really was true.)

The *Book of Mormon* is really not a story, not a novel, not a history, not a religion, not a geography, not a documentary, but rather a collection of disconnected ideas gathered and stolen from the Bible, from other books, from people living in the area at the time and based on the common belief of the people in the early 1800s that the Indians were descendants of the Jewish peoples of the Middle East. It is not a book in the sense that it has a story, a thesis, a purpose, any meaning or guidance for the reader. It could better be described as not a *Book of Mormon,* but much more accurately as a looseleaf notebook of rewritten Bible scriptures. It shows that by the tenacious efforts of a young man, Joseph Smith, who by inserting his imagination in among Bible scriptures and then copying ideas from other books and manuscripts of the period, was able to bring it together and to have it published.

How was Joseph to know that his main theme, the migration of the Hebrew tribes from Israel to the Americas would later prove to be false as scientific archaeological inquiry has done as modern civilization poured across the Americas? After all, this theory of the Hebrew tribes' migration was accepted throughout the western world in Smith's time. And how easy it was for Smith to use his newly discovered weapon of his revelation to get people to do as he wished. All he had to do was tell Martin Harris that he had received a revelation from God telling him that he must sell his farm to pay for the publication of the *Book of Mormon* or he would die. It was easy for him to tell his family and friends about his visions of God's leading him to the golden plates and to tell them that by the use of magical stones furnished with the plates he was able to translate the reformed Egyptian letters into the *Book of Mormon*. (Smith should have said he translated from Hebrew since he claimed the characters in his book emigrated from Israel.) **They believed him!!** Joseph Smith must have thought: "Look at the power and influence that I have over people. They believe that I communicate with God and that He communicates with me. I can use this great new power to influence people to follow me!! **I will be the Prophet!!**"

No doubt Smith had misgivings about how to use this new found power. And history of the Mormon Church shows the dangerous, sometimes disastrous and always uncomfortable path that Joseph was leading his members down. But by using his knowledge of Masonic Lodge ritual and his own imagination, he was always able to keep the interest and enthusiasm of his followers. As long as he claimed that he was working as a servant of God, he was able to maintain and increase his membership. For most of the followers, what Joseph said or told them to do was the word of God and should be accepted and followed and never questioned.

It is important to consider the condition of life for the New England people during the time of Joseph Smith as this provided the mechanism for the invention of a new religion. The economic existence for the vast majority of inhabitants was obtained by tilling the land that was rocky, infertile and hilly. It was, to say the least, a very rigorous life with little opportunity for improvement of one's place in life. Life expectancy was very short, with a high mortality rate of infants and children. In short, the people were ripe for accepting a religion that promised them eternal life in a blissful and harmonious " after-earth-life" that would include family members who had died at a young age. In many cases, parents were fearful to become too attached to their children since death might take them away. Because of this constant threat of death, the development of a religion that promised eternal life would thrive. The religion would flourish, especially if its inventor was a leader with charisma, intensity, great imagination, intelligence and hypnotic skill in controlling his followers as was Joseph Smith. He was the one who could build and develop his religion by convincing the Saints that with faith in God and by following his commandments, death on earth would be followed by eternal life in Heaven. Not only was this written in the *Book of Mormon,* but Smith's remarkable imagination, that he used in his sermons, writings and in the construction of his beautifully designed temples, gave his Saints a glimpse of what life might be like in Heaven. The white veil, elaborate fixtures and the luxurious decor of the numerous Mormon temples certainly emerged from the fanciful and dreamy mind of Joseph Smith. The temple indeed represented Smith's Heaven on earth.

Even though it is often agreed (even by many Mormons) that the *Book of Mormon* is not authentic, most of the faithful have been taught to want to believe it anyway. A large number accept it because the authorities say it is so, and a Mormon in good standing never questions the authority of the priesthood or what his Authorities say. A pious Mormon never questions his faith, at least not publicly, unless he or she wants to be excommunicated from the church. That the *Book of Mormon* is not authentic, one has only to know that there is no archaeological evidence whatsoever that it is true. For example, in Smith's account, it is written that horses, oxen and cows were present, but all archaeological evidence shows that they were not present during this period of history in the Americas.

Not only does Smith's *Book of Mormon* describe oxen and cows that were not in America at the time, but he claims that the ancestors of Indian tribes, the Lamanites, came from Israel. (Note: Nephites are not considered to have been "Indians," because Nephites were white. The dark skin of Lamanities came as a result of God's curse.) Smith thought that he was "safe" in this fraud since the common thinking at the time he wrote his book was that the Indians were descendants of the "lost tribes of Israel." Archaeological studies of the Indians at that time were nearly nonexistent.

And where are the cities that were developed in America by these tribes and the remains of the hundreds of thousands killed on Hill Cumorah? (See BoM, Mormon 6, p. 469) And sailing thousands of miles from Israel by wooden submarines is illogical.

Fawn Brodie and B. H. Roberts have provided evidence that Joseph Smith had access to many books and other writings. These and the beliefs of the people of his time gave Smith the ideas and material for his book. One such book, referred to before, was Ethan

Smith's *View of the Hebrews,* which was written five to seven years before the *Book of Mormon.* A summary of Ethan Smith's book appeared in the local newspaper subscribed to by the Smith family. This book was written within fifty miles of the Smith home and was known to be readily available in the area. Ethan Smith's book theorized (as did the *Book of Mormon*) that the Indians were descendants of the lost tribes of Israel, an idea that was popular at this time in American history.[14] As more archeological and DNA evidence and scientific study were completed on the origins of the American Indians, this idea was proven to be false.

B. H. Roberts in his studies of the *Book of Mormon* "presents an intense and probing evaluation of the possibility that Ethan Smith's *View of the Hebrews* furnished a partial framework for Joseph Smith's written composition, that the Mormon prophet had the intellectual capacity and imagination necessary to conceive and write the *Book of Mormon* and that internal contradictions and other defects added further evidence that it might not be of divine origin. [15]

"...during the winter of 1922, B. H. Roberts continued his search for possible explanations as to the origin of the Mormon scripture and seized the opportunities presented by his mission presidency in New England to examine early literature that could have been available to Joseph Smith during the time the *Book of Mormon* was being produced. His surprising conclusion was that the *View of the Hebrews* ... predated the writing of the *Book of Mormon* and could have furnished the 'ground plan' for Joseph Smith's authorship."[16]

Roberts made an intensive study of passages from the *View of the Hebrews* and compared them with similar material found in the *Book of Mormon* and concluded that Ethan Smith's book may "well have furnished structural outlines" for Joseph Smith's book, and he further concluded that Joseph Smith had creative and imaginative abilities sufficient to accomplish the writing of his book, using Ethan Smith's book as an outline. [17]Furthermore, since the prevailing feeling among the people at this time was that the Indians were descendants of the Israelites, Joseph Smith felt secure that time would not dispute the authenticity of his book and that he could indeed "get by" with his hoax that he had translated them from the golden plates given to him by the angel Moroni. The feeling that he was "safe" in his portrayal of the golden plates idea was also reinforced by his own family and close associates who believed young Joseph. Family members enjoyed Joseph's fantastic stories of

Indians in America, their glittering cities and his account of their immigration from Israel. This and the unfailing support of his mother Lucy, his father Joseph, Sr. and his brother Hyrum gave him great confidence that his hoax would succeed.

Other writers have provided evidence that Solomon Spaulding's manuscript, titled *Manuscript Found,* actually contained the words Nephi and Lehi used by Joseph Smith. The manuscript described the "Jewish origin" of the American Indians and the battles between the Nephites and Lamanites.[18] Walter Martin has researched the origins of the *Book of Mormon* and maintains that the historical portions of the book were transferred directly from one of Solomon Spaulding's manuscripts. This connection has been denied by Mormon Church authorities using as part of the denial a Spaulding "found manuscript" from Oberlin College in Ohio clearly showing (according to them) that there is no relationship between it and the *Book of Mormon.* However, Martin shows that Spaulding wrote many manuscripts, and he reviews the testimony of Johan Spaulding (Solomon's brother) and his wife Martha Spaulding in which they testify that the history part of the *Book of Mormon* was directly transferred from Spaulding's work. (E. D. Howe, *Mormonism Unvailed,* 1834)

According to Martin: "We know that men wrote it and these men, whoever they were, did not have God's guidance ... The *Book of Mormon* heavily plagiarizes from the King James Bible, but it betrays a lack of knowledge about the history of the Jewish people."[19]

In short, the evidence is clear that the *Book of Mormon* was not translated from golden plates using a seer stone, as described by Smith, but was the product of his boyhood and family experiences, his awareness of common thinking in the area, his extensive knowledge of the Bible and his knowledge of the Spaulding manuscript, which provided a nonreligious story as a basis for his novel. And as stated previously, Smith was aware of Ethan Smith's *View of the Hebrews,* which gave him many of the ideas for his book. Joseph Smith was surprised that he was able to influence people so easily and could use this ability to get people to accept his "revelations" as coming from God. He invented a religion, developed an organization for it and had a great persuasive ability which enticed people to follow his doctrine. He was no doubt the best missionary that the Mormon Church ever had and singularly did more than any other person to provide the church with a sizable membership foundation, as well as to insure that the church would grow and thrive by his development of the missionary organization and the priesthood. His later organization of the family visitation system insured a low dropout rate of members.

Why is it that nearly all of the revelations and doctrines of the Mormon Church were written by Joseph Smith during a short seventeen-year period? (1827-1844) These revelations and doctrines were created at a time when there were but crude communication devices. Modern conveniences such as the telephone, radio, television and computer were not available. Since that time, very few doctrines and revelations have been introduced even though communication devices have steadily improved and have developed into today's modern communication systems.

Scott further emphasizes that the *Book of Mormon* is a hoax. "Why can't the Mormons own up that the *Book of Mormon* is a fraud? If any reader be still in doubt, let him send a letter to the Smithsonian Institute with the question, 'Is the *Book of Mormon* confirmed by archaeological evidence?' He will receive a mimeographed letter that states, in essence, that the historical picture painted by the Mormon epic is totally unlike the world of ancient Americas as they have found it in extensive excavations. Mormons have in the past claimed that many other records or inscriptions "proved" the *Book of Mormon.* Among these records were the Bat Creek Stone, the Kinderhook plates, the Newark Stones and the 'Phoenician Ten Commandments' (found in Los Lunas, New Mexico). All were highly touted, but all were forgeries. Why not place the *Book of Mormon* with them?"[20]

That the writings of Joseph Smith are generally frauds and not based upon any divinity as claimed by Mormon leaders is further emphasized by Scott, who writes: "I examined the life of Joseph Smith and found him to be the antithesis of all that Mormons claim he was. Not only was his account of the First Vision unlikely and out of harmony with God's word, he himself couldn't relate the stories the same way from one telling to another. Because of reckless merchandising of men's souls, the legacy he left his people has been one of persecution, broken promises and a rash of unfulfilled prophecies. The *Book of Mormon* too has done more harm to the Mormon people than good. ...the *Book of Mormon* stands unaccompanied by even a single non-Mormon archaeological advocate."[21]

The Building of the Church

As will be described in more detail in a later chapter, the story of the building of the Mormon Church is often characterized with Joseph Smith's riding away in the night to escape the wrath of non-Mormons who believe that he and his followers have swindled them or because of their activities which they (non-Mormons) found to be oppressive and offensive. In Kirtland, Ohio, Joseph Smith had developed a large following, established a bank, built a temple and acquired large numbers of properties. Due to the failure of his bank, he was forced to leave town by militant bank depositors, who were trying to get their money out of his bank. Many non-Mormons were also upset that Smith and his followers inflated the price of the land, which made it difficult for them to buy.

Leaving Kirtland, Ohio, Mormons followed Smith to an existing settlement called Far West, Missouri. Then after a few years they were again forced by non-Mormons to leave and migrate to Nauvoo, Illinois, where they developed Illinois' largest city at this time, a city of over fifteen thousand people. Mormons were again forced to migrate after the death of their leader, Joseph Smith, on June 24, 1844. Smith was killed by a mob while he was being held in jail awaiting trial for treason.

One account of Joseph Smith's death by the mob is as follows: "Brother Stephen Markham, who had been to visit the brothers an hour or so before they were killed, gave Joseph an Allen revolver. A part of the mob rushed to the inner door of the prison and burst it open. Brother Richards parried the bayonets with his arms and hands. Joseph reached out his hand and fired his gun at the crowd, and wounded several, some mortally. While he was trying to brace against the door, he was shot in the face near the nose. 'I am a dead man,' he cried, and fell."[22]

The followers of Joseph Smith were never accepted by their non-Mormon neighbors for several reasons including: (1) the tendency to vote as a solid bloc, (2) the bringing in of immigrant Mormon converts who acquired large blocks of land among the non-Mormons, (3) the threat to establish a Mormon kingdom of God on earth and (4) socializing only among themselves. These conditions from their beginnings of 1830 to 1847 caused the non-Mormons to force the Mormon migration from Nauvoo, Illinois, to Salt Lake City, Utah, where the Latter-Day Saints, under the leadership of

Brigham Young, had a relatively peaceful ten-year period to build their kingdom of God on earth. (The "Mormon War," Mountain Meadows Massacre and the Federal government's fear that they were becoming too independent-minded led to federal involvement in the Salt Lake City Mormon affairs beginning with the year 1857.)

The largest group of the Mormon Church followers to migrate traveled from Nauvoo, Illinois, to Salt Lake City led by Brigham Young, who assumed the duties of Prophet and President of the church shortly after Joseph Smith's death. While he lacked the imagination and inventiveness of Joseph Smith, he was a leader with great organizational ability that was desperately needed to move the thousands of Mormons to their new home. Leaving Nauvoo was accomplished in a short period of time, primarily because of the constant pressure of the non-Mormons who surrounded the city and who provided a steady stream of threats and other measures to ensure that the Mormons left.

As described by DeVoto, the Mormons themselves were partly responsible for their dislike by non-Mormon frontiersmen. He writes: "...Unquestionably some portions of Israel (The Mormon city of Nauvoo, Illinois) spoiled the Gentiles (non-Mormons) by theft, burglary, and fraud, and found protection in the holy city. There was counterfeiting. There were various kinds of suckerbaiting to the greater glory of God. There was shady banking and shady credit manipulation. And wildcat real-estate operations reached as high as the prophet Joseph himself, who inflated land prices so systematically that one must not too greatly sorrow over their collapse when Nauvoo fell. (The inflation of land prices was also practiced by Brigham Young as he settled the Salt Lake Basin.)

"Finally, the greatest offense of the Mormon system was its political cohesion. The frontier took its democratic elections with the greatest possible seriousness and Joseph Smith voted his church members for whoever would pay most for the vote. The church was a bloc that could turn the balance of power. It was foolish use of this power in Illinois—quite as foolishly purchased by both Democrats and Whigs in turn—that finally exploded the dynamite which the other peculiarities of the Saints had heaped up. The one-party system is what drove Mormonism out of Illinois. (The Saints repeated this mistake blatantly in Iowa, California and Nevada. It was at least as powerful an irritant as polygamy in the conflict between Utah and the National government down to statehood. It is the principal source of friction with Gentiles today.)"[23]

The migration was accompanied by great suffering on the part of Mormons, who were forced to leave their homes in Nauvoo with only the goods that could be carried on wagons and later just what could be carried on handcarts. Many died on this trek of some fourteen hundred miles, especially those who left too late to complete the three-month journey before the arrival of cold weather. One can imagine the great organizational problems facing the leaders of this migration, such as the building of wagons, obtaining horses and oxen to pull the wagons, arranging for food and other provisions for the 10,000 travelers, as well as providing them with temporary quarters. Temporary camps were established in south central Iowa as well as a winter quarters on the west side of the Missouri River on the Iowa-Nebraska border. John D. Lee (later executed for the Mountain Meadows Massacre) was one of the leaders assigned by Brigham Young to oversee some of the migration efforts.

After temporary dwellings were built, crops were planted and irrigation systems were installed. Thousands of Mormon followers, recruited primarily in England, were a part of the migration movement along the Mormon Trail beginning in Iowa and continuing through Nebraska, Wyoming and on to Salt Lake City. Artisans and other skilled craftsmen were a priority for the recruiting efforts of the Mormon missionaries in England and other European countries. These skilled recruits were needed in the building trades, iron and metal industries as well as agricultural endeavors for Brigham Young's Kingdom of God in his new State of Deseret. The unattached females from Europe also provided the polygamists with wives to support and complete the polygamist homes.

The European Mormon converts were the poorest of the poor. They were mainly the unemployed from the dying towns of Cornwall and Wales in England. They also included Norwegians, Danes and Swedes, who would gladly trade their lowly place in life in Europe for the opportunity to go to the Promised Land, which Mormon missionaries had presented as the golden opportunity. These economically deprived people, many being threatened with debtor jail in their countries, were ripe pickings for the Mormon Church's cadre of missionaries who not only promised spiritual salvation, but a chance to farm and obtain a piece of land of their own.[24]

These European converts were anxious to leave the poverty-stricken villages; almost anything would be an improvement in the life that they were leading. The promise of opportunity in the New

America was a dream come true. However, it is likely that had they known of the great hardships they were facing and even death from disease, starvation and freezing, many would probably not have taken the plunge. But take it they did, and as a result, they probably contributed more to the success of the settling and development of the Salt Lake Valley and surrounding areas than did the original Mormons from Nauvoo, Illinois. Many did not realize when they arrived at their staging area in the Midwest, that they would have to walk all of the way and push and pull their belongings in a hand cart since wagons, horses and oxen were in short supply for this three-month journey.

Brigham Young began immediately to organize the area around Salt Lake City into a state government which included not only the State of Utah, but Nevada, parts of California, Wyoming, Idaho and Arizona. This vast territory was called the State of Deseret (a biblical term meaning honey bee). This was to be the Mormons' Kingdom of God. It began as an independent state, but it was not long before leaders realized that the United States would not permit such an independent state, and they were forced to become a territory of the United States.

The administration of the United States became alarmed that the Deseret State, organized by Brigham Young, was becoming too independent, and President Buchanan eventually sent a small army to bring the territory under the control of the U. S. government. This caused the "Mormon War" and is also said to have caused the Mountain Meadows Massacre. Contributing to the church's anger toward the Fancher wagon train party was that it was from Arkansas where revered Mormon apostle Parley P. Pratt had been killed while attempting to carry away another man's wife to join his other polygamous wives.

Mountain Meadows Massacre

Concerning the Mountain Meadows Massacre, Farkas and Reed state that "The Mountain Meadows Massacre in 1857, where about 120 non-Mormon men, women and children were slaughtered by Mormons and Indians, clearly shows that Mormonism, in Brigham Young's time, led men to do terrible things in the name of God."[25]

Jerald and Sandra Tanner write that John D. Lee, who participated in the Mountain Meadows Massacre, felt that nearly all Mormons

believed in Blood Atonement . ..it was taught by the leaders and
believed by the people that the Priesthood were inspired and could
not give a wrong order .. if Brigham Young or any of the apostles or
any of the Priesthood gave an order to a man, the act was the act of
the one giving the order, and the man doing the act was only an
instrument of the person commanding... This being the belief of all
good Mormons, it is easily understood why the orders of the
Priesthood were so blindly obeyed by the people."[26]

Lee's strong belief in Blood Atonement led to the fulfillment of
his Mormon Church leaders' wishes to carry out the Mountain
Meadows Massacre. He could not believe that church leaders in
Cedar City, Utah would ask him to lead the massacre of 120 persons
of the Fancher party in order to atone for the death of Joseph Smith
which occurred thirteen years earlier in Illinois. Yet when such an
order was given by Apostle Haight, Lee felt obliged to carry it out.
(Haight and other Cedar City Mormon Church leaders were to
escape prosecution and conviction for this hideous crime through
the protection of the Mormon Church. As will be explained in more
detail later, Lee was to take the blame for it and was tried, convicted and shot as he sat on his coffin.)

Lee was very distraught at the nature of the orders that he was
receiving and in his autobiography, wrote: "Haight (Lee's Mormon
Church superior) said: 'I expect you to carry out your orders.'"

Accompanying this train of emigrants was a small group of
Missourians, who were said to claim that they had been involved in
the killing of Joseph Smith and had the gun that was used in this
killing. It is also said that this small group of Missourians had as
Lee described it "insulted, outraged and ravished many of the
Mormon women ... as well as poisoned the water, burned fences and
destroyed growing crops."[27]

Lee continues:

"I knew I had to obey or die. I had no wish to disobey, for I then
thought that my superiors in the Church were the mouthpieces of
Heaven, and that it was an act of godliness for me to obey any and
all orders given by them to me, without my asking any questions."[28]
But Lee was not satisfied with this order and asked other leaders if
something couldn't be done to avoid the plan to destroy the Fancher
company. He also prayed that word would come to reverse Haight's
order, but no such order ever came. One of the leaders, Major
Higbee, told Lee: "I have the evidence of God's approval of our

mission. It is God's will that we carry out our instructions to the letter." After which Lee said, "My God! This is more than I can do. I
must and do refuse to take part in this matter."

"Higbee then said to me, 'Brother Lee, I am ordered by President
Haight to inform you that you shall receive a crown of Celestial
glory for your faithfulness and your eternal joy shall be complete.' I
was much shaken by this offer, for I had full faith in the power of the
Priesthood to bestow such rewards and blessings, but I was anxious
to save the people. I then proposed that we give the Indians all of the
stock of the emigrants, except sufficient to haul their wagons, and let
them go. To this proposition all the leading men objected. No man
there raised his voice or hand to favor the saving of life, except
myself."[29]

Lee, in his account, described the emigrants as strongly fortified,
with a rifle pit sufficient to hold the entire company which afforded
a shield from the incoming rifle fire. Lee was told that ten men had
been killed by the Indians, and seventeen wounded. He wrote: "As I
entered the fortifications, men, women and children gathered around
me in wild consternation. Some felt that the time of their happy
deliverance had come, while others, though in deep distress, and all
in tears, looked upon me with doubt, distrust and terror. My feelings
at the time may be imagined (but I doubt the power of man being
equal to even imagine how wretched I felt.) No language can
describe my feelings. My position was painful, trying and awful; my
brain seemed to be on fire; my nerves for a moment were unstrung;
humanity was overpowered, as I thought of the cruel, unmanly part
that I was acting. Tears of bitter anguish fell in streams from my
eyes; ...I wished that the earth would open and swallow me where I
stood. ..I knew that I was acting a cruel part and doing a damnable
deed. Yet my faith in the godliness of my leaders was such that it
forced me to think that I was not sufficiently spiritual to act the
important part I was commanded to perform. ...Then feeling that
duty compelled *obedience to orders,* I laid aside my weakness and
my humanity, and became an instrument in the hands of my superiors and my leaders. I delivered my message and told the people that
they must put their arms in the wagon, so as not to arouse the ani-
mosity of the Indians."[30]

The sick and wounded of the Fancher party were put in a wagon
driven by Lee with the women and larger children walking ahead of
the men. The smaller children mostly below the age of seven were

put in a small wagon. As the men, women and older children were walking from their fortifications, they were mowed down by rifle fire from the Mormons and Indians. Shortly afterwards Lee and others killed the sick and wounded in the wagon. The plan had been to kill all of the emigrants old enough to identify the participants in the massacre, as the Indians were to be held totally responsible. Only the wagonload of young children survived.

While more will be written in later chapters about the authority and control that the priesthood has over Mormon Church members, without the strong Mormon belief in the godliness and righteousness of church authorities, this hideous crime against the Fancher party by the Mormon Church would not have happened. Lee clearly would have saved the emigrants' lives and insured them safe passage through the rest of southern Utah. It is also probably safe to say that had the Mormons not interfered with the Indians' attack upon this party, the Indians would have abandoned the siege, since they had suffered several killed and wounded. Brigham Young and other Church Authorities, who by preaching Blood Atonement which aroused the Mormons, must be held responsible for the massacre. There is also evidence that modern day church leaders do not wish for members to learn the truth about the heavy involvement of the Mormon Church authorities from Cedar City, Utah, in the Mountain Meadows Massacre.

Juanita Brooks in the preface of her book *The Mountain Meadows Massacre* writes that "we [Mormons] have tried to blot out the affair from our history. It must not be referred to, much less discussed openly. Years ago, that might have been the best stand to take in the interest of the church, but now [1950] with the perspective of time, with the old antagonisms gone, we should be able to view this tragedy objectively and dispassionately, and to see it in its proper setting as a study of social psychology as well as history."[31] This statement by Brooks was made over fifty years ago and even today (2004) Mormon Church authorities are avoiding telling the truth to church members.

A monument has been constructed recently on the massacre site by the Mormon Church that donated $200,000 for its completion. The Mormon Church's covering up for the local Mormon leadership in this massacre has brought complaints from several descendants of the 120 members of the Fancher party who were massacred there. Following are some of the descendant's comments:

"It is time for the Church to stop stonewalling and face the truth."

"They (Mormons) have baptized all of our Fancher people into their faith (baptism for the dead) and from our point of view this is sacrilege."

"We believe that the monument should be outside the control and direction of the LDS Church."

During the planning, construction and dedication of the monument, there was much dissatisfaction voiced among the descendants. Some of them had worked hand in hand with the Mormon Church in the planning and completion of the memorial, while many others felt that the Mormon Church should not be involved in the project at all and refused to work with them. The dedication of the monument by Mormon Church President Hinckley was a carefully orchestrated affair planned and controlled by the church. Attendance at the dedication was by invitation only. Many interested and deserving parties were not invited. One would think that such a dedication that has such general public interest as the Mountain Meadows Massacre would be open to the public. Certainly, there was plenty of room around the memorial for public attendance, and those who would be special guests could have been provided with seating. Was attendance restricted to invited guests because the Mormon Authorities were afraid that in some way the awful truth concerning the massacre would get out to the public or even to the Mormon Church members?

Those who feel that the monument should be independent of the Mormon Church have formed an organization called "Mountain Meadows Monument Foundation." Questions and opposition to the Mormon involvement increased when, during the work on the monument, a backhoe unearthed remains of several men, women and children belonging to the ill-fated Fancher emigrant train. There was considerable opposition to the sending of these bones for authentication to the Mormon-controlled Brigham Young University. One descendent wrote, "It was ironic that BYU was selected as the place to check the authenticity of the remains unearthed by the backhoe. Among other things, BYU supports authenticity of the *Book of Mormon* archaeologically even though it is clearly false, including the statements that the American Indian's ancestors were the "lost tribes" from Israel. If they can't get this straight, how can the BYU archaeologists determine the authenticity of the bodies unearthed?"

Mormon Prophet Gordon B. Hinckley during the dedication

services of the Mormon Church-constructed memorial to "all who died here including the 120 murdered emigrants", said: "...That which we have done here must never be construed as an acknowledgment on the part of the Church of any complicity in the occurrences of that fateful day."[32] This statement is in opposition to J. H. Carleton's (Bvt. Major U. S. A. Captain 1st Dragoons) report of May 25, 1859, of the Mountain Meadows Massacre. Carleton reports that an Indian Chief named Jackson said: "... there were sixty Mormons led by Bishop John D. Lee of Harmony, and a prominent man in the church named Haight who lives at Cedar City. That they were all painted and disguised as Indians, ...and that Lee and Haight led and directed the combined force of Mormons and Indians in the first attack- throughout the siege- and at the last massacre. ...and nobody seemed to question the truth of it, that a train of emigrants of fifty or upwards of men, mostly with families came and encamped at ... Mountain Meadows in Sept. 1857. It was reported in Cedar City and was not, and is not, doubted, even by the Mormons that John D. Lee, Isaac C. Haight, John M. Higby, ...were the leaders who organized a party of fifty or sixty Mormons to attack this train. ...The Mormons say the emigrants fought 'like lions' and that they saw they could not whip them by any fair fighting."[33]

Also, Hinckley in his dedication remarks at the Mountain Meadows Monument (September, 1999), said that Brigham Young was opposed to the Mountain Meadows Massacre. However, according to Carleton's report, Brigham Young had turned the Indians loose upon them (emigrant trains). Jackson, a Pah-Ute chief, says that "orders came down in a letter from Brigham Young that the emigrants were to be killed, and a chief of the Pah-Utes named Touche, now living on the Virgin River, told me that a letter from Brigham Young to the same effect was brought down to the Virgin River Band, by a man named Huntindon (Huntington)."[34]

Concerning the Mountain Meadows Massacre, Quinn writes: "Brigham Young gives unsuccessful order to prevent massacre but becomes accessory after the fact. He later tells participants that he approves of the massacre and lets them know he expects them to exonerate each other in court of law. He publicly intimidates anyone who is inclined to give evidence against Mormon participants. He refuses to give federal authorities information that would implicate nearly all adults of [a] small Mormon community in the massacre and division of victims' property. Then when total denial becomes impossible, Young scapegoats three men through excommunication and arranges for participants to testify against (and jurymen to convict) only John D. Lee, Brigham Young's adopted son and a council of fifty member."[35]

Other activities concerning the Mountain Meadows Massacre include: (1) "August, 1858 Apostle George A. Smith begins conspiracy to obstruct justice in the Mountain Meadows Massacre."[36] (2) "May, 1861 Brigham Young preaches to southern Utah congregation filled with participants in Mountain Meadows Massacre: Pres. Young said that 'the company' that was used up at the Mountain Meadows were the fathers, mothers, bros., sisters and connections of those that murdered the Prophets; *they merit(ed) their fate, and the only thing that ever troubled him was the lives of the women and children, but that under the circumstances could not be avoided.* Although there had been (some) that want(e)d to betray the Brethren into the hands of their Enemies, for that thing [such] will be Dammed & go down to Hell. I would be Glad to see one of those traitors." (emphasis added)[37] (3) "October, 1870 First Presidency and Quorum of Twelve excommunicated the following leaders of Mountain Meadows Massacre: Isaac C. Haight, John D. Lee and George Wood."[38]

There are plenty of convincing documents disputing the Mormon Church media statement "that Hinckley makes it clear that the Mormon Church does not accept responsibility for the massacre." There is no question that Brigham Young's sermons on Blood Atonement, his orders to prepare for a possible war against the U.S. Army troops who were marching toward Utah in 1857, and his stirring up of the Indians to fight alongside the Mormons against the Mericats (non-Mormons) led to the Mountain Meadows Massacre. Readers who are not convinced that Mormon Church officials were responsible for the massacre are urged to read books on the subject listed in the endnotes for Chapter 1.

John D. Lee was tried and executed by a firing squad on March 13, 1877, almost twenty years after the Mountain Meadows Massacre. In his first trial, he was acquitted by the jury, with eight Mormons voting for acquittal and four non-Mormons voting guilty. However, it soon became apparent to the Mormon Church authorities that in order to avoid opening up a whole can of worms and implicating several leaders of the Mormon Church in the massacre, the best way to close the matter was to fix the responsibility of the killing of innocent men, women and children upon Lee. Having from church members the obedience and blind loyalty for priesthood authority, it was easy for Brigham Young to protect several church leaders and Mormon militia members from being indicted for this crime. Railroading Lee as the scapegoat for all of the others was very convenient for Young in removing the Mountain Meadows Massacre matter from the public eye and laying it to rest...church authorities simply told the Mormon jury members to vote for conviction, and it was done.

In Lee's first trial, obtaining Mormons to testify against other Mormons, and especially against Lee, was very difficult. However, in the second trial several Mormons came forward with their testimony, saying that Lee was totally responsible for the massacre. It has been said that Brigham Young himself ordered the Mormons to testify against Lee. According to Brooks, "the tone (of the second trial) was changed, the whole approach of the prosecution different ...an agreement with District Attorney Howard whereby Lee might be convicted and pay the death penalty if the charges against all other suspected persons would be withdrawn. This was to be done by a jury composed only of Mormons, who would bring in a verdict of guilty' if names of other participants were left out of the discussions."[39]

No doubt, District Attorney Howard was relieved that Mormons would now cooperate in bringing in a conviction against Lee since he had discovered in the previous trial that it almost impossible to obtain any testimony from Mormons. Now that church leaders were helping him to obtain a conviction against Lee who obviously was involved in this hideous crime, why not accept the cooperation that had previously eluded the prosecution. It was obvious to Howard that he could not obtain conviction for the other suspects anyway, as long as the Mormons were keeping a tight lip concerning the massacre. And as many prosecutors before him and long since after have learned: a bird in the hand is worth several in the bush.

And so it was, the second trial began on September 14, 1876, and ended on September 20, 1876. After a three and one-half hour deliberation by the all-Mormon jury, Lee was convicted. The railroading of Lee was now complete. The protection of the many other Mormons involved in the massacre was accomplished. And the church leadership has continued to cover up the truth even to this day concerning the tragedy by telling Mormon Church members that

John Doyle Lee was totally responsible, describing him as: "a zealous (fanatic) Mormon ... a rogue major in the Mormon militia."[40]

Mormon Church authorities have also shielded Brigham Young from any involvement in the Mountain Meadows Massacre. While there is no evidence that Young gave any direct orders for the massacre, it is known that Indian leaders from southern Utah made the long journey of over 300 miles to meet with Young in Salt Lake City a few days before the attack. Young described the Indians as hell bent on assisting the Mormons in the "Mormon War" against the United States, and he called them (Indians) "the battle ax of the Lord." After this meeting with Young, the Indians rushed back to harass the Fancher train as it journeyed to and through Cedar City, Utah. Since the big chief (Young) wanted them to help with the "Mormon War," they felt that the Fancher train was a good place to start. The fine herds of cattle, the excellent wagons and the fine clothes would be good rewards for the Indians' getting rid of the Mericats for the big Mormon chief.

At this time in 1857, the Mormons were being threatened by a detachment of American soldiers sent by President Buchanan to bring the Mormons into line from their much too independent stance. Brigham Young didn't foresee that this possible conflict with the United States government would be resolved peacefully. Therefore, he welcomed any assistance that the Indians could give him against the American "invaders." While Young was directly responsible for releasing the Indians to harass the emigrants, it cannot be said that he anticipated they would be involved with the Mormons in massacring the entire Faucher train. (There is some evidence that the Indians did not participate in the Mountain Meadows Massacre at all!) *(The Salt Lake Tribune,* January 21, 2001) It is also possible that Young did not anticipate that Cedar City Mormon Church authorities would commit this massacre.

The Civil War, however, caused the attention of the U. S. government to be changed from the Mormons in Utah, including the Mountain Meadows Massacre and to be focused upon the war between the Northern and Southern states. In fact, Abraham Lincoln said in effect that we have a war to fight and as long as the Mormons aren't a problem in conducting this war, leave them alone. When the war was over, the attention of the United States government again focused upon "foreign relations," and the territories became of greater importance. This was especially so concerning the State of

Deseret, parts of which were later divided to be the present day states of Idaho, Wyoming, Arizona, Nevada and California.

Readers who wish to learn more about the Mormon Church involvement in the Mountain Meadows Massacre are urged to read Juanita Brooks' book, *The Mountain Meadows Massacre* and Jerald and Sandra Tanner's account of the history and cover-up of the affair in *Mormonism, Shadow or Reality*.

Danites

The Danites, a secret organization, was a special protective police force for Mormon Church authorities. It protected the Mormon religion by removing enemies of the church by violent means and was under direct control and command of the President/Prophet. This clandestine organization began under Joseph Smith in response to attacks upon Mormons by non-Mormons, including such actions as destroying their property and even more violent acts against them.

John D. Lee, who served in several leadership capacities, was a Danite. He was assigned the responsibility for guarding Brigham Young and writes: "If any Danite was caught in a scrape, it was the duty of the rest to unite and swear him out. It was shown that the Gentiles had no right to administer an oath. The Danites might swear a house full of lies to save one of the brethren.

"Whatever the Danites were ordered to do, they were to do and ask no questions. Whether it was right or wrong mattered not to them, they were responsible only to their leaders, amenable only to God. I was among them into [to keep] the secret of all they did."[41]

In his book, Lee describes one instance of the Danites' causing a man to get drunk, digging a grave, putting him in the grave, then giving him another drink of liquor. While he was drinking, they hit him over the head, tightened a cord around his neck until he died, covered his body with dirt and covered up any evidence with a hill of corn. In another case, according to Lee, the Danites took a man out in a boat, hit him over the head, tied a rope around his neck attached to stone and threw him into the Mississippi River. Lee related other instances of atrocities committed by the Danites in the name of the church.[42]

According to Lee, Brigham Young set the tone for the Danites, when he said: "I swear by the eternal Heavens and all good

Mormons will do the same, that I have unsheathed my sword and will never return it until the blood of the Prophet Joseph, and Hyrum (brother of Joseph Smith), and those who were slain in Missouri, is avenged. This whole nation is guilty of shedding their blood, by assenting to the deed and holding its peace."[43]

Lee said that anyone who passed through their endowments in the Temple were under obligation to get revenge for the killing of the Prophet and were to teach their children to do the same.[44]

Another prominent Danite who served both Joseph Smith and Brigham Young was William A. Hickman. Hickman told Mosiah Lyman Hancock, a loyal Mormon, that Brigham Young instructed him to "kill Gentiles and take their property for the good of the Church," but Young later denies this to Hancock.[45] According to Quinn, Hickman did kill men at the request of Brigham Young as the March 5, 1853, LDS church office records the death of Luke Hatch, whom Bill Hickman ambushed in 'Big Field'.[46] Hickman later published a book describing his experiences in killing several men who Young wanted "used up." In this book, Hickman also described how he became disenchanted with Young, especially with the church leader for not being fair with him in paying his expenses for working for him.[47] In 1868 William A. Hickman was excommunicated from the Mormon Church after he tried to extort money from Brigham Young by threatening to publish Young's crimes.[48]

Polygamy

Mormons believe that the natural order of things is a patriarchy and that men are the ones primarily responsible for the administration of the universal order. A woman's role is to bear children and provide support for the administration of this order. Since women do not lead, but follow, they must be connected to a man through an official church "sealing ceremony." This allows them to be eligible for the highest degree of glory and exaltation, where they can give birth to their own "spirit children." In the early church, it has been said, while not true, the number of women exceeded the number of men. Joseph Smith, Brigham Young and many others used this as an excuse to take plural wives until the U.S. federal government banned the practice.

While polygamy became the "whipping boy" for the increased scrutiny of the United States government over the Mormon controlled territory, the fear of Mormons creating their own Zion and Kingdom of God was the real culprit that caused greater governmental territorial control. While there were several events that focused attention of the American people on polygamy, probably the most important was the case of Ann Eliza Webb Dee, inaccurately called the twenty-seventh wife of Brigham Young. This beautiful young widow resisted 65-year-old Young's marriage proposals for two years before finally succumbing after he threatened to excommunicate her brother Gilbert from the Mormon Church unless she married him. Young had contracted with her brother, Gilbert Webb to furnish telegraph poles to complete a communication line from Salt Lake City to Denver and to Montana. Gilbert was devastated by the possibility of Young's excommunicating him from the church, and to save her brother, she finally consented to his proposal.[49]

The marriage was a stormy one with Ann Eliza being opposed by many of Young's other wives and ended with Ann Eliza taking refuge in a Salt Lake City hotel. Being protected by a non-Mormon lawyer, she filed for divorce against Young. Young, in his defense, claimed that the celestial marriage through the Mormon Church was not a legal marriage, and therefore, he was not married to her at all. (Note: To a non-Mormon, this defense by Young seems strange indeed, especially since Young was the President and Prophet of the Mormon Church which holds the temple marriage as sacred and eternal.) Eventually Ann Eliza "escaped" from Salt Lake City and Utah by being secreted out by stagecoach to Wyoming and by train to St. Louis, where she began a series of lectures criticizing the Mormon Church. Her father, Chauncey Webb, who supported Ann Eliza, was excommunicated from the church. Young used the excuse that Webb, who had been a loyal Mormon, was apostatizing from the doctrine of the Church of Jesus Christ of Latter-Day Saints.[50]

Ann Eliza called Mormonism a "false religion,"[51] and in one of many of her lectures said: "It may seem strange to you that I, once a member of the Mormon Church, can characterize its leaders and usages so severely. But who could have a better right or cause than one whose entire early life was dwarfed and warped by its teachings; whose later life was embittered and blighted by its practices and who yet experiences the horror of the nightmare which rests upon the soul?... I had known no other faith and had been taught that this was heaven's last bet. I had no other standard to comparison. I dared not question. The system must be right, and my doubts arose, I must be wrong. With the spread of Gentile influences came other standards of religion. That was the time of doubt and vacillation of struggle and agony, and finally of triumph. And now, should I love the religion which tortured and enslaved me? As well expect the prisoner to love his cell and the captive to hug his chain. At last I am *free!* My bondage is of the past, and I rejoice in my deliverance. I see the false system as it is, and loathe it in all its enormities, and expect to loathe it more and more while I live. I see others in its thralldom and the public looking on in indifference, and consecrate myself to the work of exposing the cheat, and scattering the apathy, and delivering, as far as my example and voice may, those who linger in the embrace of death."[52]

John D. Lee describes Joseph Smith's leadership in the development of the principle of polygamy as follows: "During the winters Joseph the Prophet set a man by the name of Sidney Hay Jacobs to select from the Bible such scriptures as pertained to polygamy and celestial marriage to write it in pamphlet form. This he did as a feeler among the people to pave the way for celestial marriage...it met with opposition, although a few favored it.

"The excitement among the people became so great that the subject was laid before the Prophet. Not one was more opposed to it than was his brother Hyrum, who condemned it as from beneath. Joseph saw that it would break up the church should he sanction it, so he denounced the pamphlet through the Wasp, a newspaper published at Nauvoo, as a bundle of nonsense and trash. He said that if he had known its contents he would never have permitted it be published." (The evidence is clear that at this time Smith was practicing polygamy and had several celestial marriages performed for him.)

John Lee went on to write: "The Prophet Joseph anxiously desired polygamy, but he dared not to proclaim it, so it was taught confidentially to such as were strong enough in the faith to take the forward step. About the same time the doctrine of sealing for an eternal state was introduced." John D. Lee wrote that by 1847, he was sealed to his eleventh wife in Council Bluffs, Iowa, [and] in 1856 to his sixteenth wife. Brigham gave him his eighteenth wife in 1859, after which he was the father of sixty children, ten of which died, with fifty-six still alive as he was writing this book."[53] As related earlier, Lee was executed on March 23, 1877, for his role in the Mountain Meadows Massacre.

Scott wrote: "In addition, Joseph Fielding Smith, a former

President of the Mormon Church, in his book, *Blood Atonement and the Origin of Plural Marriage,* quoted an affidavit which verified that not only did Joseph have plural wives, but that he 'cohabited with them as wives'. Worst of all was that Joseph Smith married women who were married to other men, besides committing adultery himself, he used his power and influence as a supposed prophet to coerce married women to join him in sin."[54]

Scott, a Mormon apostate added: "Some Mormon Apologists shrug off polygamy by claiming, as I did, that less than 3 percent of the Mormon men ever practiced polygamy. But others, like T. Edgar Lyon have admitted that the real figure might have been as high as 10 percent.[55] Non-Mormons have estimated an accurate figure to be as much as 20 percent. A standard explanation of the necessity for polygamy is that there were many more women than men in the early church and that plural marriage was a good way to absorb the surplus women of the population. I grew up thinking that polygamous men married old or homely women just to give them a home and (if they weren't past childbearing age) a family. But John A. Witsoe, a Mormon writer affirmed that 'there seems always to have been more males than females in the church."[56]

Quinn confirms Witsoe's statement. He reported that in 1871 every national census listed more males than females in Mormon populations and that the 20-40 percent of Mormons that had several wives demographically required bachelorhood in Utah's majority population of males.[57] This would also support the contention by one of Brigham Young's sons, Seymour B. Young, who observed that there was a prostitution house on every corner in Salt Lake City in 1871.[58]

It is said that Brigham Young had as many as 70 wives sealed to him, although probably fewer than 30 had conjugal relations with him. Since Mormon polygamous marriages were often not recorded, it is difficult to establish anything but an approximate number of such marriages in Young's time. Probably 20 to 30 percent of the Mormons had more than one wife before polygamy was officially abolished by the church leadership (in order to gain statehood in 1896). The granting of wives to church members was in the hands of Brigham Young, but he undoubtedly delegated some of this responsibility to other church authorities.

There are many instances of unhappiness and conflict in the polygamist households, including jealousies among the wives and

among the children. One obvious problem of a polygamist husband
(for example, John D. Lee with 56 children) would be not only to
remember all of their names, but to provide for or give them any real
sense of love and attention. And as one can imagine, the relationships and the family names given to children would be very confus-
ing. Was the boy born to eighth wife Poly Ann Workman called John
D. Poly Ann Workman Lee, Jr. and the girl born to eighteenth wife
Teresa Morse called Alice Teresa Morse Lee?

Ex-Mormons

As can be imagined, the Mormon Church throughout its history
has been plagued with disagreement and apostasy. Joseph Smith was
able to build the church and hold it together by timely "revelations."
As stated earlier, when it appeared that the *Book of Mormon* could
not be published, he "received a revelation from God" threatening
death to Martin Harris that God would kill him if he did not pay for
the first printing. When he was threatened by his wife Emma, concerning his polygamous relations with younger girls and women,
Smith "received a revelation from God" threatening harm from God
if she (Emma) did not become a good wife and accept Smith's other
wives. As a reward for this acceptance, He (God) would make her
the "Executive Lady" of the church.

Brigham Young, who did not have the imagination that Joseph
Smith had to invent revelations, took a different approach, such as
"excommunication from the church for apostasy." Present day
Mormons have learned that in order to prevent excommunication
from the Mormon Church one must never do anything that would
oppose the doctrines of the church or the teachings of church authorities.

As has been previously stated, the General Authorities expect
Mormon Church members to be obedient to church teachings and
doctrines, as the following statement illustrates:

"When our leaders speak, the thinking has been done. When they
propose a plan—it is God's plan. When they point the way, there is
no other way that is safe. When they give direction, it should mark
the end of controversy."[59]

"...learn to do as you are told, both old and young; learn to do as
you are told .... None of your business whether it is right or wrong."[60]

Apostates who did not agree with the doctrine and control of church authorities included Elias L. I Harrison, William Godbe and others associated with the *Utah Magazine* in the 1860-70s. The *Utah Magazine* promoted reform within the Mormon Church which met with great opposition from Brigham Young. Concerning this, Taves writes:

"Of the problems facing the church in the post-Civil War years, we shall begin with that posed by several Mormon intellectuals and relative sophisticates, men (and at least one woman) more in tune with the outside, contemporary world of ideas and thinking than their brothers and sisters. These were church members who liked to think for themselves and who became increasingly uneasy about accepting the absolute authority imposed upon them by their church. Two of these men were Elias L. T. Harrison and William Godbe, both British converts."[61]

Elias Harrison wrote in his *Utah Magazine:*

"There is one fatal error which possessed the minds of some... that God Almighty intended the priesthood to do our thinking...our own opinion is that, when we invite men to use free speech and free thought to get into the Church, we should not call upon them, or ourselves, to kick down the ladder by which they and we ascended to Mormonism. They should be called upon to think on as before, no matter who has or has not thought in the same direction... Think freely, and think forever and, above all, never fear that the 'Ark' of everlasting truth can ever be 'steadied' by mortal hand or shaken."[62]

When Brigham Young was shown the article that contained the above quote, he was furious and sent the following message to Elias Harrison and others involved with the *Utah Magazine:*

"Dear Brother: I hereby inform you that a motion was made, seconded, and carried by a unanimous vote of the School of the Prophets today, that you be disfellowshipped from the Church until you appear in the School and give satisfactory reasons for your irregular attendance there."[63]

Harrison and others responded by refusing to give up the "liberties of thought and speech to which the gospel entitles us..."[64]

Harrison and the others involved with the *Utah Magazine* were excommunicated from the church. The Mormon Church hierarchy of today still maintains the authority of the priesthood as it did in the days of Brigham Young. This is illustrated in a statement by Elder Bruce R. McConkie on October 7, 1987:

"On every issue it behooves us to determine what the Lord

would have us do and what counsel He has given through the appointed officers of His kingdom on earth.

"No true Latter-Day Saint will ever take a stand that is in opposition to what the Lord has revealed to those who direct the affairs of His earthly kingdom. No Latter-Day Saint who is true and faithful in all things will ever pursue a course or espouse a cause, publish an article or book that weakens or destroys the faith."[65]

Mormon Church authorities from their very beginnings have ruled with an iron fist, beginning with Joseph Smith in the 1830s, by making the rules that were enforced with unbending loyalty by the Prophet's Quorum of Twelve and all the General Authorities. This organizational structure of the authorities (which Sonia Johnson describes as the **Old Boys' Club**) carries through to the present time, as is most eloquently reinforced and confirmed in her book, *From Housewife to Heretic,* which describes her excommunication from the church for her activities in support of the Equal Rights Amendment to the United States Constitution. While Johnson's work, manifested through speeches and organizational activities in support of the Equal Rights Amendment, led to her excommunication, the reasons given by the church for this excommunication were generally due to doctrinal practices and beliefs. These included: (1) "encouraging members not to follow the leadership and teachings of the authorities (appointed leaders of the church), (2) encouraging people not to take the counsel of the President of the church seriously and (3) that she did not believe that God has set up His work upon the earth in the way the church teaches."

On the third charge as grounds for excommunication, Johnson writes: "This obviously means that I do not believe in patriarchy. It means also that my repentance was not acceptable because they needed evidence to oust me before more Mormon women started thinking they could oppose the Brethren openly with impunity. Why didn't the men who wrote the press release have the courage to come right out and say, 'You are excommunicated because you do not believe in the divinity of male supremacy?' Because, I think, none of the leaders of the church want widely understood either outside or inside the church that it is necessary to believe in the rule of men in order to be a member of the Mormon Church. ...The church, while beating its PR drums across the land in support of equality, might find it awkward to explain why, if they believe in equality, they are excommunicating people who will not accept males as God's only divinely chosen rulers."[66]

Johnson's husband Rick made the following comment to his wife: "I'm ashamed of men; I'm ashamed of us all ... We're all bastards, Sonia. All of us. Do you know what they tried to do as they were leaving tonight? [The leaders from Sonia's Mormon Church ward who were delivering a message to her from the church bishop about her excommunication trial.] 'You know, Rick, we men in the priesthood have to stick together,' the implication being against the women. Can you imagine? They tried to buddy-buddy me; they tried to turn me against you! ... I'm ashamed of what I witnessed in that room tonight. I'm ashamed of what happened in the kitchen on their way out. You're right, you know. Men do hate women. They're afraid of women. I saw it."[67]

Johnson described one of the Mormon men guarding the church where her trial for excommunication was held as an "Avenging Angel." This Avenging Angel was an FBI agent, as so many Mormon men are. Many Mormon men work for other governmental agencies such as the Secret Service and the CIA. As stated earlier, they are in these agencies in large numbers, much greater than their proportion to the general population.

Johnson's excommunication trial was held in the Mormon Church Sterling Park Ward meeting house which she describes as "'suburban tacky,' the tasteless sort of building the church is now erecting everywhere. Except for the spire, it could be a ranch-style office building. Rapidly disappearing are the church's truly lovely and distinctive buildings, such as the Logan First Ward meetinghouse in which I spent so many hours of my youth."[68]

The ward meeting houses in the southern Utah city of St. George reflect the same type of building as described by Johnson. They can be seen by driving not more than ten blocks in any part of the city, all with the same drab architecture, usually brown, contrasting sharply with the individual homes surrounding it. It is true that the church buildings reflect the authoritarian nature of the Mormon Church, allowing little deviation in design, just as there is no deviation from its doctrine that provides little individualism in church affairs by its members.

"Her gentle hands darted beneath my sheet to bless the parts of my body. ...She intoned, 'I wash you that you may be clean from the blood and sins of your generation.' She touched my head ('that your brain may work clearly'), my ears ('that they may hear the word of the Lord'), my mouth and lips, my arms, my breast and 'vitals,' my loins ('that you may be fruitful in propagating of a goodly seed'), my legs and feet."[69]

Chapter Two
Mormon Doctrine and Beliefs

In the previous chapter, logical and scientific evidence was presented that shows that the *Book of Mormon* was not written by Joseph Smith's using seer stones to translate from the golden plates as he claimed. And court records prove that he had long been using seer stones in an effort to locate buried treasures and was indicted for fraud in a public court for taking money for these services. Also in the previous chapter, evidence was presented revealing that Smith had used over three thousand phrases in his book copied directly from the Bible and had used the book, *The View of the Hebrews*, as a guide for the writing of his manuscript.

Since the *Book of Mormon* has been proven to be false, it is reasonable to assume that the beliefs and doctrines that Smith wrote for the Mormon Church are fraudulent as well and were not received by divine revelations as he claimed. Smith used his keen imagination to write the basic philosophy of the church, including its doctrines and beliefs.

Several of these beliefs and doctrines are summarized as follows:

1. Baptism for the Dead

Baptism for the dead is a ritual invented by Joseph Smith for the purpose of allowing dead people into heaven who did not have the opportunity or who did not take the opportunity to join the Mormon

Church. According to Tanner, "Even though the *Book of Mormon* is supposed to contain the fullness of the gospel, it **never** mentions the doctrine of baptism for the dead, **not even once**. The word 'baptism' appears 25 times in the *Book of Mormon*. The word 'baptize' appears 28 times. The word 'baptized' appears 85 times, and the word 'baptizing appears 6 times, but the doctrine of baptism for the dead isn't even mentioned once."[70] If the Mormon Church claims that the *Book of Mormon* contains the fullness of the gospel, then why are Mormons doing baptisms for the dead when it is not mentioned in the *Book of Mormon*?

As described by Scott, the baptisms were performed in the Mormon temples in a special baptismal font room, "...which held an immense bowl-like metallic font which was supported on the backs of statues of twelve life-sized brass oxen, symbolic of the twelve tribes of Israel. A platform extended along one side of the great bowl..."[71]

Scott, who performed in several baptisms for the dead continues: "...One by one we were called by name to descend into the font. A recorder sat on a high stool, not unlike a lifeguard's stand, at one side of the font, and witnesses watched. An elder stood in the font in garments like ours and beckoned for each participant as his or her turn came. He spoke the baptismal prayer in a hurried, monotonous voice, stopping only to lower a proxy into the water.

"I sat on the platform, looking furtively for the angels I had heard often appeared in temples. When my name was called, I went down into the water. The baptizing elder turned me around so that he could see a large screen, something like an electronic football scoreboard, which he looked at over my shoulder. On top of the screen was my name, and below it a name I don't remember, but which I'll say was Elizabeth Anderson.

"'Sister Celester Latayne Colvett,' he said, looking at the screen, 'having been commissioned of Jesus Christ, I baptize you, for and in behalf of Elizabeth Anderson, who is dead, in the name of the Father, and of the Son, and of the Holy Ghost, Amen.' Then he quickly dropped his right arm from the square and lowered me beneath the water. As I was regaining my footing he had already begun the same prayer, inserting this time the name of another dead woman which had flashed onto the screen behind me. Fifteen consecutive baptisms were performed with me as proxy in a matter of about three minutes. As I left the font, another proxy was preparing to be baptized."[72]

This ceremony is completed in the confirmation room and goes on daily in the temples for thousands of dead ... Millions, probably billions of the dead have been baptized including "deceased presidents of the United States and other prominent persons of the past including Catholic popes and saints...Wilford Woodruff, a President of the Mormon Church during the turn of the century, said that on April 10, 1898, all of the signers of the Declaration of Independence, along with George Washington, appeared to him in the St. George Temple two nights in a row, begging that vicarious ordinance be done for them. Woodruff obliged, and also did the proxy work for Christopher Columbus, John Wesley, and other prominent men of the past, one hundred in all."[73]

Unbelievable? Can one believe that the Mormon Church is credible when a President (Prophet) of the church claimed that he actually talked to George Washington and all of the signers of the Declaration of Independence almost one hundred years after they were dead? Baptism for the dead is one of the most ludicrous and disconcerting practices of the Mormon Church. It has been said that the Mormon Church spends millions of dollars on researching genealogies in order to do proxy work. Scott writes for example "...the LDS church spent over 125 million dollars [in 1975] on genealogical and proxy work, employing over eighty camera crews just to keep up with microfilming the bales of documents which pour in daily."[74]

The majority of the members of the Mormon Church have no idea how their money is spent, since the Church Authorities do not release their budget for perusal and approval by the membership, as do most other churches. So the General Authorities are free to spend the money as they please. No doubt, releasing general budget expenditures would be shocking to outsiders as well as to the members themselves because they are so huge. Later in this book we will discuss the vast holdings of the Mormon Church, including several corporations, as well as innumerable tax-free buildings and temples. Decisions on church expenditures are made by the Presidency, the Quorum of the Twelve Apostles and the Presiding Bishopric.

It would seem to this author, that with all of the ways to use money to enhance the quality of life in the world, such as schools, housing, food and recreation, not only in our country, but in countries through out the world, using vast amounts of money to baptize the dead is wasteful and senseless.

2. Celestial Marriage (Marriage in the Temple for Time and all Eternity)

"In the celestial glory there are three heavens or degrees, and in order to obtain the highest, a man must enter into this order of the priesthood [meaning the new and everlasting covenant of marriage]; if he does not, he cannot obtain it. He may enter into the other, but that is the end of his kingdom; he cannot have an increase." (D&C 131:1-4)

Joseph Smith's imagination invented three main kingdoms of heaven: Celestial, Terrestrial and Telestial. Those who accept the teachings of the Mormon Church and remain faithful reach the Celestial, while those who do not accept Mormon Church teachings while living, but do so after death reach the Terrestrial kingdom. The third kingdom of heaven, the Telestial, is reserved for persons who committed adultery, murder and were social Misfits.[76]

Joseph Smith also imagined that some did not deserve heaven at all including all ex-Mormons, whom he considered enemies of the church.[77] Smith's casting of all ex-Mormons into outer darkness forever should be a clue to Mormon Church members that his writings and work in the church were not of divine nature. Surely a righteous, moral and law abiding person even though he may disagree with the church doctrine, would deserve a better place even in Smith's afterlife.

Laake writes that the only way for a woman to gain entry into the highest level of heaven (Celestial) was that she marry a worthy priesthood holder and be sealed to him in a temple ceremony. "I knew that my success in this life and the next was dependent upon it (marrying a worthy priesthood holder).

The importance of such a marriage was the primary lesson of my Mormon girlhood when it had been repeatedly impressed upon me that if I failed to marry a faithful Mormon man in a ceremony performed in a Mormon temple, I would be denied access to the highest level of Mormon heaven."[78]

Early marriage for Mormon women is encouraged by the authorities of the Mormon Church. This is so ingrained in the minds of young girls that they are constantly on the lookout for "the one".

Laake was so indoctrinated in the idea of early marriage that when she became a sophomore at Brigham Young University, she was embarrassed that she was one of the few girls in her circle who was not wearing an engagement ring. Because of her desperation to find "the one," two of her marriages were failures because she had no real love for her mates. In order to make a decision about marriage to one of her suitors, she asked that he get a revelation from God. When she was told of the revelation from God by her prospective marriage partner, she was stunned to hear, "Well, it wasn't a burning bush or anything, it was a just a good warm feeling that said it was the right thing for us to get married."[79]

"The information paralyzed me. I thought he was telling me the truth, of course. It didn't occur to me that a righteous priesthood holder would use the sacred tradition of revelation toward his own ends."[80] After Laake spent many days praying for her own revelation from God concerning her marriage, she finally concluded: "I'm not feeling anything, except that I seem to be floating in space whenever I talk to God about you. It's a most terrible feeling." To which her fiancé replied, "I know what this is, that's just Satan trying to inter fere with what the Lord wants us to do. Satan is doing that to you."[81]

Laake, because of her strong belief in the Mormon concept of Satan and her respect for her fiancé's position as a priesthood holder believed that Satan was indeed trying to keep her from marrying and asked that her fiancé and her brother come and give a blessing to remove Satan from her. (All priesthood holders, according to doctrine, have the power to bless and heal non-priesthood holders, which includes all Mormon women, boys under the age of eighteen, or males who have not received the priesthood, and all non-Mormons.)

Laake writes: "My dreaded sweetheart and my brother stood on either side of me, pouring a few drops of olive oil onto my head out of a tiny bottle 'consecrated' oil that had been blessed for this purpose and that priesthood holders keep on hand in the medicine cabinet. They laid their hands on my head and with the power of all Mormondom behind them rebuked the devil, commanding him to leave me."[82]

Mormon women are taught that men, through the power of the priesthood, also provide the path for them to communicate with God. Men, who are the priesthood holders, according to doctrine, have mystical powers not given to women, to heal the sick and to remove evil spirits from them. Men have the authority in the home and generally lead all prayer there, lead all church services and others such as funerals, weddings, etc.

With this "power" over women and the family, it is no wonder that there is abuse and supremacy toward women in Mormonism. Authority in the Mormon Church runs from the top down, that is from the Prophet (the President) to the Counselors, the Quorum of Twelve, the Quorum of Seventies, the stake presidents, bishops, priesthood holders and finally to the father of the family. This authoritarian structure is extremely strong, with little room for variation. In a later part of this book, we will discuss the organizational structure of the Mormon Church. Bishops, for example, issue temple recommends, which allow worthy church members to enter the temple. Before the issuance of these temple recommends, bishops ask many personal questions of members to determine their worthiness. Bishops do counseling which often gets into areas for which they have no training. They are not professional people who have extensive education and training in mental health. Deborah Laake, the author of *Secret Ceremonies*, is one example of a Mormon who had been driven to serious mental problems in trying to cope with pressures and some of the questionable doctrines fostered and taught by Mormon General Authorities, bishops and stake presidents. It is surprising that many bishops and other priesthood leaders who have attempted to provide counseling and healing through the laying on of hands, etc., have not more often faced serious legal problems in practicing without a license in psychiatry, healing and counseling. Who knows how many thousands of Mormons have suffered serious emotional problems by being counseled by men lacking professional training.

3. Word of Wisdom

Joseph Smith introduced the Word of Wisdom into the Mormon Church in 1833 that provided for abstaining from tobacco, harmful drugs, coffee and tea. A member who does not follow the Word of Wisdom is not in good standing in the church and cannot enter the temple.[83]

4. The Life Before, Mortal Life, Life Beyond

Mormons believe that in addition to mortal life upon earth as human beings, prior to coming on earth they existed as spirit children of God. These children of God do not remember their premortal life "...since a veil of forgetfulness is placed over their minds" before they have a human life on earth.[84]

Mortal life is the second phase of a Mormon believer's life; it is to gain a physical body and experience. It is a life not only filled with happiness, but also with pain and suffering. A major purpose of mortal life is to prepare oneself for eternal life by living within God's instructions according to the Bible and the *Book of Mormon*. The better that one fulfills God's wishes, the better his life will be in the life beyond. Who defines what God commands? Most of these commands came from the imagination of Joseph Smith. As the Prophet of the church, according to Smith, only he was able to receive revelations from God concerning the organization and doctrine of the church. Today, the President of the Mormon Church, who is the current Prophet, interprets God's commands to members. However, he generally continues the interpretations which Smith had written more than a century and a half ago.

The third component of existence according to Mormon belief is the life beyond mortality, that is, eternity. Mormons are taught to believe that upon dying, one is reborn into immortality which is an eternal life of a finer and more blissful existence.[85]

5. Spirits

As previously indicated, Mormons believe that spirits have three forms in life or existence: (1) pre-existence, (2) in the human body while alive and upon this earth and (3) in life after death. All persons on earth had a pre-existence and will have an after death existence. In order to go to heaven, a pre-existence spirit must enter a human body and live on earth before that can occur. The highest level of heaven is Celestial to which all Mormons aspire. They must perform righteous duties throughout their lives while upon earth to get there. Some of the duties that will lead to the highest level of heaven include: serving on a two-year mission, serving in all callings, i.e., as a ward bishop or other priesthood callings. A woman must marry a worthy priesthood holder in a temple and perform her duties and callings at home and in the church. This is why in the days of polygamy, young girls often would readily marry an older man as long as he held one of these high offices even if he already had several other wives, since this would assure them a place in the highest level of heaven. Women had no ways of their own to reach heaven except as a servant and had to be sealed to a husband to insure their admittance into the Celestial kingdom. Even today, Mormon women often push their husbands to take on high church positions, temple assignments or other duties, so they may be "pulled through" to higher levels of heaven with their husbands.

Turner adds: "One underlying belief of the Saints is this: They are now living a mortal existence which was preceded by an existence in the spirit world and which will be followed by life in the spirit world. During this mortal life, a person may be able to improve his status in the spirit world, or he may be able to worsen it. Where some Christian sects have a doctrine of pre-ordination, i. e., that all events of a person's life are established in heaven before his birth, the Mormons have a doctrine of 'free agency.' They hold that a soul in its mortal existence is continually confronted with choices and that it is completely free to pick among the alternatives. Thus, the mortal has a chance to better his soul in the spirit world, to enhance his exaltation to the Celestial kingdom which follows life on earth.

"A certain broad code of conduct is set out to govern the Saint in his mortal existence. The sum of this is that he must always strive for betterment."[86]

With the teaching by the leaders of the Mormon Church that pre-existent spirits are waiting for a chance to have a human body, pressure is put on female members to bear children in order to provide these pre-existent spirits with the opportunity to have human bodies in order to fulfill the requirement that they live a mortal life in order to advance into the Celestial kingdom. Utah, with a large majority of Mormons, has the highest birth rate of any state in the nation. According to Mormon theology, woman's primary purpose in life is to bear and raise children. This is partially based upon the need to provide a mortal life for pre-existent spirits. This Mormon concept is deeply rooted in Mormon history as shown by the following that appeared in *M'Clure's Magazine* in 1911 "... unless they come to earth, reborn, these souls are doomed to an eternal life as homeless spirits....Every woman is constantly surrounded by thousands, millions of them, pleading for an opportunity to get into the world."[87]

Spirits waiting to enter mortal existence was another one of Joseph Smith's creations arising from his remarkable imagination. The idea, no doubt, had the ulterior motive of increasing membership in his church by encouraging members to have large families.

This desire of Smith to expand the membership of his church has resulted in great burdens being placed upon young married women, who need this time to gain an education or training for a vocation that would improve their economic positions in life. Instead, they are tied down to bearing and raising more children.

This belief in spirits and emphasis on motherly duties resulting from the Mormon teachings has retarded women in their freedom and advancement. Modern society in the United States has generally accepted the equality of men and women. If a couple wishes to have children, then the male has the same responsibility for rearing the children as the female. Today's woman has as much right to a career as a man, and home responsibilities should be shared. The Equal Rights Amendment (ERA), defeated in 1982, was considered by the leadership of the LDS church as a threat to male control of their church, and they fought vigorously for its defeat. The tactics that the Mormon Church used in this defeat are vividly described in Sonia Johnson's book, *From Housewife to Heretic*. Johnson was one member of the Mormon Church, who believed very strongly in the Equal Rights Amendment and was a leader in a national movement to get enough votes to obtain two-thirds majority of the states to insure its passage. As a result of her involvement in this national movement, she was excommunicated from the church.

Laake made an observation that illustrated the great hardship that young women endured by following church doctrine of early marriage and large families: "As I cut across Center Street (Provo, Utah) [Brigham Young University], again and again into rows of old, dark, brick houses, I was startled that even in the unsparing light of Provo's sunniest season, the neighborhoods were dingy. The houses were very small—just one story and a full basement—and appeared unfinished and half sunken. Some of them also had whole conventions of weeds sprouting in the yards. The entire scene bespoke neglect and a mild desperation that I couldn't fathom at first in this town that was about strong religious hearts finding their true courses. And then when a young Mormon woman surfaced out of the basement apartment of one of the houses, clutching her baby, I realized that this was a neighborhood of married students, whom I knew to be impoverished creatures.

"Every day hordes of women like this one—wives—hiked onto campus with their babies on their hips. They streamed into the student center, plopped their children into booster chairs and shared

between-classes burgers with their husbands. They were part of the
college landscape of young women with bright, lipsticked mouths
and long eyelashes and pressed dresses. As I passed them on the
sidewalks, where they often stood holding their husband's hands
before the men dashed back to classes, I believed that they led perfect lives. Yet this woman, the woman who was climbing out of the
stairwell that led to her apartment was not thinking about true love.

"She was a couple of years older than I, with blond, unstyled hair
and a slight figure that had gone slack in the middle with either an
early pregnancy or the remnants of her last one. She was wearing a
pair of old-looking cotton pants and a shapeless shirt in an artificial
green that would have looked characteristic only on a matron. Her
remarkably pretty face was not only pale with exhaustion but was as
unadorned as though it had just been whipped clean in the shower...

... "As though it took all of her strength, she was completely
absorbed in trying to get herself up the stairs with the baby and dia-
per bag ... I saw that marriage could be deadening.

"Was this the paradise of married life, the exalted dream of every
Mormon girl?"[88]

And the author believes that still today Mormon leaders perpetuate false doctrine that makes marriage a drudge for young families
and too often pushes promising young people into lives of poverty.
Marriage should be a happy experience, one in which the partners
are able to plan their families and postpone child bearing until their
incomes can provide properly for them.

Married couples, alone, should make decisions about when they
will have children. Spirits waiting for mortal life as a basis for large
families, is another fabrication by Joseph Smith, and has no logical
or scientific basis, and is certainly not in the best interest of our
country's social or economic welfare.

Apparently the church authorities have received much criticism
for encouraging large families and have recently modified this doctrine of the Mormon Church. This change recently reported in The
Salt Lake Tribune includes the following: "...sexual relations within
marriage are 'divinely approved' even if procreation isn't the aim ...
The decision as to how many children to have and when to have
them is extremely intimate and private and should be left between
the couple and the Lord. Church members should not judge one
another in this matter."[89]

The article in *The Salt Lake Tribune* further reports on the new

Church Handbook of instructions for bishoprics and stake presidencies that a "two paragraph entry on birth control marks a significant break from a past in which Mormons practiced polygamy for more than 50 years, with some men fathering dozens of offspring, and in this century large families have become a trademark of faith. ...With unusual candor, the new handbook makes clear that sex is an important ingredient of happy marriages. The handbook states: 'Married couples also should understand that sexual relations within marriage are divinely approved not only for the purpose of procreation, but also as a means of expressing love and strengthening emotional and spiritual bonds between husband and wife.' ...The Mormon Church's position on birth control today appears to reflect the prevailing attitude in America as portrayed in a 1995 National Survey of Family Growth conducted by a branch of the government's national center for health statistics as follows:

"Of 20,378 pregnancies charted nationally, 80.5 percent of the mothers had used birth control sometime before conception. That percentage was exactly the same for the 520 pregnancies of Mormon mothers in the survey", said BYU sociologist Tim Heaton. "...Though modern Mormons are having fewer children than their parents, they remain far more prolific than the nation as a whole.

"...From 1990 through 1997, the national birth rate has declined steadily from 16.7 births per 1,000 population to 14.6 births. In Utah, where more than 70 percent of the population is Mormon, the 21.0 birth rate last year was 44 percent higher than the national average."[90]

6. Sacred Undergarments

Sacred undergarments are worn by all Mormons, male and female, who have received recommends to enter temples and have been endowed there. These garments, white in color, have markings of a compass and a square on the left and right breasts and one mark embroidered over the navel and a mark over the right knee. These are Masonic markings copied by Joseph Smith who initiated the idea of the garments. They are to be worn 24 hours a day throughout life, supposedly since they protect the wearer from Satan and harm. Laake tells about one of her embarrassing moments with "the garment." "That night the other girls and I lined up on the tile ledge surrounding the whirlpool. ...One of the attendants, a girl with black hair to her waist and legs like a Barbie doll's was shoving hairpins into her ponytail in order to get it off her neck. Then she stepped out of her blue slacks and the other girls all followed suit, tugging at their pants or kicking their way out of them until they were a wall of bare young legs forming a complete ring around me. The girls pulled their shirts over their heads. Wielding spitting hoses, they stood hip to hip in their bras and panties, squealing and with their eyes gleaming, wordlessly ready for the water fight of their lives.

"I couldn't see a way out of it. While my co-workers waited, I very slowly pulled my own slacks down to the floor and stood revealed in the baggy, knee-length lower half of my garments. In the back, I could feel them flapping open at the crotch and exposing my buttock to the fetid air. In the front, they parted so that the other girls could see my pubic hair.

"What are those?" somebody asked into a moment of sudden silence.

"They're my underwear, I mumbled ...I broke out of the circle and fled into a dressing booth, where I sat on the narrow bench, my heart pounding. ...I stayed there, very still, as the shrill sounds of the water fight gathered force, until the sounds died out altogether and I heard the girls chattering, emptying out the dressing rooms. Finally the lights went out and yet I continued to sit alone in the dark, too humiliated to move.

"I never went back to the spa again, except to get my check. It wasn't just that I didn't want to face the other girls. It was that I couldn't feel I belonged there with them, since they hadn't yet thrown away their lives."[91]

The garments pose many problems for those who wear them. For one, Mormons have been so indoctrinated in the importance of wearing them at all times except in special situations, decisions as to when not to wear them are unnerving. Secondly, they are ugly for fashion-minded women, since fashion clothes often are incompatible with the garments. And for Mormons who leave the church, the greatest joy often is getting rid of the garments. Laake was finally able to get rid of her garments and writes: "I was very frightened on the day I finally relegated my garments to the past in a ceremony of prayer and voodoo that I hoped would appease any heavenly onlookers. — I gathered them into a soft pile and carried them out onto the little concrete porch that adjoined my apartment. I mounded them together on the concrete and crouched down beside them, clutching a pair of scissors and a book of matches."[92]

After burning the garments Laake writes: "It was over, and I was more elated than I could have imagined. My heart and loins pulsed with a thrill of danger that was almost sexual, but I also felt utterly helpless and unprotected, as though I were a soft, stripped sapling an inch thick that could be snapped in two by someone's hands. That sensation of vulnerability would last for years."[93]

Another young Mormon woman who had received her endowment and had to wear her garment was in tears when she said that her garment was uncomfortable and hid her breasts, as it was necessary to put her brassiere over them.[94]

While still another young Mormon woman's marriage ended in divorce when her husband insisted on keeping garments on at all times.[95] Some Mormons do not remove them ever, although removal is allowed on certain occasions, as when swimming or in some sports, etc.

Sacred garments are worn after a person has received his or her first temple "endowments." During this ceremony, a person is given a "new name," is taught the story of the creation of the world (from the Mormon perspective), makes vows promising to live according to the Mormon Church's requirements, learns how he or she can enter the Celestial kingdom, and is given instruction in Mormon doctrine. The garments are to be worn under one's clothing at all times, except during times (to be determined by the member's own prayerful discretion) where the garments would be exposed to nonmembers as in the armed forces or would hinder a worthwhile activity. Some examples whereby garments can be removed are bathing, activities such as swimming and for visits to the doctor's office or hospital, where they could easily be seen by nonmembers. The temple workers explain that there are other situations where the garments may temporarily be removed, subject to the wearer's judgment, but that the garments are a source of both spiritual and physical protection and should be worn continuously.

The garments look somewhat like short versions of "Long John" underwear. The men's garments have a top with short sleeves and a neckline that is a bit more "scooped" than a typical man's T-shirt. The bottoms reach to just above the knees. Women's garments are similar except there is a choice of different necklines (scooped, V, or square), and the sleeves are shorter than the men's, sort of like "cap sleeves." The bottoms also reach to just above the knees. Both men's and women's come in either one-piece or two-piece styles, and in a variety of fabric weights and blends, such as nylon, cotton, and cotton/poly. Members are informed that they are not to cut, sew or alter the garments in any way. For example, they cannot be shortened, pinned up or rolled up to allow for wearing a shorter dress or pair of shorts.

7. Temple Recommend

Temple recommends, which worthy Mormons may receive from their bishops, and are also signed by their stake presidents, are mandatory for admittance into the Mormon temple. As stated before, endowment ceremonies, marriages, baptism for the dead and other sealing ceremonies are performed in the temple. "The 'temple recommend' is a cherished slip of paper which gives its holder the right to enter the temple and participate in its ceremonies, including marriage. Mormons 'pass stringent demands of dietary laws, tithing, sexual orthodoxy and others requirements for a 'temple recommend'. These recommends are printed forms which, when filled out by the bishop, provide a copy for the church headquarters files, one copy for the ward's records and a third for the holder to present at entrance of a temple for admission.

"Since the church believes that one must be 'temple worthy' in order to attain the Celestial kingdom, having the power to grant or withhold recommends gives the local bishops immense power. Furthermore, in predominantly Mormon areas the lack of a recommend can often mean the loss of a job or being shunned by one's neighbors. These slips of paper are most valuable."[96]

It is possible to "borrow" someone else's temple recommend and gain entry into the temple, as well as to forge one. However, only a very daring individual would attempt to enter the temple without his own official temple recommend. Laake, for example, indicates that she knew of only one person who entered the temple without his own temple recommend.

In applying for the temple recommend a Mormon must be interviewed by his/her bishop (or the bishop's first or second counselor) and is asked such questions as:

(1)   Do you attend meetings?
(2)   Are you a full tithe payer?
(3)   Do you support your church leaders?

(4) Do you avoid tobacco, alcohol, coffee and tea?

(5) Are you morally clean?

(6) Do you wear the sacred garments?

(7) Do you keep the Word of Wisdom?

(8) Have you ever been divorced?

(9) Will you regularly attend church including sacrament, priesthood and other meetings?[97]

(10) Will you follow the church rules and doctrines?[98]

(11) Are you involved with, or have sympathy for any apostate groups?[99]

8. Priesthood

The priesthood is the life and soul of the Mormon Church and as such establishes the authority for and control of Mormonism. This was the most important invention that came out of the superior imagination of the church's founder, Joseph Smith. By creating the priesthood, Joseph Smith was able to provide a framework from which the church would grow and also prevent defectors. Within this organization is a system that provides constant vigilance upon members to pressure them to remain in the church. It is not unlike the Communist spying system which held the Russian and surrounding smaller nations' peoples under the Communist dictatorship of the Proletariat for almost a century, only to be broken when Mikhail Gorbachev destroyed the spying system in his attempt to democratize the Communist Party.

The priesthood includes the top leaders of the church called General Authorities, district leaders, stake presidents, bishops and all worthy male church members. According to Scott: "All authority in the Mormon Church comes directly from the top; that is, the Prophet who expects (and generally gets) obedience to his edicts. Much of the high leadership of the church has for its 150 years of existence been in the hands of about twenty families—the Smiths, Romneys, Kimballs, Cannons, Richards, Bensons and others.

"These leaders, along with all other priesthood authorities in the church are regularly 'sustained' by their followers. Several times a year Mormons are called on to show a vote of confidence in their leaders by raising their hands in public worship. In ten years as a Mormon, I never saw a hand raised to oppose a single one of my leaders."[100]

Laake writes about the power that the priesthood holder wields:

"...that all Mormon men are 'priesthood holders' anointed with the literal, supernatural, nearly unlimited authority to act for God on earth, and are headed into an eternal life where they will themselves become gods who rule entire worlds. It's a theological concept that, tucked into a brain that's egotistical or unbalanced, is [like] a match to dynamite."[101]

Since all worthy Mormon men are priesthood holders, it is no small wonder that they feel that they have supernatural powers, and as Laake writes: "All men are ordained to the priesthood—a designation that they believe has been passed down to them directly from Christ's apostles, one that endows them with mystical and supernatural powers, such as the ability to perform miraculous healings and exorcism."[102]

9. Second Coming of Christ to rule the Kingdom of God on Earth

The name of the Mormon Church, The Church of Jesus Christ of Latter-Day Saints, portrays the belief that its role is to prepare the earth for the coming of Christ to rule the kingdom on earth. Therefore, as Coates wrote in 1991... "as the years tick off toward A. D. 2000 the Mormon Church emphasizes survivalist with increasing ardor. These are, after all, the Latter Days, the final dispensation before the events foretold in the biblical Book of Revelation are at hand. ...The church's work is to establish the appropriate set of moral, social and political conditions necessary before Jesus Christ can return and usher in the final thousand years."[103] Happily, the year 2000 arrived with no fulfillment of the Mormon Church's expectations for a calamity on earth.

The Mormons are taught that prior to the second coming of Christ, there will be a period of upheaval and trauma upon the earth, and to deal with this, survival kits and food storages are homemade, while others may be purchased already made. They include granola bars, nuts, dried fruits, dried meats, small pots, spoons, forks, paper towels, can openers, camp stoves and matches. Tents, blankets, flashlights, candles, first aid kits, aspirins and battery operated radios are also included. In addition, families are urged to keep a bag of several hundred dollars in bills, a quantity of postage stamps, insurance policies, stocks and bonds, deeds, wills, immunization records, LDS documents, genealogy lists, lines of priesthood authority and pedigrees. [104]

Some Mormons even go as far in their preparations for this day that they actually practice an imaginary disaster drill and find their "72-hour kit" is too heavy and cannot be moved.

This is another creation emanating from the fantasy of Joseph Smith, the founder of the Mormon Church who had at one time predicted that End-times would occur within his lifetime, sometime around the 1880s. Smith's prediction, like many other beliefs of the Mormon Church, is based upon faulty thinking and reasoning. While it is probably true that such catastrophes as a nuclear war, a large comet striking the earth or global warming could greatly alter the way of life, none of these is very likely to destroy all human life. It is an illusion practiced by cult-religions that has no scientific or rational basis. Scientists have estimated that the sun will burn up to the point that in four billion years the earth will not be able to sustain life. However, it is much too early to prepare a "72-hour kit" for this event which will occur millions of generations into the future.

10. Temple Ceremonies

The temple ceremonies were largely copied from the Masonic Lodge by Joseph Smith. Scott writes that "Any Mason who reads even such an abbreviated account of the temple ceremony as I have outlined will be amazed at the similarities between temple ordinances and Masonic Lodge ordinances. Joseph Smith claimed that he got much of the substance of the temple ceremony from the Book of Abraham papyri. The truth is that Joseph Smith was himself a Mason of the sublimest degree."[105] The Masonic lodge resents the use of Masonic symbols in Mormon temple ceremonies, so much so that the Grand Lodge of Utah (1979) has refused initiation to known Mormons and denied admission to any Mormon Mason who was initiated in any other state.[106]

The pilfering of the temple ceremonies from the Masonic Lodge discredits the claim of the church hierarchy that the Mormon Church is divine. The Masonic Lodge, whose rites include memorizing long statements which are recited in the induction ceremonies, and if one ever reveals any of the secrets of the ceremonies he has received within the lodge, he is to have his throat slit and bowels cut out of his body. The oath that Masons take "to have my throat slit and bowels cut out of my body if I ever reveal any secrets of the Masonic Lodge" was, until recent times, (1990) a part of the oath of the

Mormon temple ceremonies. If the Mormon Church is the true church established by Joseph Smith from instructions given by God, why was it necessary to copy Masonic rites for Mormon Church ceremonies? If the temple ceremonies were required by God, wouldn't He have provided Smith with revelations of his own to guide him in devising the ceremonies? As has been shown in other parts of this book, many of Smith's writings were counterfeit. One can, therefore, come to the conclusion that the temple ceremonies are fake.

The Mormon temple rites are secret, but as Laake writes: "Although the most significant rituals of Mormonism go on within its temples, and although the *Book of Mormon* itself warns against secrecies in religion, the temple ceremonies are, nonetheless, top secret outside temple walls, lest their sacred strangeness be ridiculed and defiled by non-believers."[107]

It is understandable that a primary purpose of the secrecy of the temple ceremonies is to prevent embarrassment to the Mormon authorities and members from outsiders who would contend that they were strange. Perhaps in the 1840s, the time of Joseph Smith, such ceremonies were necessary to attract members and to hold them together, as this gave them some cohesion. Also in Smith's time, there was no television, no movies and as a result the church was the entertainment center. But today, with the varied choices of entertainment, education, the automobile, travel and other human fulfillment activities, secret ceremonies such as those held in the Masonic Lodge and the Mormon temple seem to be completely outdated. Why is it necessary to have secret ceremonies in the Mormon Church when most other religions are open? Could it be that if the Mormon Church had a policy of openness, too much would be exposed and the religion would die?

Endowment ceremonies with oaths are administered to Mormons in the temple. According to Laake: "These are sacred ordinances and promises that make a person eligible for the highest heaven, and the Mormons partake of them on their own behalf during their first visit to the temple. In the years to come, I would be expected to run through the same ceremony again and again as a proxy for dead ancestors whose names had been discovered through the Mormon pastime of genealogy. (The idea behind the temple is that certain ceremonies, such as baptism and marriage and the 'endowments,' are vital to a person's placement in the hereafter and yet can be performed only on earth. Unless conscientious mortals turn their attention to the graceless states of those who've gone on, scads of wishful spirits will flap around in limbo for eternity.)"[108]

The temple depends on numerous workers, generally volunteers, usually elderly men and women who have time to devote to the temple. In the temple are workers who rent the white costumes for the ceremony, and workers who anoint those who are to receive their endowments with washings and anointing. Most of the presentations in the temple are on video, excepting the Salt Lake temple that still has live actors (Mormons, of course) playing the various parts in the ceremony.

The temple ceremony may last as long as five hours in live sessions. Initiates are first greeted by temple workers and separated into men's and women's locker rooms. They are given temple clothing, and all parts of the body are washed and anointed with oil by the temple worker. Initiates are told that it will clean them from the blood and sins of this generation.

Members are told that they must not reveal what they are told or what takes place in the temple and they must take oaths to that effect. Many feel after completing the ceremony: "Why should they not keep it a secret. If they ever complete the ceremony, they would be too ashamed to tell anyone what they had participated in." Many often feel defiled, ashamed and bewildered while going through the ceremony. Some women who complete the ceremony are embarrassed by the "five points of fellowship" embrace by the male temple worker. One complained that the temple worker held her too close which was embarrassing and much too intimate for a stranger.[109]

Laake describes the washing and anointing ritual that happened on her wedding day as follows: "Her gentle hands darted beneath my sheet to bless the parts of my body. ...She intoned, I wash you that you may be clean from the blood and sins of your generation.' She touched my head ('that your brain may work clearly'), my ears ('that they may hear the word of the Lord'), my mouth and lips, my arms, my breast and genitals,' my loins ('that you may be fruitful in propagating of a goodly seed'), my legs and feet. Her chanting and her cool fingers were both song and dance, and I was caught up calmed. When she had finished the first round she began again, replacing the water with oil from a dropper that anointed me head to toe ... Finally the temple worker leaned to my ear to whisper my 'new name': Sarah.

"...I didn't know what this new name was for, and the conditions attached to it disturbed me. I must reveal it to no one, not ever, except at the one proper moment during today's ceremony, the temple worker told me.

" ... I was coming up now on the only part of this morning that I'd been truly dreading. It was time to climb into my first pair of regulation Mormon underwear, an unlovely wardrobe item that, during their first temple visit, Mormons agree to wear for the rest of their lives and that they refer to ever after as their 'garments,'... One of the purposes of the 'garments' is to make sure that Mormons eschew daring clothing. ...Women's garments were slit in the crotch, very generously, so that they flapped open and left a girl's greatest fascinations exposed ... I was wearing long johns."[110]

Mormons are admonished to wear their garments next to their skin (girls under their bras) as protection from Satan while they complete their work on earth. Both Laake and her mother hated the garments, as they often prevented them from wearing fashion clothes since the garments would keep such clothes from fitting properly. Laake writes: "...I figured that from this moment on I was a freak."[111]

Some of the other ordinances and secrets of the temple include:

(1) Women learning to obey their husbands in all things so long as their husbands obeyed God.

(2) Men receiving a special secret handshake (the first token of the Aaronic Priesthood).

(3) Men receiving the second token of the Aaronic Priesthood and the first and second tokens of the Melchizedek Priesthood with their signs and penalties.

Laake, in her 1972 ceremony (as all Mormons are required to do, when going through the ceremony), was asked to make a sign, "as though we were slitting our throats 'from ear to ear,' to signify the penalty for revealing this handshake to anyone on the outside."[112]

11. Passing through the Veil

Joseph Smith invented the ceremony of passing through the veil. It was to show what he imagined would take place when one dies and enters heaven. Smith created a veil which was like secret huge white bed-sheets, with slits in them large enough to put hands through for testing the knowledge of signs by veil workers on the other side, representing the Lord. After testing, initiates pass through the "sheets" to the "Celestial room," representing the Celestial kingdom. Part of the ceremony is taking someone through the veil, which signifies entering heaven from earth. During the marriage ceremony when the new bride is "sealed", not only for time (life on earth) but for eternity (life everlasting) to her husband, she is taken through the veil by her future husband. It is ironic that should this sealing of the wife to the husband later result in divorce, the woman often cannot get her temple marriage annulled and remains a wife "for eternity" to her ex-husband even if their marriage for "time" on earth has ended, but the husband can remarry in the temple and have another wife (and another ...) for eternity. And when he enters the Celestial heaven after his death, he will have two or more women sealed to him (depending upon how many divorces he had) thus having polygamous marriages in his Celestial heaven. Women, on the other hand cannot be sealed to more than one man in the Mormon "eternal life".

Laake tells about her temple experience in being taken through the veil by her husband. She writes: "As I moved with the others toward the bed-sheet, we were told that it symbolized the veil that separates this life from the next. ...The person who took his place on the other side of the veil was Monty [her future husband]. It was he who would usher me into heaven. It always happened this way for brides, who unlike the men had made their temple covenants not to God but to their own husbands.""[113]

The temple rituals of Celestial marriage and sealings for young brides often shatter their expectations of an enjoyable experience. Many young Mormons joke about the ceremonies, wondering what a secret handshake or wearing the "garment" has to do with eternal marriage. Laake writes: — The mysteries of the world were fraternity rituals (Temple Celestial marriage ceremonies). A wild bewildered giggle was forming in my throat.

"What in the world was everyone doing? Did all the whitesuited glorifiers in the room unquestioningly accept a ritual of nutty gestures from the pseudo-occult as a sacrament?

"These were the first moments when I viewed Mormonism with suspicion...[114]

12. Tithing

Mormons are expected to give ten percent of their earnings to the church. If they do not, they are not allowed to participate in temple ceremonies or to receive callings as bishops, high priests and other important high positions. Many Mormons are faithful to the ten percent tithing, even giving ten percent of the money earned on the side. When the author bought a television set from a private home, a neighbor with a pickup was asked to haul it for which he paid her twenty dollars. She said at the time, only eighteen dollars would go to her, with the remaining two dollars going to the church. Other churches would be rich if members paid ten percent of all their earnings or profits to the church.

And so the Mormon Church is rich, worth an estimated fifty billion dollars in assets that include the thousands of church buildings, 100 temples, (2001) a worldwide television network for Mormon Churches and nationally organized business corporations, etc.

According to Scott: "The Mormon Church does now or has recently owned hotels, department stores, newspapers, bookstores, publishing companies, a funeral home, farms, canneries, mills, factories, salvage stores, food-producing industries, cattle grazing land, banks, mines and much of the land and buildings in downtown Salt Lake City. It finances supermarket chains and food processors and controls the copper and sugar beet industries. Mormons own automobile factories and control paper mills and newspaper chains."[115]

Tithing and corporation income are used for promoting the Mormon Church and for increasing membership. This is accomplished by a large publishing division that develops and prints faith-promoting literature, a number of television and radio stations and state and national advertising. Tithing and corporation income of the church are also used to support its vast programs of genealogy and as noted earlier, baptism for the dead. Special welfare funding collected from members in addition to regular tithing is used for welfare programs, especially where such welfare programs will promote the church, such as in recruitment areas of Mexico, Central and South America. Nearly all of the Mormon "welfare" assistance is for Mormons, who are expected to repay for any welfare they receive when they find themselves economically able to do so.

Scott writes: "Now Mormons are expected to give one-tenth of their clear profits after doing business, or ten percent of salary before deducting taxes or living expenses, plus one-tenth of any interest earned on funds or investments. A rough estimate of the amount that a faithful Mormon will give annually, including tithe, ward quotas, contributions to welfare projects, and the cost of sending children on missions would average about twenty-six percent of his income... However, it is estimated that only one in four Mormons pays a full tithe."[116]

13. Blood Atonement

Blood atonement is the Mormon doctrine of killing by spilling of one's blood upon the ground for sins such as murder, adultery, stealing, apostasy, taking the Lord's name in vain and breaking covenants. Scott states that blood atonement was never widely practiced, but was endorsed by Brigham Young. She writes "...Brigham Young taught that the doctrine had two purposes: (1) to allow a sinner to atone for his own sins and (2) to put fear into the hearts of any who might contemplate such a sin. He taught, too that shedding a sinner's blood for him was a way of showing your love for him.

"...Mormons have gone so far as to say that blood atonement was never practiced, but Gustive O. Larsen documented a case where a man, Rosmos Anderson, who was guilty of fornication, allowed his throat to be slit so that his blood ran into an open grave in which he was subsequently buried. This was done by his bishop and two counselors, who hoped to save his soul. ...But blood atonement is taught and believed in modern times, too; for apostle and church President Joseph Fielding Smith once stated that the only hope of a person who committed the unpardonable sin was to have his blood shed. The Mormon Church no longer serves as executor in such cases, but it heartily approves capital punishment of murderers."[117]

In Utah, (the only state that allows execution by firing squad) those convicted of murder are given a choice of capital punishment, and one of these choices is death by a firing squad. It is presumed such a death will result in blood being spilled upon the ground, atoning for one's sins.

Scott believes that many Mormons still believe in blood atonement. She relates a story about a friend who was very distressed to find out that a mutual friend had stabbed to death his teenage wife and also her premature unborn son and said: "He can atone for killing one person by facing a firing squad, —but not two! There's no forgiveness for that!"[118]

14. Family Home Evening

The family home evening provides another opportunity for increasing LDS members' commitment to the church. In addition to lengthy three hour Sunday services in the wards, regular family visits by priesthood holders, called home teachers and other planned church and social activities, the family home evening provides the active Mormon more time each week for indoctrination into Mormonism.[119] Monday family home evenings were established by the church hierarchy in the 1960s.[120]

In addition to the several hours spent in the various Sunday church activities, family home programs are held at home on Monday nights. Family home evenings are conducted by the father, or in his absence, by the mother. Sometimes, the Monday night sports program in predominantly Mormon communities conflict with the family evening programs. In an April, 2000 report by the Associated Press, as appeared in the St. George Spectrum, basketball, soccer, baseball, softball practices and games continue to he held in these communities, despite a letter from Gordon B. Hinckley, church President reemphasizing the importance of staying home on Monday evenings. Some mayors have attempted to ban sports activities on Monday nights but have been warned by the ACLU, that such bans would be a violation of the First Amendment of the separation of church and state.

15. Burning in the Bosom

In the introduction to the *Book of Mormon* it is written: "We invite all men everywhere to read the *Book of Mormon,* to ponder in their hearts the message it contains, and then to ask God, the Eternal Father, in the name of Christ if the book is true. Those who pursue this course and ask in faith will gain a testimony of its truth and divinity by the Power of the Holy Ghost."[121]

The church teaches that if a person receives a burning in the bosom after reading this book, and has prayed to God, this will prove that the *Book of Mormon* is true. However, in reality, burning in the bosom hardly provides the reader the scientific evidence that the book is true. In addition, many Mormons say they did not get the emotional feeling of "burning in the bosom," no matter how hard they tried.

Following are some comments of Mormons who have left the LDS church concerning burning in the bosom: (Summarized from *"Recovery from Mormonism"* website).

"Who said any feelings were fake? Feelings are feelings nothing more. ...If I have a good feeling (a burning in the bosom, if you will) while at a baseball game, at a concert or while eating at a nice restaurant, does that make baseball true, the rock band true, or the restaurant the only true restaurant on the face of the earth?

"No one's burning bosom is ever fake. It was and is very real. What the real pain comes from is that you burned from something that was false, that came from the outside instead of from within, and that your deepest devotion was betrayed. That you were brought to a place where you didn't matter anymore, and as a result, you betrayed your own self. It makes it very difficult to trust yourself or others ever again. My burning bosom is still there, but now it burns for things that I believe, that I have determined for myself. Like the song from Van Halen, "It's mine, all mine, all mine...

"As for me, I never did receive a 'burning in the bosom' when praying about the *Book of Mormon* or any aspect of Mormonism. I sought this "burning" earnestly, but it simply never happened. I was happy and excited when I first read the *Book of Mormon*. It made me feel good. This was simply my emotions at play and not a divine confirmation of the truthfulness of Mormonism. For me, Moroni's Promise failed. I usually either felt nothing at all or sometimes complete emptiness when praying about Mormonism, particularly the subject of Blacks and the Priesthood. Some Mormons will claim that I did not recognize the burning. Either you have it or you don't.

"I'm sure many Mormons will claim to have received this "burning in the bosom." I found it interesting that no Mormon I associated with had ever told me he had received such a burning. They all claimed I would, though. Most Mormons I knew claimed that the Holy Spirit had revealed to them over a period of time, bit by bit, that Mormonism is true. To me, this does not meet the criteria for the "burning in the bosom." It is more like a gradual convincing of one's self based on Church indoctrination and a desire to believe. Our friend Moroni has quite a dilemma. Hypothetically, if God were to give a 'burning in the bosom' to a hundred million people and then decide not to give it to one poor soul among us, then Moroni's Promise fails for all of us. Would God pick and choose among those who try the Promise?

"I believe there are two possible explanations for the results of
Moroni's Promise:

(1.) All people who have sincerely tried Moroni's Promise did in
fact receive a 'burning in the bosom' and a knowledge that
Mormonism is true. Several of these people, myself included, have
since left Mormonism and are denying ever having had that experience.

(2.) Of all the people who have sincerely tried Moroni's Promise,
some have reacted emotionally and claim this emotional response to
be a 'burning in the bosom'. Others felt nothing at all and have left
Mormonism because of it or are still participating in Mormonism in
spite of it.

"Personally, I support explanation number two. Number one is
quite a stretch, and if number one is true, I am lying about my experience with Mormonism.

"It is important to realize that the Mormon Church teaches
(either directly or indirectly) that the human heart is a spiritual truth
detector while the human brain is of flesh, will only confuse the
truth, and cannot be trusted. Any person in any religion can tell you
that he "knows in his heart" that his religion is true. Contrary to popular belief, the Mormons do not have a patent on that phrase. In reality, the human brain, though imperfect, is a much better detector of
truth than the human heart. After all, God did give us a brain and He
expects us to use it. The Mormon Church fears those who step
beyond the limits of sanitized information imposed by the great
Mormon propaganda machine. In other words, they fear those who
use their brains. They fear those who are not content with a warm
and fuzzy feeling about Mormonism.

"I would like to share this experience with you. I remember a
conversation between a young Mormon man and his bishop. The
young man told his bishop that he had read non-Mormon material
which made him doubt Mormonism is true. The bishop told him to
read the non-Mormon material for fifteen minutes and then read
Mormon material for fifteen minutes. After having read both, he was
to decide which material made him feel better. Since the Mormon
material would make him feel better, the Mormon material was the
"truth" even though the non-Mormon material may have made better sense. This is hardly an exercise in truth detection."

Other Mormons question the burning in the bosom:

"I first questioned the 'burning in the bosom' when I noticed that

I felt it in connection with many different emotional experiences. I felt it more at times of intense emotion than as a confirmation of belief. I felt it most strongly when I prayed to ask God if I should leave the Mormon Church. I have since found the burning to be a good guide to an especially emotional experience, but a poor indicator of "goodness" or "truth."

"Like another person here, I never received a burning of the bosom. However, this was certainly not for lack of trying. I read the *Book of Mormon* several times and prayed each time. Nothing.

"I also read the book *"Drawing Upon the Powers of Heaven"* which provides a kind of step-by-step approach for receiving answers to prayers. I fasted and prayed a number of times with the intent of gaining a testimony and that burning. This was an extreme sacrifice for me; I love to eat! I made bargains with the Lord. In one case, I promised to sing in both the ward choirs if He would just give me a testimony.

"I wrote in my journal. I paid my tithing. I tried to keep the Sabbath Day holy. I tried to perform all my callings. I went to BYU. I was honest. I didn't steal, didn't drink, didn't have premarital sex, didn't smoke ... the list goes on and on. It finally dawned on me that after many years of never getting a burning in my bosom I wasn't going to get one. That realization precipitated my departure from the church, and I took steps to remove myself shortly thereafter."

This former member of the Mormon Church concluded that the *Book of Mormon* is not a divinely inspired history of real people, but only a 19th century product, fiction written by Joseph Smith using books and other written materials available to him. (Rauni Higley from *Recovery from Mormonism*)

Chapter Three
Ex-Mormons and Excommunication from the Mormon Church

Because of long indoctrination, frequent social interaction in the church, and overseeing by the priesthood, former members find leaving the Mormon Church accompanied by trauma, psychological problems and social disorganization. This is especially so if a member of the church has been born into a family that is active in the church, and has grown to adulthood while a member. To understand why it is so difficult to leave the church, even if one has a strong desire to do so, it is important to know about the intense propagandizing reinforcement, social controls and the priesthood "watch" that insure that members "toe the line" regarding church regulations and doctrine.

As stated earlier, when a family is active in the church, family members are subjected to many weekly activities designed to draw them strongly into Mormonism. These activities include three hours of church attendance on Sunday, during which time members give testimonials, hymns are sung and prayers and "talks" are given. Also on Sundays, meetings are organized for different groups. The children attend Sunday school for their age groups taught by members of the priesthood or experienced female Sunday school teachers. Adult Sunday school is also divided into groups based on their knowledge of the Mormon gospel. After Sunday school, women

attend the Relief Society meetings, the youth attend Mutual and
boys over twelve attend their respective priesthood meetings.
Children under the age of twelve attend the Primary. These various
groups use materials that have been prepared under the direction of
the church's General Authorities.

The church has developed materials to fit the needs of each
group, including elaborate books for children's groups and teaching
manuals for Aaronic and Melchizedek priesthood classes. These
materials are produced by the vast publishing department of the
Mormon Church and financed not only by the tithing of church
members, but by income generated from the profits of its fifty billion dollar corporate church empire. Monthly periodicals are published for each age group of the church. *The Friend* is published for
young children, which contains articles written by General
Authorities. *The Friend* has cutouts, puzzles and short articles, all of
which are designed to reinforce church teachings. *The New Era* is a
monthly periodical for the youth of the church reinforcing church
teachings at their level. The *Ensign* periodical reinforces church
teachings for adults and also contains articles written by one or more
of the apostles of the church and other General Authorities. All three
of these periodicals are attractively illustrated which not only promote the church's image, but its content further indoctrinates church
members.

If any family is discovered to be waning in its attendance at
Sunday meetings, or in some other way seems to be drifting from the
church, it will receive special attention from the bishop and other
local priesthood leaders. Someone from the leadership will visit the
family's home more often and provide the necessary "incentive" to
bring them back to regular attendance. The watchful eye of the
Mormon local priesthood looks for possible tendency for apostasy
and works to prevent anyone from leaving the church.

In addition to the regular church services and the weekly family
home evenings, the local church sponsors basketball leagues for
youth, the Boy Scout troops, dances and other social activities, making the church not only the religious center for its members, but the
social center as well.

Having been in this way propagandized and integrated into
Mormonism, it becomes very difficult for members to leave the
church even though they may no longer believe in its teachings and
tenets. The evidence that proves that the instruction given to church

members may be false is readily available in most libraries, but most Mormons are "intellectually unprepared to see the evidence. ...But first [one] must be predisposed to truth getting by thinking for one's own self. The Mormon faith has a strong cultural tenet of denial of the free will to think, and those that do are cast aside from the community of Mormonism and are seen as having lost the faith. ...For Mormons to accept the truth...would be equal to banishment from the tribe of old and left without social connections that make life meaningful. That is the truth for most Mormons and in the light of that, the real truth is simply unimportant" (Larry N. Jensen—March 5, 2000 letter) Therefore, many non-believers simply ignore the truth or keep it within themselves in order to avoid controversy with their Mormon community.

A mother whose son had become a Mormon convert was very upset as she told the author that she was losing her son to what she called the Mormon cult. The son's wife was a member of the Mormon Church, who had influenced her son to join the church. The mother said that her grandchildren were also receiving rigorous teaching in church tenets, and she felt that she was losing them, too. Her son had been married in the temple "for time and eternity," having his wife and children sealed to him. The mother explained that her son was immersed in the Mormon community as well as the church. He was attending church for three hours every Sunday and holding family home evenings on Monday nights. They were having monthly visits by home-teachers assigned to them from their ward, etc. The propagandizing of Mormon Church tenets is so ingrained in the minds of members, that most have accepted it as true even though all research and logic show it to be false. The son's teaching by the Mormon Church will be difficult for him not to accept unless he is exposed to truthful literature to read from outside the church.

The Mormon Church hierarchy, in its 174 years of existence, has developed a remarkable method of indoctrinating the minds of its members. In general, this intense indoctrination produces a closed mind for many members, so much so that, as mentioned previously, they are unwilling to read anything but their own "faith-promoting" literature. Since they are unwilling to read the truth about the Mormon Church and read only literature that the General Authorities write and approve, it is almost impossible for the members to have open minds about the church. The priesthood leadership, including the General Authorities and the First Presidency, continually remind

their members that they are not to read books that are not "faith promoting." Scott writes: "—complete obedience is essential, and that
individual thinking is not necessary." As one Mormon publication
put it, 'When our leaders speak, the thinking has been done. When
they propose a plan, it is God's plan ... Satan wins a great victory
when he can get members of the Church to do their own thinking."[122]

As has been estimated earlier, only one-fourth of the members of
the Mormon Church pay their full (ten percent) tithing. Scott writes:
"Many Mormons have in conscience 'left' Mormonism while still
remaining on church rolls. Some do not want to hurt relatives with
the public scandal of excommunication. Others, especially in Utah,
want to preserve business connections. Still others who no longer
recognize the authority of Mormon leaders over them have seen no
need to initiate the formal name removal procedure, which in itself
could be a frustrating and harrowing experience.

"It is interesting to note that almost every vocal ex-Mormon of
today started out by trying to disprove the claims of those who wrote
or spoke against Mormonism. ...Melanie Layton looked into
Mormonism's past to investigate charges against her church and
found more questions than answers. Jerald Tanner, too, tried to
defend the LDS Church against charges made by one of its first
apostates and now is himself perhaps one of the most influential
apostates of all time."[123]

The propagandizing program of the Mormon Church which
includes the Primary, Mutual, Seminary and Missionary training
systems in addition to regular Sunday school classes makes it
extremely difficult for one to remove all Mormonism from his brain.
Few Mormons have read anything but faith-promoting materials
that have been laundered to remove any and all information that may
be harmful to the church. Since the church is promoted as the "only
true church" with the *Book of Mormon* as "the most correct book on
the face of the earth," only materials that support these contentions
by the church hierarchy are permitted to be taught by LDS teachers.
Reading materials are carefully prepared so that the reader would
believe that these contentions of the church hierarchy are well documented. Most Mormons who are immersed in carefully laundered
faith promoting materials for a period of years and are later handed
materials that provide evidence contrary to "official"church tenets,
will most likely throw them away rather than read them. Or if what
they do read is upsetting to them, they will most likely resolve never

to read non-faith promoting literature again. However, a few free-thinking individuals will not only read the materials but will read further and check the documentation of the presented information.

The author believes that throwing away or not reading "anti-Mormon" literature is exactly what the leadership of the church wants members to do. In fact, many church priesthood holders will do everything possible to keep anti-Mormon literature from getting into the hands of church members or other readers, including trading anti-Mormon library books for faith promoting books with unwary librarians, keeping anti-Mormon books checked out from the library so that others cannot read them, and finally "losing" them.

Leaving the Mormon Church does occur, however, generally by thoughtful members who have had some unfortunate experiences with the church such as a guilt complex arising from a failed marriage. Some members, who have seen doctrinal errors may leave after an attempt to reform the church and to give it some sort of correctness in doctrine which was rejected. Others may leave because they believe in an important principle that would improve society but which is opposed by the General Authorities.

Ex-Mormons

Some of those who have left the church or have been excommunicated include:

Elias L. T Harrison and William Godbe who were excommunicated from the church in the 1860s because they thought that God Almighty's giving of priesthood power to do their thinking for them was a fatal error that possessed the minds of some. They promoted use of free speech and free thought within the church, liked to think for themselves and did not wish to accept the absolute authority imposed upon them by their church. When Brigham Young read some of their writings concerning free thinking, he had them excommunicated from the church.[124]

Sonia Johnson was excommunicated from the Mormon Church for her activities in support of the Equal Rights Amendment (ERA) to the Constitution. The Equal Rights amendment was opposed by the Presidency and other General Authorities of the church since it would give equal rights to women, including rights to the Mormon priesthood. The First Presidency, through local priesthood leaders, organized a campaign to defeat the amendment in several key states, especially in states with sizable membership in the Mormon Church. Johnson was asked to repent after her excommunication, but she wondered why she should repent and wrote: "Repent of what—Of being happier than I have ever been in my life—Because as I look up from my typewriter at the snowy woods outside my window in the Virginia winter of 1979, I realize that I never have been happier."[125]

Jerald and Sandra Tanner, former members of the Mormon Church, have compiled an encyclopedia-like book of Mormon documents containing information on: Archaeology and the *Book of Mormon*, Joseph Smith, the Danites, blood atonement, temple ceremonies and sacred temple garments. Their book, *Mormonism, Shadow or Reality,* contains many copies of original documents, such as Brigham Young's speeches on blood atonement and original checks from Joseph Smith's failed bank in Kirtland, Ohio. These famous ex-Mormons operate a bookstore in Salt Lake City and the Utah Lighthouse Ministry. The historical documents of the Mormon Church that the Tanners have collected, have gained so much prominence, that even Mormon writers have used their collections as references for their works.

Deborah Laake, a renown writer is a well-known ex-Mormon who wrote the book, *Secret Ceremonies.* This book outlines her frustrations as she attempted to live a Mormon life, including her haste to become married in order to fulfill her role as a Mormon woman. As mentioned earlier, because of the pressures that she felt from the priesthood and the Mormon community she married without love, became disillusioned with Mormonism and eventually left the church. This freeing of Laake's mind from the control of the church and priesthood is dramatically portrayed in her book as bit by bit she was able to free herself from the grip of Mormonism, to plan and to lead her own life, as defined by her own individual personality, interests and desires. She loved the freedom and independence that she had won by leaving the Mormon Church.

Another ex-Mormon, Fawn Brodie, a talented and noted writer and historian, was excommunicated from the Mormon Church after she published the most authoritative work on the life of Joseph Smith ever assembled, *No Man Knows my History.*

Mark Hofmann

Probably the most embarrassing excommunicated member for

the Mormon hierarchy was Mark Hofmann, a forger-bomber. This is because the current President of the Mormon Church, Gordon B. Hinckley, was directly involved in the Mormon document forgeries. Hinckley served as a second counselor of the church's First Presidency when he made arrangements through intermediaries to purchase historical documents from Hofmann. Unbeknownst to Hinckley was the fact that the documents he purchased for the church were forged by Hofmann. Hofmann, who had lost faith in the church and had a deep resentment toward it, developed a clever scheme to destroy the church that he hated as well as to become rich through it. His scheme was first to forge faith-promoting documents and thus gain the confidence of the church hierarchy. Then he followed up by forging documents that if they became public, would destroy the faith of many. He became skilled at developing paper through the use of chemicals that gave his documents the appearance of old writings. Some of these that he forged appeared to be in Joseph Smith's own handwriting.

After Hofmann had convinced the Mormon leadership that he had indeed found authentic Joseph Smith writings, he began to develop documents, as if written by Smith, that would be damaging and that would expose the *Book of Mormon* and the church as frauds. Subsequently the church purchased them in order to keep them hidden from the membership. Since Joseph Smith was their prophet, any negative writings by him such as these would undermine the credibility and power of the church leadership.

Gordon B. Hinckley fell into Hofmann's trap and directed the buying of both the faith-promoting as well as the faith-destroying documents. Large amounts of money were paid to Hofmann for these. News conferences were arranged by the church to publicize the best of the faith-promoting documents since they supported the teachings of the church based on the Joseph Smith story. The Mormon Church bought many potentially damaging documents, *but did not publicize them, and hid them from the public and from its membership*. The Mormon Church was greatly embarrassed when the truth became known about the purchases of the forgeries.

The purchase of the Hofmann forgeries by the Mormon Church was brought to the forefront in 1985, after a bomb built by Hofmann was sent to Steven Christensen, one of the purchasers of the false documents. Christensen had been meeting with Hofmann and paid him for the forgeries to be given to the church. Christensen, a

Mormon bishop, "a wealthy and well connected Salt Lake investment counselor who had numerous dealings with Hofmann, arrived before 8:00 A. M. at his office . . . and found a package
addressed to him leaning against his office door. Seconds after he
touched the box, it exploded, killing him."[126] Hofmann's motive
for sending the bomb to Christensen was that he was afraid that
Christensen was about to expose him as a forger. Later on that
same day another person was killed by a bomb sent by Hofmann.

In an interview as part of a plea bargain, "Hofmann told how
he had held Mormonism in utter contempt through the years of
garment wearing, temple going and food storing. He studied LDS
scriptures and history deeply, but he did so with a secret agenda
of destruction. Hofmann had lost his faith in Mormonism at age
fourteen in a particularly eerie fashion, considering his enchant-
ment for explosives that took two lives. As had many a preco-
cious adolescent before, Hofmann found the chemical recipe for
gunpowder in the family *World Book Encyclopedia*—charcoal,
saltpeter, sulfur ...and mixed up a batch in his basement. During
one experiment ... to produce a bomb, it detonated in his face, seriously burning him and leaving a scar on his chin as a lifelong
reminder of his ill-fated flirtation" with making a bomb.[127]

This incident convinced Hofmann that there was no God,
otherwise if there were, He would not have allowed this to happen,
and so he became an atheist and secretly an anti-Mormon. While
he secretly abhorred the Mormon Church, he forced himself to act
as an upright Mormon, always wearing his garments, keeping his
food kit, bearing his testimony at ward meetings and keeping a
journal. His objective was to damage the Mormon Church as much
as he could. With his skill in developing forged documents, he had
found his weapon to undermine the church. This weapon was used
to expose the falseness of Joseph Smith's writings and teachings.

Hofmann had a great knowledge of Mormon Church history, but
he concealed this knowledge so that nobody would suspect that the
"documents" he had "found" were forgeries. "Each time he churned
out a fake, he knew well the content and purported significance of
each piece. For example, when forging a fake letter in Joseph Smith's
hand, he first performed enough historical research to find other
evidence that Smith was, in fact, present at the time and place
where the letter purportedly would be written."[128] Hofmann also
became well-acquainted with Smith's spelling errors, his practices

and his writing style. His documents were so skillfully crafted that the Mormon authorities gave him nearly a million dollars to purchase the documents so that they could be kept secret and not be exposed to the members of the church and public.

One of the faith-promoting documents was called the "Anthon Transcript," which Hofmann had carefully concocted, containing Egyptian hieroglyphs which Joseph Smith had claimed were the characters that he had copied from the "golden plates" in translating the *Book of Mormon*. In addition to them, Hofmann attached to these hieroglyphs a note purportedly from Joseph Smith to Professor Anthon as follows: "These caractors [sic] were diligently copied [sic] by my own hand from the plates of gold and given to Martin Harris who took them to New York City..."[129] The members of the First Presidency of the Mormon Church were eager to purchase these forgeries as they were convinced they were authentic. They wanted them because this would help prove Smith's story that he had indeed translated these Egyptian hieroglyphs through the use of his seer stones.

"[church] Historians called in to authenticate the document were particularly impressed that the note contained misspelling of several words that Smith apparently carried throughout his life. These experts also commented that the writing was typical more of a young man's robust hand than were the many works of the older Joseph Smith at Missouri's Liberty Jail and in Nauvoo....

"Selling the faked 'Anthon Transcript' as his first major deal with the First Presidency, Hofmann received as payment a rare five dollar Mormon gold coin dated 1850, a first edition of the *Book of Mormon* and numerous bank notes printed by church elders in the early years in Utah. These items were worth at least $20,000."[130]

The First Presidency was so impressed with Hofmann's "discovery" of the "Anthon Transcript" that they called a press conference, at which they announced the new "discovery" and commended Hofmann for his efforts. Hofmann followed the Anthon Transcript with several non-faith-promoting forged documents, which were quickly bought by the First Presidency and were hidden from the membership and the public. One of these forged documents included one that linked Sidney Rigdon (second in command to Joseph Smith) to Solomon Spaulding. This was significant since many people had suspected that Joseph Smith had used the Spaulding manuscript in writing the *Book of Mormon*. The Spaulding manuscript could have provided the basis for Smith's book, rather than the golden plates which Mormon Church authorities claim angel Moroni had delivered to Joseph Smith.

Hofmann was growing bolder and planned to forge the "lost" 116 pages of the *Book of Mormon* that Smith claimed he had translated from the golden plates. This would have been extremely valuable to the Mormon authorities, especially if they contained what Joseph Smith had claimed. However, Hofmann, with his intense hatred for the Mormon Church, was probably going to forge a non-faith promoting 116-page novel, rather than a religious book, that would prove that Smith was the author of, rather than a translator of the "divine" *Book of Mormon*. As discussed in Chapter One, these pages were lost after Smith reluctantly loaned them to Martin Harris so that he could show them to his wife, who was upset with her husband's selling of their farm to pay for the printing of the *Book of Mormon*. The 116 pages were never seen again after Harris' defiant wife took them to read. If Hofmann could forge the original 116 pages, he would have received a handsome sum (estimated in the millions) from the Mormon Church.

So far Hofmann had received almost a million dollars for his forgeries. (A total of forty-eight forged documents were obtained from Hofmann by the Mormon Church.)[131] He was expanding his forgery efforts to "discovering" early documents of American history, etc. Because of his success, he quit his studies in medicine at the University of Utah and was developing a comfortable lifestyle from the profits of his forgeries. But the successful forgery business of Hofmann was soon to come to an end since one of his proposed forgeries, the "McLellin Collection," from which Hofmann obtained a large amount of money in advance, would be exposed if Steven Christensen continued to represent the Mormon Church in Hofmann dealings. This was because Hofmann knew that Christensen would use Kenneth Rendell, an expert in historical documents, to authenticate this forged collection. Because of this, Hofmann dared not let Christensen be the church's representative with him so he sent the bomb that killed Christensen and sent another, to distract police investigators, to Christensen's associate, Gary Sheets. This resulted in a police investigation, which led to Hofmann's arrest. Hofmann had hoped that the income from the McLellin forgeries would solve his deep financial problems.

The Hofmann forgeries purchased by the Mormon Church

caused the deaths of their representative, Steven Christensen, and of the wife of Gary Sheets, who had opened the package intended for him. The resulting publicity in national headlines was devastating to the Mormon Church. The trial of Hofmann brought out the desperate desire on the part of Mormon authorities to prove the authenticity and divine nature of the *Book of Mormon*. It exposed their willingness to withhold the truth of the origination of Mormonism from members which they knew some of the Hofmann documents could reveal. It gave the many critics of the church a new platform from which to launch attacks on the church leadership for continuing to impose false doctrines upon their generally obedient members. It also shows that the church leadership was unsure about the truth of doctrines that it teaches and was willing to grasp at any straw that will, in some manner, give them some credence. In addition, it shows the relentless leadership of the church in promoting principles that they knew may be false.

At least one Mormon who left the church over its involvement in the Hofmann forgeries writes about his growing sense of discontent with the premise of divine revelation coming through the dark-suited prophets and apostles in Salt Lake City after discovering the behavior of many of them in their dealings with Mark Hofmann. When he realized one man who is currently the Mormon Prophet, manipulated the Utah legal system and otherwise obstructed justice, he was outraged that such violations of morality go unrecognized by the world. As he thought further about this incident, the passage from 1st Nephi, 'It is better that one man should perish than that a nation should dwindle in disbelief' took on special significance. The deaths of two faithful Mormons were allowed to pass unpunished to protect the Mormon Church from further public embarrassment.

And so the prosecuting attorney of Salt Lake City allowed Hofmann to escape the most serious charges through plea bargaining. The result was to send Hofmann to prison with the possibility of parole, rather than to death row which he rightfully deserved. As a prosecuting attorney, there clearly should have been only one decision to be made, insist that he receive the death penalty for the two murders. (Summarized from "*Recovery from Mormonism*" website)

Another, who was excommunicated from the church, is D. Michael Quinn. Quinn is an excellent writer and accomplished author of several outstanding books on Mormon history. Since he was unwilling to "launder" his historical research to reflect the teachings of the General Authorities, he was forced from the church. Quinn's voluminous notes from his research contained information which the Church Authorities did not wish church membership and the public to know. Two books, *The Mormon Hierarchy, Origins of Power,* and *The Mormon Hierarchy, Extensions of Power,* contain nearly two thousand pages of valuable information concerning the history of the church.

Stories of Ex-Mormons

Following are several excerpts from recent former members, citing their reasons for leaving the Mormon Church (summarized from the Website: "*Recovery From Mormonism*")

This former member of the LDS Church did translation work which gave her an opportunity to study Mormon history from many books not generally available to the membership of the church. She started to wonder about the credibility of the church because she saw so many changes in the church doctrines and contradictions between its scriptures and the writings of the Prophets and the top leadership. She was concerned, because it was obvious to her that the church was hiding a lot of important information from its membership. This was a serious question because if Mormonism was not the truth, then she felt that their (she and her husband's) eternal life and salvation were in danger.

Here are some of the problems she found that caused her eventually to leave the LDS Church:

Joseph Smith claimed he had a visit from God, the Father, and His Son, Jesus Christ, in 1820. During this visit, Smith (according to Smith) was told that all churches were wrong and that he should not join any of them. After informing several in his community of this, Smith claimed that he received intense persecution. Smith also claimed that he was given the golden plates which he said he had translated as the *Book of Mormon* by use of a seer stone.

After informing his community about a visit from God, the Father, and His Son, Jesus Christ, and who, he said, had told him that all churches were wrong and that he should not join any of them, this former member wondered why all the commotion and persecution which Smith claimed were caused by his message, was not written in the newspapers of the time. Nothing of the vision or about the persecution that supposedly had followed, is acknowledged by his own family, and it is not mentioned even in his mother's autobiography of him.

One wouldn't really even have to dig deeper than the First Vision and the *Book of Mormon* to find out that the claims of the LDS Church regarding the visions are not true. This former member concluded that the *Book of Mormon* is not a divinely inspired history of real people, but only a 19th century product, fiction written by Joseph Smith using books and other written materials available to him. She also concluded, based on documented evidence about the so-called *Book of Mormon* witnesses, that they were not reliable men, but unstable and easily convinced. Most of them ended up leaving the LDS Church, and like Martin Harris, for example, who changed his religion at least eight times, testified of their new religion's truthfulness as fervently as they had of Mormonism.

Some of her other conclusions that caused her to leave the Mormon Church included:

1. Joseph Smith claimed that the golden plates were written in "reformed Egyptian language." If this were a history of Jewish people coming from Jerusalem, it most certainly would have been written in their own language, Hebrew! Joseph Smith more than likely chose "reformed Egyptian" because such a language does not exist, and showing "characters" from that language to those who questioned would not expose him as a fraud.

2. Smith writes in his book about ample timber to build a ship to sail to the Americas. Ample timber was not and still is not available on the Sinai Desert. He also describes fruit and wild honey as being products of the Sinai Desert which is not possible. Wheat, barley, olives, etc., are described in the *Book of Mormon*, but none of these were in the Americas at that time. The following animals were listed as being in North America in Smith's book: cows, asses, horses, oxen, lions, leopards, sheep and elephants. No such animals have ever been found in archaeological diggings relative to the time period described in the *Book of Mormon*. The *Book of Mormon* mentions lions as "beasts of the forests." Lions are found only in African grasslands, not in forests. Smith also mentions butter in his book, but no milk-producing animals lived in the Americas at the time.

Following are some of the other absurdities in the *Book of Mormon* which caused a former member to disbelieve and eventually leave the LDS Church:

(1) "Furious winds" propelled the barges to the Promised Land

for 344 days! If the winds blew only 10 miles per hour, the distance traveled in 344 days would have been 82,560 miles rather than the 4,000 miles from Israel to the Americas.

(2) According to the *Book of Mormon*, Lehi's group had only about 20 people when they arrived, 600 B.C., to the Americas, but the *Book of Mormon* reports that already in about 588 B.C., they were building a temple that "construction was like unto the temple of Solomon" (BoM, 2 Ne. 5:16). It took a lifetime of King David to collect materials for the temple and years of Solomon's reign to add to them. When Solomon built the temple, he used tens of thousands of skilled people and seven years to construct it. (I Kings Chapters 5-6.) This *Book of Mormon* story is impossible in more ways than just a lack of workers! They could not have had the materials nor the manpower to do it.

(3) The *Book of Mormon* teaches that Indians originated from these Jewish settlers. Indians are distinctly Mongoloid—they have the "Mongoloid" blue spot, specific blood traits, and their facial features are typical of Asian origin, not Semitic at all.

(4) Near the end of the *Book of Mormon*, a great battle is described that took place on Hill Cumorah about 385 B.C. (near Palmyra, N. Y.), where hundreds of thousands of people were killed. (See BoM, Mormon 6:1-20.) No evidence of it, no breastplates, helmets, swords nor any signs of human remains have been found on that relatively small hill.

(5) Thomas S. Ferguson's archaeological studies, under the New World Archaeology Foundation, also added to the reason why this former member left the LDS Church. Ferguson, early in his career, firmly believed that the *Book of Mormon* was true and that it could be proven to be so. In 1955, he received $250,000 from the LDS Church to start the foundation, and the Church continued to support his efforts financially, even if somewhat reluctantly, for many, many years. Ferguson became disillusioned due to the fact that in spite of efforts, nothing was found that had any connection to the *Book of Mormon*. He finally had to admit that Joseph Smith and his *Book of Mormon*, and consequently the LDS Church, were frauds.

(6) B. H. Roberts, noted scholar and a General Authority of the Mormon Church, also came to seriously question the authenticity of the *Book of Mormon* after completing his comparison of the *Book of Mormon* and a book, *The View of the Hebrews*, written in 1823, near

Joseph Smith's hometown by a minister named Ethan Smith, seven years prior to the *Book of Mormon*. As a matter of fact, Ethan Smith's book was so popular that two years after its publication, a second edition was published (in 1825). B. H. Roberts wrote over 400 pages of typewritten research that was later published as *Studies of the Book of Mormon*. (First ed. 1985, second ed. 1992.) Roberts' conclusions were that given Joseph Smith's creative imagination and materials available to him, it is highly possible that he wrote the book himself.

(7) The *Book of Abraham* which Joseph Smith claimed to have translated from ancient records, was also discovered to be false. Joseph Smith had claimed that it was a translation he made from Abraham's writings. When the papyri he had "translated" it from was found in 1967 and compared to Smith's translation of it, it proved to be nothing more than a portion of a pagan burial record, called the *Book of Breathings*. While the Utah Mormon Church has not removed this book from its scriptures, the *Reorganized Church of Jesus Christ of Latter-Day Saints* has. (The Reorganized Church of Jesus Christ of Latter-Day Saints was established under the guardianship of Emma Smith, Joseph Smith's first wife, after Brigham Young had led the main group to the Salt Lake Basin.)

(8) This former LDS member suggests that it was polygamy that led to the killing of Joseph Smith in Carthage, Illinois in June of 1844. There was a furor building up in Nauvoo because Joseph Smith was not only marrying many very young single women, he was also taking married women as his wives, while denying the polygamy issue altogether. (He had married 33 women with an additional 15 claiming marriage to him also.) Joseph Smith had ordered the destruction of a printing press in Nauvoo that was exposing his affairs. He was arrested for that crime. While in jail with his brother, Hyrum, they were shot to death. The records show that Joseph Smith and his brother both had guns smuggled into the jail. Joseph did not die a martyr's death, but was killed in a gunfight. Before Joseph Smith was killed there, he had shot and killed two men and wounded a third one.

(9) This former member of the LDS Church learned through her research that Joseph Smith had copied his temple ceremony from the Masons. Joseph Smith had become a Mason in early 1842, and within a few weeks after learning Masonic ceremony and its tokens, signs and penalties, he introduced them to the Mormons as

"revelation from God." It was pretty obvious that a secret man-made organization's rituals did not have anything at all to do with the God of the Bible and what He requires of men.

Authority, false documents, including the *Book of Mormon*, hiding the truth, restricting freedom of thought, glossing over important concepts, inability to answer questions about the authenticity of the Mormon doctrine and beliefs, are some of reasons that Mormon members become apostates. Leaving the church often results in serious emotional stress for former members. Following are excerpts from former Mormon Church members expressing this great stress.

* * * *

Recovering from Mormonism means removing one's self from the Mormon cultural life and the noxious belief system. You have come to the realization that everything that you have known and believed in is a fraud. How do you correct that?

This young person faced many serious problems in the first several years of her marriage, many of which were directly caused by her membership in the Mormon Church. Like many in the Mormon Church, she grew up in a very traditional Mormon family whose ancestors crossed the plains and settled in Utah. Her relatives assumed various positions in the church including stake presidents, bishops, patriarchs, mission presidents and relief society presidents. In her early years, she attended Primary, and four years of early morning Seminary. She had many wonderful experiences, attending youth conferences, performing in road shows, talent shows, going to dances and performing in dance festivals.

She attended BYU and married a returned missionary in the temple. She became the mother of several children, but gradually her dream of a blissful marriage was falling apart. Since her husband was a priesthood holder, she felt that she deserved the abuse that he poured upon her, hitting, kicking, punching, and in some cases, spitting on her. Gradually she got enough nerve to talk to her bishop about her problems, but he and other bishops that she talked to later always told her: "It's up to the woman to save the marriage. You need to pray more, you need to try harder."

Her husband told her that she was lazy, even though she was giving music lessons, feeding and caring for her children, delivering newspapers, nursing a baby and at the time, pregnant with another.

She was wondering if she would ever make it to the Celestial kingdom. With all of the abuse from her husband, she was starting to hate him. Finally everything came to a head when he beat her child. He kicked him, punched his face and screamed at him.

In desperation, she called the police. They supported her husband. She turned again to the bishop, and he advised her to try to make up with her husband and to pray more and try harder. She started going to the temple more, but things didn't get better. Finally, after a nasty fight, she packed up and left for a few days, taking her children with her.

She opened up her own checking account, rented a post office box and began depositing her own money into her account in the bank. She began reading about family violence and asked her husband to seek help. The bishop decided that her husband didn't need help and that it was she who was causing all of the problems. In her reading she began to see a parallel between the Mormon Church and problems in her marriage. Something was beginning to click in her brain, and she determined that the control and oppression of the Mormon Church were in some way responsible for the control and bullying by her husband.

After receiving counseling from outside of the church, she was told that this could be a divorce situation. She began to realize that she was okay and that she had a way out of her dilemma. The bishop of the Mormon Church, that she had spoken with, wanted a signed release so that he could learn from the counselor "our confidential conversations." The bishop was conducting an "investigation" of her life. The counselor wrote the bishop a letter advising him to leave her alone. She was beginning to have some real doubts about the church. She saw her husband as a pathetic victim of his family and of the Mormon Church.

She began seeing friends from her growing-up years. One couple had left the church, and they gave her articles and books to read. Other people came into her life who had left the church, and she noticed that they were all happy. She quit wearing her garments and quit attending church. She is no longer afraid of church authorities. She is now a product of the choices that she makes and is responsible for them.

* * * *

This ex-Mormon left the church when she became convinced that it was not right for her to indoctrinate her son into the false teachings of the Mormon Church. At one time she was very active in the church although she was raised only as a "cultural Mormon." She was married in the temple, accepted many "callings" and chose to accept church doctrine although her heart and mind did not believe. She lived by the teachings of the church even though she did not believe them. At times she wished to be free from Mormonism and was unhappy, but she did not think that she would ever leave the church. However, as her son reached the age that he should be baptized, she decided that she could not allow her son to become indoctrinated into church beliefs. She realized that many Mormons who go through the indoctrination program of the Sunday school, the High School Seminary and the Missionary training school generally cannot escape from the church's control. She would not sentence him to a life of imprisonment in the church.

Before making this decision not to have her son baptized, she was unaware of all the documentation that proved Joseph Smith was a fraud and that the church authorities are still covering up the changes and the lies contained in Joseph Smith's writings. She is happy that she avoided putting her son under the power of the priesthood and that he is able to avoid the anguish that she faced as a Mormon. She is still frightened that she allowed the priesthood to hold power over her mind. The freedom over her own thoughts that she has gained since leaving the church are indescribable, especially when she remembers that for a large part of her life she allowed the church to control her thoughts. She continues to search for the truth concerning the Mormon Church and is always adding to her research library.

* * * *

Following is a story of an ex-Mormon who like others went through all of the usual indoctrination programs of the church. However, unlike most Mormons, while believing deeply in the doctrines of the church and especially in the Joseph Smith story, he read widely not only of faith-promoting literature, but non-faith promoting literature as well. While he was originally convinced that the Mormon Church was a true religion, by reading literature obtained from the Tanners (Sandra and Jerald) he soon discovered that many questions were raised in his mind about the church. He read some of these materials while on his mission for the Mormon Church.

Early study failed to alter his beliefs during his college years and during his mission. He tended to take the attitude that if so many people were attacking the church, then it must be true. In fact, many of the writings caused him to have greater belief in the church since they seemed to support the persecution complex of the church. He was most impressed with Tanners' book, especially in reference to Joseph Smith's First Vision. Smith's First Vision, as explained by the Tanners, had gone through many revisions. The most disturbing aspect of the First Vision was that it was not recorded until 18 years after the visit to the fourteen-year old Joseph Smith. This report was also quite different from earlier reports of the visit by the angels.

When he read the information provided by the Tanners about Joseph Smith's fraud in claiming that he had translated the *Book of Abraham* from an ancient Egyptian papyrus, the young Mormon's belief in the church became confused. He could not rationalize away the attempt by the Mormon Church to disregard Smith's fraud and to call the fragment of Egyptian papyrus (a pagan funeral text) the inspiration that Smith used to compose the *Book of Abraham*.

After discovering Smith's *Book of Abraham* hoax, this ex-Mormon's reading expanded into other literature that convinced him that Smith was not a prophet of God but an opportunist intent upon spreading his religious magic as far as people would allow. He began to look at the Mormon God that wanted to exchange eternal life for his intellect and sense of reason. The Mormon God, through the church hierarchy with their fine business suits, was losing this ex-Mormon's trust, respect and admiration as they were promoting church doctrine and history that had too many questions about its authenticity.

He began to make a decision about whether to leave the church or to forget his doubts about the church. He recalled his first visit to the temple which he thought to be comical, bizarre and frightening. The temple ceremony was not dignified, divine or inspiring. The temple clothing, with the little apron and hat, gave him a feeling of guilt, unworthiness and embarrassment which further added to his doubts about the church. The Mormon Church had tried to hide the true history of the Brigham Young and Joseph Smith years, and in its place had created a huge dreamy church empire with great programs for everybody. He finally became convinced that General Authorities had hidden and still are today attempting to cover up doctrinal and historical problems of the church by carefully laundering all teaching and learning materials to insure that only favor-

able history and doctrine are presented. He has also decided that
rational thought is discouraged by the hierarchy of the church, especially if it conflicts with the church's teaching. "God's ways are not
man's ways" and "In the last days, even the very elect will be
deceived" are words often used by Mormon Church leaders to prevent rational thought and to keep members under church control.

* * * *

Another ex-Mormon was concerned that members made their
testimonies about how they felt and not upon their own logical reasoning. He said that they let their hearts do the thinking for them
rather than their brains. He grew irritated at the testimonies of these
people who "knew the church was true," that "Joseph Smith was
true," that their bishop was a holy man and "true." He decided that
his intellect, what his brain told him, was more important than what
several years of Mormon indoctrination had tried to tell him.

What did this ex-Mormon lose after spending so much time
and money on a religion that he later found to be false? His greatest
loss was faith and confidence in human nature. He confesses that
discovering that the Mormon Church is based upon a false premise
introduced by Joseph Smith, and his decision to leave, have been
difficult and stressful. He is sorry that he spent two of the best years
of his life engaged in such a useless activity as a missionary in
Europe. This activity introduced several people into the Mormon
religion and caused them to lose control of their own lives and the
ability to do their own thinking. He is sorry for that. He regrets that
he attended Brigham Young University instead of attending a different one where he believes he would have received a more well-
rounded education. He suggests that Mormonism maintains control
of its members by providing the "elect" with a blissful, eternal life
that Church Authorities claim is waiting for them in the Mormon
Celestial kingdom. The Church Authorities are confident that this
promise will discount the assaults on logic, and that members will
remain faithful. Obedience, worship and sublimation of will are the
earthly tests for eternal companionship with the Mormon Cosmic
terrorist known as Eloheim. He says that Mormons are fighting for
your eternal soul, and in the process, they cause many people to experience a loss in the richness of "here and now" of this earthly life.

* * * *

Mormonism—is like a cancer that has invaded my body, even my very soul. When I left the church, I removed a large lump, only to find that the cancer had spread. But day by day and bit by bit I am removing that which would prevent my body and soul from living free.

* * * *

The following ex-Mormon is concerned that the Mormon Church is becoming more prominent and more powerful in our society. He says that Mormons are occupying influential positions in state and national governments far out of proportion to their population numbers. The church has become a megawealthy financial enterprise, worth billions of dollars with money-making businesses and property all over the country. These wide-ranging (and usually unseen) enterprises influence many aspects of American life and are unknown to most non-Mormons. Income has been reliably estimated to be millions of dollars **per day**, not only from the many businesses but also from faithful members, who are required to donate a minimum of ten percent of their gross income to the church.

The Mormon Church, according to this ex-Mormon, boasts of its rapid growth which is a result of not only its tradition of large families but also its large voluntary corps of full-time missionaries who are a well-trained and thoroughly indoctrinated sales force whose primary purpose is to bring more people into the church. While many of these innocent young missionaries do sincerely believe that their purpose is to save souls, to help people and to enrich the lives of their converts, the results of their efforts is not to convert, but to enroll, not to enrich lives, but to baptize, not to save sinners' souls, but to enlarge membership rolls. This missionary force is not directed by caring clergymen, but by successful businessmen because the Mormon missionary effort is a business, and a very successful business, when judged by business standards. Another reason for the rapid growth of the church is the supporting role of a vast television and radio network, bombarding the airways with constant propaganda from the church leadership. Since every Mormon is taught to gain members, the home folks obtain a sizable number of new members, more than the full time missionaries.

He feels that the ultimate goal of the church, as practiced publicly by early leaders, Joseph Smith and Brigham Young, was to

establish the Mormon kingdom of God in America and to govern the
world as God's appointed representatives. (The present leader of the
church, Gordon B. Hinckley, and other leaders before him, probably
have been ordained King of this kingdom.) He adds that this goal
has been kept quiet by the church leadership. He says the church is
far more influential in state and national affairs than its number
would indicate. (They often vote and act as a bloc, which makes
their voices and actions more powerful than they would otherwise
be in individual actions.) And he says that the long range goal of the
church leadership is to gain control of the United States and ultimately of the world.

After being taught the age of the earth, he asked a professor, a
member of his ward, how he reconciled the teachings of his science
with the teachings of the church (which said that the earth was created only 6000 years ago). The professor replied that he had two
compartments in his brain: one for geology and one for the gospel.
They were entirely separate, and he did not let the one influence the
other.

After graduation from Brigham Young University he attended
a university to work on his Master's degree. His association with
non-Mormon fellow graduate students led to discussions about religion and especially about the Mormon religion since many students
were not familiar with it. At first he felt confident that he could
answer the students' questions about his religion, but eventually,
questions were asked that he could not answer about the Danites,
Brigham Young's blood atonement doctrine, and Joseph Smith's
claims of the divine nature of the *Book of Mormon.*

This ex-Mormon was able to find both faith-promoting and
non-faith-promoting literature in his search to find answers to the
questions posed by his fellow students. When he returned to Utah,
he read extensively in the *Journal of Discourses*, which contains
most of the sermons preached by church leaders during the reign of
Brigham Young. He had noticed that the non-faith-promoting literature often referred to these sermons but that the present day church
leaders almost never referred to them. He wondered why.

His research into Mormon history brought him to the conclusion that the church was hiding the truth about such events as the
Danites (or the Avenging Angels) and the Mountain Meadows
Massacre. While the church kept quiet about the murders committed on behalf of church leaders by the Danites, it was clear that the

leaders encouraged and organized the enforcer gangs of the Danites. He also concluded that the Mormon Church hierarchy was hiding the truth about the Mountain Meadows Massacre that happened in September of 1857, where LDS Church leaders of Cedar City, Utah, led fifty Mormon militia and a group of Indians to murder about 120 members of the Fancher emigrant train.

After all of his reading and research, this ex-Mormon concluded that the Mormon Church was just another man-made institution and that the church wasn't true. Unfortunately, he had not included his wife in all of this research, and she refused to believe him and remained loyal to the church. He finally left the church since he had learned that the Mormon Church is not led by God, and it never had been. He concluded that it was a religion of 100 percent human origin.

All of his Mormon friends predicted that since he had left the church he would live a short life and die an alcoholic. However, his life without the Mormon Church has been rich and rewarding. He remarried and raised two sons without religious training who turned out to be fine young men. He has no fear of death and feels sorry for Mormons who desperately worry that their work for the LDS Church on earth will not be sufficient to qualify them for the Mormon Celestial kingdom in heaven.

Getting out of Mormonism has greatly helped this ex-Mormon to appreciate and enjoy fully the here and now rather than frantically working towards a possible reward to join Eloheim (a Hebrew name for God), Brigham Young, Joseph Smith, et. al in the Celestial kingdom. The price of such an eternal reward includes many weekends of boring priesthood meetings, working at the ward meeting house every now and then, paying the church ten percent of your income, pretending the king is in fact fully clothed while donning the funny little costume in the heavily marbled and chandeliered palace called the house of the Lord, standing up in sacrament meetings a couple of times a year to parrot the thoughts and admonitions of the brethren, testifying in Fast and Testimony meetings every couple of months that you know your leaders are 'true', and making obligatory ten minute monthly visits to other eternally aspiring families. The other part of the price of working towards such a reward is not at all easy, the general sublimation of your will to a Cosmic Terrorist who expects you to Obey, Follow and Worship rather than think, with all the tremendous cognitive dissonance this creates.

"...we document that the Mormon belief that God's providence is that they assume political and economic control of the United States is still alive and well in the late twentieth century. More important, this goal is being actualized to a much greater extent than most people realize."[132]

Chapter Four
Organization and Finance of the Mormon Church

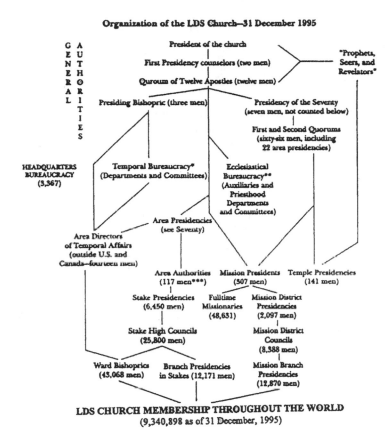

Organization of the LDS Church—31 December 1995

LDS CHURCH MEMBERSHIP THROUGHOUT THE WORLD
(9,340,898 as of 31 December, 1995)

Source: D. Michael Quinn *The Mormon Hierarchy Extensions of Power* Signature Books, 1997 p 161

As discussed earlier, when Joseph Smith finished writing the *Book of Mormon*, he coerced Martin Harris into financing its publication. After the *Book of Mormon* was published, Smith told the story that he and Oliver Cowdery were given the authority to baptize by John the Baptist. At the same time, Cowdery and Smith, according to Smith's story, were given the Aaronic Priesthood by John the Baptist. The story of this authority given to Joseph Smith and Oliver Cowdery by John the Baptist was necessary in Smith's eyes in order to make him the Prophet and the official communicator with God for his new church. Since this incident would validate his divine connection to God, Smith could anoint and baptize others into the priesthood and give them the right to administer church ordinances and sacraments including baptism. Male members of the church were and are today considered by the church to receive their priesthood authority from John the Baptist through Joseph Smith.

Priesthood

The organizational structure of the priesthood arose soon after Smith's book was published when he developed the concept that all male members twelve years of age or older could have Mormon priesthood. The twelve-year-olds are ordained into Aaronic Priesthood as deacons. When they turn fourteen, they may be ordained in Aaronic Priesthood as teachers, and at sixteen, as priests. Upon passing certain requirements at the age of eighteen, they can be ordained as elders in the Melchizedek priesthood, with such privileges as the laying on of hands (to heal the sick or afflicted), serving as missionaries and participation in other more important functions of the church.

The priesthood which is the basis for the organizational structure of the church, provides the manpower necessary to administer the many programs of the church. As related earlier, in the Mormon Church the power comes from the top starting with the Prophet and his two Counselors and the Twelve Apostles to the Presidency of the Seventy to the First and Second Quorum of the Seventy to Presiding Bishopric, to the area and regional representatives to stake presidents and ward bishops and to the Melchizedek priesthood holders down to the Aaronic Priesthood. They administer each in their own sphere their given assignments and programs of the church, which include the Boy Scouts, Beehives (for girls), the recreational and social functions, the home teachers, etc. The priesthood provides the church with men for many appointments and responsibilities, as well as officers for the many businesses that are run for the profit of the Corporation of the President, i.e., the Mormon Church.

While the Mormon Church claims a membership of more than 11 million (St. George *Spectrum* 4/7/00) throughout the world, with fewer than one-half residing in the United States, only about one in four of these members is active or worthy enough to receive appointments with church responsibilities. The callings (as appointments or assignments are called) for positions in the wards and stake levels of the church are made locally, although the missionaries are called on missions by the President/Prophet after he has received recommendations for them by the local bishops and stake presidents. Many positions do, after local recommendations, receive an official call from the General Authorities and even from the President himself.

The Mormon Church does not operate democratically, although leaders pretend to be democratic in some matters. For example, bishops and other appointed officials are periodically presented to members for their approval or consent. When a vote on this request is made, all hands are raised, indicating unanimous approval. Secret ballots are never used in making appointments and decisions of the church.

All authority and, therefore, power within the church evolves from the President of the church. The President is assisted in his decision-making by his two Counselors and the Quorum of Twelve Apostles. In reality, there are fourteen apostles in the Mormon Church, in addition to the President, who, prior to becoming the President of the Church, was the President of the Quorum of the Twelve Apostles, or oldest member (not by age, but by position) in the Quorum of the Twelve. The President and his two Counselors, the Quorum of Twelve, the Presidency of the Seventy, the Two Quorums of the Seventy and the Presiding Bishopric are known as General Authorities of the Church. From them the authority goes to the area and regional representatives and then finally to the stake presidents and bishops who are leaders in the local levels of the church who, in turn, give authority to various quorums and priesthood leaders in the wards and stakes.[133]

Democracy, in its highest form, promotes freedom of thought, protection of individual rights and encourages a well-read and literate society. Censorship and restriction of reading materials in a democracy are generally not practiced except in cases of national security or in the case of pornographic materials for children. However, in the Mormon Church, members are cautioned not to read non-faith promoting materials. As Scott writes: "—Those wavering in the faith who sneak furtively off to a public library to check out a book critical of Mormonism will find many such listed in card catalogues but few, if any, on the shelves. One Mormon missionary explained this phenomenon by saying that in his area it was common practice for missionaries to keep anti-Mormon books checked out of the libraries continuously until the book got 'lost'."[134]

This is tantamount to the burning orgy by the Nazis under the leadership of Adolf Hitler, who was attempting to create a one-minded society, one that was more susceptible to totalitarian leadership. Is it the purpose of the Mormon Church hierarchy to keep the membership ignorant of the true history of Joseph Smith? Documentation reveals that the *Book of Mormon* is a hoax, that Smith's revelations from God were fraudulent, that his temple ceremonies were copied from the Masonic lodge, and that his leadership often resulted in great and unnecessary hardship and suffering for his followers. Smith's inventions of baptism for the dead, male members becoming gods of their own planets and the wearing of sacred garments have no theological or scientific foundation or merit.

Scott writes that: "...The priesthood holders have become the network holding this vast religious empire together, and the means of communication between leaders and members.

"In any community where Mormons worship together, they meet in congregations of 250 to 500 people, known as wards. Up to ten wards in a given geographical area form a stake. Usually two or three wards will share a meetinghouse, and attend worship services in shifts."

Scott continues: "Whenever Mormons worship together in wards or branches, they subdivide themselves for the tasks at hand. There are committees to take care of the aged, to do genealogical and welfare work, and even to determine musical selections for worship services. The Sunday school has a superintendent, greeters, organists and pianists, choristers, a secretary, teachers, teacher trainers, media aides, supervisors and more."[135]

Church Hierarchy

According to Coates, in 1995 there were 160,000 high priests in the Mormon Church holding offices ranging from the President down to the bishop. Coates writes that: "While all Mormon men are priests, the best-connected soon become bishops. Bishops from several wards (parishes) convene at stake houses (dioceses) where they spend much time deliberating on the devotion of individual priests and their wives to the 'United Effort', Brigham Young's term for the uniquely Mormon approach to community affairs. Priests tend to be blue-collar workers, clerks, farmers, computer programmers or school teachers, while bishops tend to be auto dealers, chiropractors, store owners, plant managers, school principals and, of course, doctors and lawyers. Priests are Jaycees, while bishops belong to the Chamber of Commerce.

"Bishops move up by aspiring to a place on the Quorum of Seventy, the body of elders who manage the Mormon empire's assets, handle its massive stock trading, administer its vast news and entertainment media assets, oversee its many agribusiness operations, real estate holdings and other ventures. Within the Quorum, seventy aging men vie for openings on the Council of Twelve Apostles, the dozen old men who move according to strict seniority onto the three-member First Presidency—patterned after the Holy Trinity — and ultimately to the Presidency itself, the role of Mormondom's 'prophet, seer and revelator.' The church teaches that the President receives direct revelations from God and is not to be questioned on matters of belief.

"...These geriatric Mormon hierarchical systems have been oppressive and intolerant of those who raise only the mildest of questions. In politics, rule by seniority is dangerous enough, but in religion it can become disastrous."[136]

Priesthood Rule

Joseph Smith's development of the priesthood rule in the Mormon community was greatly enhanced by Brigham Young's thirty-year reign as the President and Prophet of the church from 1847 to 1877. Young admired autocratic government and felt that qualified men should remain in office for life. Quinn writes: "Nineteenth century Mormon leaders argued that factionalism, contending political parties and more than one candidate for political office were contrary to righteous political order. In the kingdom of God people exercised freedom by sustaining their leaders' decisions and by voting unanimously for the candidates presented to them."[137]

Young's followers had been well indoctrinated into the practice of bloc voting during Joseph Smith's reign over the Mormon Church from 1830 to 1844. Young preached that he was continuing Smith's church doctrine and practices and maintained that Smith's teachings were absolutely correct. As with most authoritarian leaders, complete loyalty was expected from his followers, especially those who were appointed to leadership positions. Young demonstrated his devotion and loyalty to Smith and in this he encountered no risk that such loyalty could ever diminish his own authority since his "beloved" Prophet was now dead.

The success of the "bloc vote" was astounding, as the negative Utah territorial vote in 1852 against church candidates was only .49 percent, .3 percent in 1861, 6 percent in 1862, .1 percent in 1864, .3 percent in 1865, and .3 percent in 1868. Gradually, the percentage of negative votes against church candidates increased, for in 1882, 17.4 percent of the voters voted against church candidates in Utah.[138]

The result of bloc voting by the Mormons in Utah and some surrounding states resulted in great apathy by the Utah Mormons, since many felt "Why vote?" since the "election" was prearranged by the priesthood and there was no contest. The voters were described as 'too lazy or indifferent to walk or ride to the polls.'[139]

As a result of the "common consent" practices of the priesthood rule of the Utah territorial legislature, for 30 years Utah legislators passed all bills as laws or tabled them unanimously.[140]

Theocracy in Utah Ends

In order to convince the Congress of the United States that Utah was no longer a theocracy, Mormon Church authorities began to encourage their constituency to vote for both of the major American parties. This would make Congress more favorable toward the admission of the Utah Territory as a state in the Union. The theocracy of the Mormon Church in Utah ceased functioning in 1887 after Mormon President John Taylor's death. And for a period of about sixty years, from 1900 to about 1960, Mormon Church members were free to campaign and vote for whom they pleased without any guidance or pressure from the church leadership. In fact, under the leadership of President Joseph F. Smith, the church adopted a... "doctrine of the separation of church and state; the non-interference of church authority in political matters; and the absolute freedom and independence of the individual in the performance of his political duties. If at any time there has been a conduct at variance with this doctrine, it has been in violation of the well-settled principles and policy of the church."[141]

This declaration of the church led to relative freedom of Mormon Church members in political activities in the first half of the twentieth century. It was also a policy that would make many apostles turn over in their graves, since they believed that absolute power given to one man was the best and most efficient human government and that a people obedient to a theocracy provided prosperity and happiness. In order to assume statehood and to prove that Mormon Church leaders believed in individual freedoms outside of the church, the Church Authorities had temporarily abandoned the theocracy that they had planned for the United States and the world in the first fifty years of the twentieth century. However, after 1960, there is evidence that shows church leaders began moving away from the policy of separation of church and state and individual political freedom. This is indicated by the following.

To illustrate the freedom that church members had in politics Utah Senator Reed Smoot, an apostle, disregarded President Joseph F. Smith's instructions to vote to sustain President Taft's veto of an immigration bill, and despite the First Presidency's public opposition to Franklin Delano Roosevelt, nearly 70 percent of Utah's Mormons voted for him during the four times that he ran for president. Church President Heber J. Grant had spoken for years favoring prohibition, but in 1933, Utah Mormons overwhelmingly voted for anti-prohibition candidates.[142]

Political freedom for the members of the Mormon Church continued up to the election of Dwight D. Eisenhower as U. S. President in 1952. After the election of a Republican president, the Church Authorities gradually increased their control of the church members' votes, which culminated in the Mormon campaign to defeat the Equal Rights Amendment and more recently (1999) when Mormons campaigned in Hawaii and California to defeat same sex marriages in these states.

Quinn suggests that the "adoration" campaign of the Mormon

Church General Authorities has "increased political allegiance of
rank-and-file Mormons to political direction by the First Presidency.
It became more difficult for the majority of faithful Mormons to dissent politically from the Presidency than it had been in the first half
of the twentieth century. For example, 88 percent of students at
Brigham Young University in 1973 valued 'obedience to [church]
authority above own desires,' compared with 41 percent of BYU students who held that view in 1935."[143]

According to Quinn, the "adoration campaign" for the General
Authorities has made it unlikely that faithful members will dissent
(even privately) from the political counsel of Mormon Church headquarters. In Utah, for example, 86 percent of the state legislators in
1993 were Mormon, and legislative leaders meet periodically with
the church's council of four members of the Twelve Apostles to discuss legislation.[144]

Wealth of the Church

The Mormon Church has enormous wealth to use in financing
the well-organized proselytizing, public relations and maintenance
organizations of the Mormon Church. The complete control of the
spending and income budgets are in the hands of the fifteen Higher
Authorities of the church, the First Presidency (the President and his
two Counselors) and the Twelve Apostles. Decisions upon spending
the money are based first of all upon promoting the empire which
these fifteen individuals control, namely the Mormon Church. Since
the President is the final authority for making all major decisions
within the Mormon Church, he controls the financial decision making.

Because of the church's large empire, the President, of necessity, calls upon his two Counselors and the Twelve Apostles for guidance upon the spending plan. They, in turn, seek guidance from the
First and Second Councils of Seventy who have knowledge of
regional needs. The two Councils of Seventy, in turn, seek guidance
or recommendations from local stake presidents and bishops in
spending for local needs. Nevertheless, the ultimate and final decisions on financial affairs rest with the President of the Mormon
Church. The President of the church and other General Authorities
often appoint their own family members to important positions, and
for this reason, many of the current leaders of the church are descen-

dants of the founders and early leaders, including the Youngs and the Smiths. In fact, many of the past Presidents of the church were related to Joseph Smith, its founder. The top leaders of today descend from about twenty families who were active in the church in the early 1830s.

Secrecy in Financial Control of the Church

The income and expenses of the Mormon Church are kept secret by the General Authorities, and presumably the budget of the Church is approved by their common consent. "Common consent" in the Mormon Church means that the President presents the budget to the other Authorities, listens to their suggestions, after which he approves or disapproves of such suggestions, and then submits the budget for "common consent." A show of hands is unanimous in their "common consent" for the budget. According to Shupe, "... control of the Mormons' vast wealth is concentrated in the hands of a small group of directors. We know from the structure of the church hierarchy that no more than a dozen men really make significant decisions about investment policies and priorities. As we saw from recent changes made in the church's stock investment plans, religious outlooks and preoccupation of just a relatively few key persons can affect hundreds of millions of dollars and indirectly, the lives and careers of millions of church members tied by employment and investment of those monies."[145]

Shupe collected a vast amount of data and estimated the total assets of the church as early as 1983 to be almost eight billion dollars.[146] Considering the enormous growth of the church's stock portfolio due to favorable economic conditions in recent years, favorable tax exemptions from local, state and federal governments and the doubling of church membership, it is reasonable to estimate that these assets have increased by more than six times since 1983. The value in temples and ward buildings alone is estimated at twenty billion dollars. (In 1997, *Time* magazine reported that the Church owned fifty temples and 11,575 meetings houses.)[147] As cited earlier, the news media show the church with plans for additional temples which will increase the total temples to more than 100. (The 70th Mormon temple was dedicated on January 23, 2000, in Kona, Hawaii.) Meeting houses added in recent years would bring the total to at least 13,000. The Salt Lake City temple had a valuation of $79 million in 1983, with others ranging down in price to $2 million.[148] The value of its business corporate empire is estimated at $25 billion and miscellaneous holdings of $5 billion. Annual ten percent tithing by twenty-five percent of its five million church members in the United States is estimated at $5 billion per year. Gifts and other tithing by members is estimated at about $2.5 billion yearly. Income from investments and non-religious corporations is estimated to be $5 billion per year.

In a more recent analysis (1999) of Mormon Church income and expenses, it was stated: "The talented church managers run a tight and profitable financial ship and can spend the cash any way they choose. They are not held accountable to the unquestioning flock in any way. The officials make their investment decisions in secret and report no dollar figures to anyone outside of white-haired, life-tenured gentlemen at the top. One thing, however, is known. The church is on a building binge of historic proportions, part of an attempt to match its burgeoning global membership. It is building 350 meeting houses or chapels each year and has more than a hundred of its trademark temples in operation, under construction or announced. Large temples cost $18 million or so a pop. All of this is financed with cold hard cash. The church tells its members to avoid debt, and it practices what it preaches."[149]

The Balance Sheet of the Mormon Church

Since the Mormon Church keeps financial matters secret, it is not known the amount of its income and expenses. The total wealth of the Mormon Church is estimated to be $50 billion. One periodical in 1999 estimated the church's wealth to be more than $30 billion. (Economist, February 13, 1999, p. 34) *Time* magazine had a ten-page report on Mormonism in its August 4, 1997 issue. Under the title: "MORMONS, INC. The Secrets of America's Most Prosperous Religion," Time reported the Mormon Church's assets to total a minimum of $30 billion with an annual income of $5.9 billion. According to the Time report, "THE TOP BEEF RANCH IN THE WORLD IS NOT the King Ranch in Texas. It is the Deseret Cattle & Citrus Ranch outside Ireland, Fla. It covers 312,000 acres; its value as real estate alone is estimated at $858 million. It is owned entirely by the Mormons. The largest producer of nuts in America, AgReserves, Inc., in Salt Lake City, is Mormon owned. So is the

Bonneville International Corp., the country's 24th largest radio chain, and the Beneficial Life Insurance Co., with assets of $1.6 billion. There are richer churches than the one based in Salt Lake City: Roman Catholic holdings dwarf Mormon wealth. It should be noted that the Catholic Church has 86 times as many members and is about 1400 years older than the Mormon Church!!! There is no major church in the U. S. as active as the Latter-Day Saints in economic life, nor, per capita, as successful at it... Last year (1996) $5.2 billion in tithes flowed into Salt Lake City, $4.9 billion of which came from American Mormons." Time reports also while other churches spend most of what they receive in a given year, the LDS Church puts nearly $6 billion yearly into investments. Time estimated that the Mormon Church's investments alone equaled at least $11 billion.

Tithing members of the Mormon Church would rightfully be concerned about the Time report and the above estimates of the Mormon Church's income and wealth if they knew of them. However, few members are aware of the great wealth of the Mormon Church and its expenditures. In addition to putting all of the corporate financial income back into investments, the General Authorities are funneling over $1 billion of the tithing income into investments. The Mormon Church members who are struggling to meet the church's demand for ten percent of their incomes would wonder why this income is not spent for church (religion) related activities. The church leaders seem to be unconcerned about the financial needs of the large concentration of Mormons living in mobile home communities throughout the State of Utah populated by people who are barely able to make ends meet. Faithful as they are, these poor souls are encouraged by the church to raise large families, and they are barely scraping together enough to feed, clothe and house their children. Given the opportunity, they surely would question the siphoning off of their tithing dollars for lucrative business deals made by the church hierarchy. They would surely wonder if some of the church's money could be used to improve their lot.

One example of the wealth and centralized nature of the Mormon Church is illustrated by their common practice of financing ninety percent of local ward churches while ten percent is paid for by raising money from local members.

All of the income of the Mormon Church is funneled into the

Salt Lake City central office and managed by the General Authorities (the President and his Two Counselors, the Twelve Apostles and the Presiding Bishopric). A portion is returned to local leaders, (bishops and stake presidents) to finance wards and stakes with their programs. However, a large amount remains in Salt Lake City for promoting the church and its proselytizing activities. Some of these activities include: (1) Supporting the vast public relations programs, including television and media advertising, (2) Maintaining its missionary centers in the United States and around the world, (3) Maintaining and expanding its vast network of television and radio stations throughout the United States and the world, (4) Operating and expanding its network of satellite programming in the United States and the world, (5) Providing "instructional" materials for local wards, (6) Financing "faith promoting" books and materials, (7) Operating and expanding its missionary training centers (8) Providing "flip charts" and instructional materials for the church-claimed sixty thousand missionaries (note: missionaries have to buy them from the church with their own monies) and (9) Maintaining the large central office staff to administer the church as approved by the General Authorities.

Understandably such a large organization as the Mormon Church with its massive holdings (not only religious but corporate), would be entangled in a constant string of lawsuits. According to Shupe, "Most of the church's legal fees are paid to the Utah law firm of Kirton, McConkie and Bushnell. Oscar McConkie, a senior partner in the firm, is the brother of the late Apostle Bruce R. McConkie. He also married one of the daughters of the late LDS President, Joseph Fielding Smith. Smith was instrumental in having Bruce R. McConkie 'called' to the First Council of the Seventy and late to the apostleship on the Council of Twelve.

"...KM&B's forty-one attorneys handled an estimated 3,000 lawsuits, both in the United States and overseas. The lawsuits we reviewed fell into four categories, listed in order of relative frequency before 1980:

1. *Disaffected Members and Others.* These included members who voluntarily left the church or were excommunicated for whatever reason as well as ordained ministers and others outside the Mormon faith.

2. *Business-Related.* Here we include suits both when the church was a plaintiff and when it was defendant. On occasion the

church has also been a third party in a suit (such as a beneficiary to the estate of a deceased person).

3. *Discrimination.* The LDS Church has been involved in numerous cases involving alleged racial, religious and sexual discrimination.

4. *Government Tax Status.* The Internal Revenue Service and State, County and City governments have on occasion challenged the tax-exempt status of church lands and enterprises."[150]

Several suits have been brought against the Mormon Church, including: (1) from members who have been excommunicated from the Church, (2) from employees who have been fired in church related businesses for not tithing and for not attending church regularly and in some cases for not receiving temple recommends to be able to participate in the church's temple work and (3) from local, state and national governments for non-payment of property and income tax.[151]

Local, state and national governments often grant tax exemptions for religious organizations, for churches and properties used for church purposes. The Church Authorities have often been involved in "politics" to help preserve their tax exempt status. "... Henry D. Moyle, first counselor to the Church President," was sent to London to help preserve the tax exempt status of the London temple. A church attorney, Oscar McConkie "recalled with pride" in a speech that he was able to persuade the Oregon state senate not to remove the tax exempt status of church properties in Oregon. The church has won some of the efforts to preserve tax exempt status for its properties even though it was making a profit. Church officials have often used the claim that the profits of their properties were being used primarily for "welfare services."[152]

Other church profit-making enterprises such as Brigham Young University's Polynesian Cultural Center in Hawaii were forced by the IRS in 1983 to pay income taxes on their profits. The church claimed that the PCC was a student welfare program, since University students were employed by the center so that they may be able to finance their school expenses. However, the IRS disagreed since the center had accumulated more than $10 million in profits, some of which had been sent to the Corporation of the President of the Church of Jesus Christ of Latter-Day Saints for investment purpose.[153] In 1997, according to a Time report, the Polynesian Cultural Center of Hawaii, owned by the church was

Hawaii's main attraction, with annual revenues exceeding $40 million.[154]

Many questions arise about the tax exempt status for a church that has more than $50 billion in assets controlled by a few individuals in the church hierarchy. Should a tax exempt status be continued for an organization that does not make its financial affairs known to its members? A tax exempt status of the church puts more of the financial burden for supporting government activities such as the military, welfare, roads, schools, etc. upon the general public. How much of the billions of dollars collected in tithing from members each year actually goes into profit-making corporations rather than church or religious activities? The Mormon Church is using tax exempt dollars to finance millions of proselytizing and church promotion activities throughout the United States and the world, Except on rare occasions, missionaries' expenses are not paid by the church, but are either paid by the missionaries themselves or their parents. Parents of missionaries send their support monies to the church, and the church forwards the money to the missionaries. This is done so that parents can deduct money that goes to their children for missions, as tax deductions to a "charitable organization," the Mormon Church.

Shupe puts it very mildly when he writes: "In short, because the church's millennial vision includes earthly economic and political power, it continues to establish and run profitable businesses while claiming the tax-exempt status accorded non-profit religious organizations. We are not the first to note this aspect of Mormonism, but it is a subject rarely dealt with by the national press."[155]

Add to the above statement that: The church's millennial vision includes economic and political power. And that Presidents of the Mormon Church have been ordained Kings in secret ceremonies and that they are said to maintain a special Council of Fifty charged with the responsibility to run the government of the United States and the World, to usher in the "Mormon kingdom of God on earth." Supposedly, this Kingdom of God on earth, which the church would establish is to be given to Jesus Christ who is to govern the earth for one thousand years. Do you suppose that the President of the Mormon Church who has been ordained King would voluntarily turn his country or his world over to Jesus Christ? Why would they have themselves ordained Kings, if they do not intend to be Kings?

Let us now look at the progress that the General Authorities have made in achieving what the author believes to be their goal: controlling the United States and the world.

1. The Mormon Church has (according to its own published figures) more than doubled its membership from five million in 1983 to over eleven million in 2000.

2. The assets of the Mormon Church have been estimated to have increased from about $15 billion in 1983 to over $50 billion in 2000.

3. Satellite dishes to receive Mormon Church messages by television have been installed in local ward and stake buildings throughout the United States and the world.

4. Sixty thousand fully trained, adequately financed and prepared Mormon missionaries are serving in all parts of the United States and in over 125 countries around the world.

5. Because young Mormon men have served in and studied the languages of foreign countries throughout the world, large numbers of them have been hired by the federal Central Intelligence Agency and therefore are in control of a significant number of CIA activities.

6. Many Mormon men have been hired by the FBI, a preponderance when considering their proportion to the percentage of the population.

7. In year 2000, a Mormon, Orrin Hatch, a United States Senator from Utah, ran for president of the United States. He was chairman of powerful senate committees.

8. The Mormon General Authorities were successful in opposing the Equal Rights Amendment by organizing members to lobby key state legislators to vote against the amendment (even though the vast majority of the United States people supported it). Sonia Johnson has written an excellent book: *From Housewife to Heretic* describing tactics used by the Mormon Church leadership in obtaining the ERA rejection in several key states.

To emphasize a point, the author repeats the following:

A famous Mormon saying should scare free-thinking Americans about the kind of government that the author believes that the General Authorities have planned for the United States is: **"When our leaders speak the thinking has been done. When they propose a plan—it is God's plan. When they point the way, there is no other way that is safe. When they give direction, it should mark the end of controversy."**

9. A Mormon Church radio network is in operation that is both

national and worldwide. The Mormon Church-owned Brigham Young University airs church promoting broadcasts throughout the world. The basketball games of BYU are especially attractive to South American listeners.

10. The Church owns several television stations, including KSL-TV of Salt Lake City, KBYU-TV in Provo, Utah and KIRO-TV in Seattle, Washington.

11. The church utilizes radio and televisions stations throughout the United States to broadcast "Home Front Series" offering to send listeners free copies of the KJV of the Bible or the *Book of Mormon* and family value videos. They are given toll-free phone numbers to call for these. When they arrive, they come with two Mormon missionaries "attached," wanting an appointment to talk to families. These radio and television commercials are professionally produced and designed to enhance the public image of the church. (For anyone who orders these free materials from the Home Front, the Mormon Church has a professionally organized follow-up program. In addition, after the missionary visits, the mission president's office of the district follows up these proselytizing calls.)

12. Devout Mormons have been chairmen of the Federal Communications Commission (FCC) and have been influential in approving the Mormon Church expansion of its radio and television stations. One FCC commissioner (Nicholas Johnson) who opposed further granting of radio and television licenses to the Mormon Church wrote:

"Bonneville International Corporation receives approval today from this Commission to add to its stable of industrial and mass media properties an AM radio station and an FM radio station in the second largest market in the United States: Los Angeles — a city in which it already has a $20 million interest in the prestigious and dominant *Los Angeles Times*.

"This action is taken without a public discussion of the principle issues raised by this case: the conflicts with the public interest in granting ever—increasing mass media power—with all it economic, political and social implications to large industrial conglomerate corporations in the United States, in this case an industrial conglomerate that is inexorably intertwined with a religious sect, the Mormon Church."[156]

13. In 1983, Shupe estimated the grand total of all Mormon Church communications properties to be $547,640,000. Today by

interpolation these properties are estimated to be valued at $4 billion. Since media is an enormous tool for enhancing control of public thinking (as political campaigners and advertisers have learned by showing their willingness to spend huge sums on radio and television commercials), the Mormon Church has a tremendous advantage in the aim to build its Mormon kingdom of God on earth.[157] The FCC must be careful to insure that the Mormon Church is not gaining control of public opinion and that the church is not hampering the free dissemination of news. Democratic principles and individual freedoms cannot endure if an organization that, as documentation shows, fosters an authoritarian theocracy, a religion conceived from the figment of the mind of a mystical, magical, treasure digger, gains control of public opinion and has free dissemination of news to the public of the United States and the world. It should also be emphasized that the current President of the Mormon Church, 94-year old Gordon B. Hinckley has had a lifelong career in public communications and public relations in the church.[158] This may explain why the Mormon Church has put so much emphasis and money into media and public relations in recent years.

Because of the financial growth of the Mormon Church, the management of the $50 billion empire has forced the development of a large bureaucracy within the church. As many as 10,000 people are employed full time to administer the business of the church such as financial affairs, keeping track of present and new members, the assignment of the sixty thousand missionaries, supervision of its vast communications network, administration of its large genealogical division and insuring that church doctrine is being followed.

Tithing in the Mormon Church was implemented by Joseph Smith shortly after it was established in 1830. Smith's tithing was set as ten percent of a man's surplus property, but not on his basic property. Brigham Young "placed great emphasis on tithing and donations, making this obligation a deciding factor even in how members could enter into fellowship with their neighbors."[159] Many members today give more than ten percent, feeling that "if they give more, the Lord will be more generous in return." About "one-third of Mormons [1985] pay at least a full tithe (ten percent of annual income before taxes)."[160]

According to Shupe "...All church employees are expected to pay a full tithe or face immediate termination. How would the church know if a member had not tithed? In the same way it learns of fornication, adultery and the other sins it is determined to stamp out: through the rigorous questioning of members seeking temple recommends and through the reports of ward bishops and other local officials as well as the payroll records of Mormon companies."[161]

Tithing is not the only way that Mormons support their church. Many donations in addition to tithing are made to the church in estate property grants and company executives' granting of company stock to the church. A very important contribution is that nearly all of the 60,000 missionaries pay for their own expenses while on two-year missionary assignments. Mormon families often establish a "mission savings account" for their children who eventually will serve a mission. Part of the earnings of their children is put into the "mission bank" as they grow older, so that many have a sizable savings account when they are old enough to go on their missions. Parents pay donations to the church for any additional money that is needed for the missionary to pay his expenses while on the mission. This is in addition to their regular tithing and other donations to the church.

Since the Mormon Church Authorities teach that service and financial support for the church is important in attaining a higher level in the Celestial heaven, many Mormons sacrifice greatly through volunteering of their time and in tithing to the church.

Tithing in the Mormon Church has vacillated between voluntary contributions with no suggested amounts in its early history, to giving the church all of the members' property, except a portion for the member's own living and well-being.

Brigham Young estimated that his members were paying only about one percent of their incomes for tithing.[162] It was reported that in 1910, 16.5 percent of the Mormons in that year paid a full ten percent tithing. But when wage earners were placed into the statistics, in 1915, 73 percent of the wage earners paid some tithing.

Tithing in a Big Way

In 1962, the per capita tithing payment was $56 (about $253 in 1990 dollars). Thus an average tithing family of six would pay $1,518 (1990 dollars). Today most devout Mormons, define full tithing as ten percent of gross earnings. In the 1990s estimates of $5 billion (probably much below the actual figure as noted by Quinn) was received from tithing by the Church Authorities each year.[163]

This calculation was also reinforced by an *Arizona Republic* report in 1991 which estimated that the church collected $4.3 billion from its members.[164] At the time of the Arizona newspaper report, the overall membership of the Mormon Church was estimated to be 7.8 million, compared with today's membership estimates of 11 million. This should provide a tithing increase of 74 percent if one also adds to the 29 percent increase in membership a 45 percent (5 percent per year for nine years from 1991 to 2000) increase in member earnings, or $8.7 billion in tithing income for the church. Discounting any revenue received from foreign Mormon Church members and considering only the five million "claimed" members in the United States, this amounts to $1,740 per capita, which is a very significant amount, far higher than any other church in the United States. About 25 percent of the Mormon Church membership in the United States is active in the church and paying full tithing. Therefore, many devout Mormons are paying $6,960 per capita each year if the estimates are true that the church receives $8.7 billion per year from tithing. In order to meet the per capita payment average, many higher income families ($100,000 or more) are contributing at least $27,840 in tithes. Tithing is also ballooned by wealthy members who often leave large amounts of their estates to the church. A report in *The Arizona Republic* also confirms that well-to-do church members pay thousands of dollars in tithing every year.[165]

That foreign countries with Mormon members contribute little to the Salt Lake treasury of the church is described by Quinn: "...it is important to recognize that tithing from Mormons outside the United States has rarely ever been transferred to church headquarters in America. Except for the early years of the British Mission (established in 1837) and the Canadian settlements of Mormons (begun in 1887), Mormon tithing funds have remained in the countries of their origin. The first reason for this is that foreign outposts of Mormonism have been financial drains on the church's general funds, which typically supplement local tithing collected outside the United States. In the nineteenth century it was more practical to use foreign tithing for the immediate needs of the missions and branches in each country where it was collected. Physical transfer of overseas funds required months of travel to and from headquarters in the United States."[166]

Tithing is not a casual matter for the Mormon Church members, for they must meet annually with their bishops during which time a tithing "settlement" is made with them. During "...this meeting members are privately told what they have donated during the year and then asked two questions: whether they wish to submit extra donations, and whether they are full tithe payers. Normally the conversation ends at that point, left to the member's own conscience."[167] Since full tithing is also a requirement for a temple recommend from the bishop for a family who wishes to witness their daughter or son married in the temple, it (full tithing) is very important for the head of the family. Marriage in the temple is an important social achievement for both Mormon parents and for their offspring, and because of that a temple recommend from the bishop is a cherished piece of paper.

Quinn quotes information that supports his contention that the Mormon Church is unlike most other churches, especially those in the United States, since the Mormon Church leaders state that the money management's goal is the expansion of the church "as [a] temporal structure whose major goal is spiritual—the building of the kingdom of God on earth in preparation for the millennial reign of Jesus Christ."[168] It is temporal as well as spiritual, while most other churches are concerned only with the spiritual, leaving man's economic and political affairs up to the individual, without undue interference. Mormon religious leaders' involvement in members' political and economic affairs as well as spiritual affairs, is clearly shown in the early history of Mormonism under the leadership of Joseph Smith and Brigham Young. As previously mentioned during these years (1830 to 1877) total religious and economic domination was practiced in members' lives. However, in the period of intense federal intervention (about 1877 to 1896) and the period of political and economic freedom for Mormon Church members (about 1896 to 1960), control of political and economic freedom by church leaders was relaxed. And, as stated earlier, since the 1960s, General Authorities have become more involved in the economic and political affairs of church members.

Freedom to Spend

Very few organizations in the world can get by without some accounting of their income and expenditures to members of the organization, and until about the 1960s the Mormon Church was generally accountable to its members for its financial affairs. Around that time, the General Authorities decided that reporting their financial affairs to church members was an unnecessary restriction upon their freedom to "do the will of God" to establish the "kingdom of God" on earth. In order to attain this "kingdom," they had to be able to spend freely to proselytize and expand church membership throughout the United States and the world. As stated previously, Mormons are taught that the church General Authorities, since they are God's appointed representatives, are infallible and incapable of making mistakes or wrong decisions for the church.

And make decisions, they do. They decide where temples will be built, how they are to be built and when. They approve the design and location of new local stake houses. They decide where money will be spent for proselytizing, in what countries, in what areas of that country, and in accordance with where proselytizing will be the most successful. Their recruiting machinery includes a world-wide network of radio and television stations, assisted by a vast array of satellite receivers.

Decisions are made concerning what are the most effective media and public relations devices to reach out and gain converts. Free copies of the *Book of Mormon* are found in many public places, especially in Utah and surrounding Mormon country. In Utah, the *Book of Mormon* replaces the Gideon Bible in hotel rooms, and Joseph Smith's book is even found in the waiting rooms of auto repair shops, doctors' and dentists' offices, etc.

Financial decisions are also made as to the payment of salaries of full time church leadership and General Authorities. Generally those who have an outside income from investments, etc. are not paid or do not accept salaries. Those who do not have an independent income generally receive income necessary for them to fulfill their duties properly. Other officers like stake presidents and bishops do their work as volunteers, most of whom retain their regular position of employment. This was not always true in early Mormon history, as during the reign of Brigham Young, ward bishops "drew at will from the primarily non-cash tithing Mormons donated." Young was able in 1859 to claim property for himself of $100,000, worth almost as much as the entire Mormon Church's holdings and in 1875 he estimated his wealth at $600,000.[169]

Bishops, under church President John Taylor, in 1884, were allowed to retain eight percent of what they collected in tithing from members, while stake presidents were allowed to keep two percent of the bishops' receipts from church members. However, this practice was eliminated in 1896 after it was decided only to pay the Twelve Apostles of the church.[170]

As reported by Quinn, First Presidency's counselor, Gordon B. Hinckley, in 1985 reported that General Authorities received a modest amount for their services and that the source of their modest amount was not from tithing but from business income. According to one source about one-fifth of all tithing income is put into business investments, which would provide some of the business income used to pay General Authorities for their work with the church. Quinn also questioned what Hinckley meant by modest, since President Joseph Fielding Smith died at age ninety-five in 1972 with an estate worth $496,262.[171]

As the great Depression was catastrophic to the economy, it was likewise catastrophic to the Mormon Church. The church had made several bad investments as well which led to deficit spending amounting to almost $900,000 in 1938. Because disclosures of deficit spending and large losses from investments were embarrassing, the church discontinued giving complete financial reports to members and finally in 1959, financial reports were discontinued altogether. Financial matters were kept strictly secret within the leadership. Deficit spending increased to almost $32 million in 1962, which put the church in such bad financial straits that it was barely able to meet its church employees' payroll in 1963.[172]

If the Mormon Church was in such poor financial shape, with deficit spending in 1963, how did it become worth almost $50 billion in the year 2000? A large amount of the credit is given to N. Eldon Tanner who introduced the church to corporate financing. Tanner canceled new building projects until a reserve could be built up and invested money in lucrative stock deals.[173] Another explanation of the church's great increase in wealth is the great improvement in the national economy in recent years, which increased the amount of tithing of Mormon wage earners.

The Mormon Church has gained its financial strength through tithing of over $5 billion annually and investment in industry which provided an additional $5 billion of income each year. This has given the church enormous amounts of money to use in reaching the church's goal of establishing the "kingdom of God" on earth.

The state legislature in Utah and the Utah federal congressional delegation in Washington D. C. are controlled by Mormon Church authorities. Control of the Utah state government and the Utah federal congressional delegation, while an important accomplishment for the Mormon Church leadership, is only one step toward the control of the political process in United States and the world. Growth toward the "kingdom of God" on earth is a gradual expanding process. Quinn writes: "On the eve of the twenty-first century, many outsiders in the United States and other countries regard the LDS Church as engaged in colonialism and religious imperialism." To accomplish the "colonialism and religious imperialism," General Authorities no longer fill the Utah state legislature in person; instead, the hierarchy orchestrates a political agenda through loyal Mormon proxies, as well as fellow travelers of various religious persuasions who share specific political goals with the LDS hierarchy. Mormon lock-step partisanship and interfaith partnership also operate in every large satellite population of Mormonism throughout the United States. It will undoubtedly continue wherever international Mormons gain a population sufficient to wield political power within democratically governed regimes."[174]

The CES (Church Educational System) and the higher education system which are shaping church members and church leaders to be "obedient, intensely loyal, disciplined, submissive to ecclesiastical authority, committed to official orthodoxy as defined by the hierarchy," are just what the Church Authorities intend.

Chapter Five
Indoctrination, Activities and Social Pressure

Church Activities

From the days of Joseph Smith to the present time, the Mormon Church has developed an extensive social and peer group organization to keep members in the church. The active Mormon spends several hours a week in church-related activities that include church attendance, volunteering and social activities. Everyone in the family is immersed in Mormon-sponsored activities, which include volunteer service as home teachers (men), as visiting teachers (women), as members of a church basketball league, attending Boy Scout meetings, acting as Boy Scout leaders and for adults serving on the various auxiliaries. Other jobs in the church include bishops and their counselors, stake presidents and their counselors, Elders' Quorum presidents and their counselors, teachers in Relief Society, Mutual Youth Organization, Primary (for children under 12), etc. All of these programs are directed by local volunteers, who receive their direction from Salt Lake City. Since time commitment to the church and church activities is very heavy, little time is left for activities other than one's job. The sacraments, testimony and preparation for class instruction take up a good portion of Sunday which is supposed to be a day of rest and free from any kind of work. The freedom from work is substituted for work performed in church buildings, buildings that would be recognized by those familiar with Mormonism. They are without flair, of plain construction, low and long buildings with white steeples rising several feet over the rest of the buildings. Inside is found a small gymnasium, used as a gathering room for dinners and receptions, with a kitchen close by. They usually also have a stage for presentations and entertainment. Most of the stakes built in the second half of the twentieth century have the same design, with the only variation found in outside coverings, some with brick and some with wood. Often stakes serve two different wards on Sundays due to the large membership in the area.

The men have priesthood meetings on Sundays, while the women have Relief Society meetings. During the Sacrament meetings (communion), bread and water are passed, and assigned "talks" are given by members of the ward. They also have singing, and necessary announcements are made about upcoming events, etc. The first Sunday of each month is called the Fast and Testimony meeting, where there are no assigned talks, but members are encouraged to "bear their testimonies," saying "they know that the LDS Church is the true church and that Joseph Smith was a Prophet, and that the current President is likewise a Prophet of God and that the *Book of Mormon* is true," or something similar to that. "Ward, stake and regional levels encourage a wide variety of social opportunities for members of all ages, including theatrical projects, youth orchestras, athletic competitions, choirs, mini-trek campouts, square dances and devotional or 'Fireside meetings,' where talks are often given by visiting scholars or General Authorities."[175]

Boy Scouts

The affiliation of the Mormon Church with the National Boy Scouts, provides an excellent opportunity to recruit members into the church. Boy Scouts is a very popular organization since it offers camp-outs and other interesting activities that attract boys. In states with a high concentration of Mormon Churches, nonMormon boys who want to participate in Boy Scout activities often must join the Mormon Church sponsored group, as there are no other sponsors, especially in areas with a low population density. In these areas the Boy Scout troops become important recruiting prospects for the Mormon Church. Because the Boy Scouts have a "God and Country" award, for those performing their duties well, it connects

Scouts with a religion, and thus Scout programs become also an important proselytizing and indoctrination tool for the church. The First Presidency of the church reported in December, 1967 that they were reaching 80 percent of available boys in Cub Scouting, Boy Scouting and Explorers.[176] In February, 1973 Boy Scouts of America reported that one out of every twenty Boy Scouts is a Mormon, which indicates that Mormons form a much larger size of the membership than their proportion to the total population of the United States.[177] The Mormon Church affiliates with the National Boy Scout movement, but does not affiliate with the National Girl Scout organization, apparently because the National Girl Scout organization promotes women's independence. The Mormon leadership expects women to be dependent upon men.

Seminaries across the Street from Public Schools

The Utah Mormon teenager attends a "Seminary" during each school day, where classes are held in a small building across the street from the local high school. In the "Seminary," teenagers study the teachings of the "living prophets," as well as the *Book of Mormon* and other scriptures and writings of Joseph Smith and other church leaders, past and present. These writings are approved by the General Authorities and published by the church. Special materials such as workbooks that explain the doctrines of the church are used in the "Seminary." Books and materials used there include such titles as the *Book of Mormon* Stories and the *Book of Mormon Student Manual*.

The *Book of Mormon Student Manual* published by the church is typical of church-published materials about the *Book of Mormon* in that it attempts to show that the book is true and that it is divine in nature. Evidence has been presented in other chapters of this book to show that many of the ideas presented therein have been copied from other authors, as well as from the Bible. Smith's writings were based upon archaic notions prevalent in the first half of the 19th century, including the ancestry of American Indians and other disproved beliefs. It is a travesty that highly impressionable youth are encouraged to spend so much of their valuable time studying false premises.

In addition, placing the seminaries across the street from high schools is against the concept of a free pluralistic American public school system. A non-Mormon student in a school with a majority of Mormon students would find it difficult enough to remain a non-Mormon even without having a Seminary across the street from the high school. Observing Mormon students receiving released time every school day would naturally cause the non-Mormon student to want to obtain released time as well. And the peer pressure that is strong in teenagers will provide great incentive for them to become Mormons. Teenagers longing for acceptance from their peers want to be members of popular groups like the Boy Scout troops, the Mormon league basketball team, dances, field trips and Seminary classes.

The Mormon hierarchy realizes the power of peer pressure and with what the author perceives as its ambition to encompass the world with Mormonism, it is not bashful about utilizing all the weapons it has, including control of the Boy Scout troops and spon- soring many fun youth activities in order to accomplish their indoc- trination and proselytizing goals. As far as the youth are concerned, they could care less about the doctrine of the church as long as it helps them to be accepted by the group and provides them with enjoyable companionship. So the full immersion of the Mormon Church membership in such activities as dances, hikes, sports leagues, homemaking meetings and other church youth activities is a two-way trade off. In order to gain these fun and fulfilling activi- ties, all the young person has to do is accept the teachings of the Mormon Church. It is a high price to pay in order for the active Mormon youth to receive these benefits. This high price includes: (1) ten percent tithing of family gross income, (2) many hours spent weekly in church activities, (3) acceptance of false church doc- trine, (4) loss of free individual thinking, (5) obedience to Church Authorities and (6) control by the local church and priesthood leadership.

Keys to the Temple Controlled by the Church Hierarchy

Another way in which the Church Authorities maintain control and obedience from members is by allowing only worthy and faith- ful members to enter the temple; that is, they must be loyal to church leaders, be faithful to church teachings, pay ten percent tithing, be obedient to the Word of Wisdom, lead a clean and moral life and, as mentioned before, wear their sacred undergarments. Having their children married in the temple is a socially important goal of Mormon families. Young and old among Mormons are told to marry "within the faith," and not to marry, or even date outsiders.[178] Since the General Authorities "hold the keys to the temple," members must remain loyal and obedient to the church in order to get a temple recommend that allows entrance therein. Even parents of the bride and groom must have a temple recommend to attend the weddings of their sons or daughters.

And since members must have a temple recommend from their bishop (a trusted, faithful servant of the church), also signed by the stake president in order to be allowed to enter the temple, a recommend becomes a powerful tool that the Authorities use in obtaining compliance with the laws and rules of the church, including the required ten percent tithing, This explains why Church Authorities have been building temples at a record pace in recent years. Temples are located in several countries of the world including Hong Kong where a member of the Presidency assured Tung Chee Hwa, the People's Republic of China administrator over Hong Kong, that Mormon Church members accept the rule of kings, presidents and magistrates, regardless of where they live.[179]

Indoctrination Program Misses few Opportunities

The Church indoctrination program misses few opportunities. It begins almost from the time a Mormon child is born and continues until death. The program begins with Sunday school classes for the very young and attendance with parents for church services. The ward arranges for regular home visits to all members and extra home visits for those members who have missed church meetings and who may seem to be weakening in their commitments to the church. For high school youth indoctrination continues during school days for several hours each week in the Seminaries, as has already been mentioned. Many young men and some young women have saved enough money from early childhood to go on a two-year mission after graduation from high school. (For young women, a mission is for eighteen months.) For those who have the financial resources, either through savings or from parents, the indoctrination continues in the Missionary Training Center, MTC. This in a boot camp-like school lasting about two months that prepares young men and women for their missionary assignment either in the United States or in a foreign country.

The indoctrination program has an element of fear and intimidation. The August, 1992, Salt Lake Tribune reported that the First
Presidency's spokesman acknowledged existence of a special
"Strengthening the Members Committee" that keeps secret files on
church members who are suspected or regarded as disloyal. Due to
publicity about this matter in the New York Times, the Presidency
issued a statement "defending organization of this apostle-directed
committee as consistent with God's commandment to Joseph Smith
to gather documentation about non-Mormons who mob and perse-
cute the LDS Church."[180] This file is now said to include names not
only of Mormons, but also non-Mormons, those who are critical or
in any way questioning of the church and its teachings.

Brigham Young University

For many Mormon youth, the indoctrination program continues at Brigham Young University, the largest church-sponsored university in the United States, with thirty thousand students. Of these
thirty thousand students, 98.6 percent are Mormon who arrive on
campus with an average high school grade point average of 3.74.
More than 73 percent of the male students and 26.6 percent of the
female students have served their full time missions either before
they arrived on campus or will do so at sometime before graduation.
Only .4 percent of the enrollment at BYU is black.[181]
    Students who attend BYU must follow a strict honor code that
includes following a dress code, forbidding sex outside of marriage,
requiring clean shaven men, disallowing multiple earrings, maintaining a clean and neat appearance, prohibiting use of alcoholic
beverages and no visiting of dorm rooms of the opposite sex.
Occasionally the media reports prominent athletes at BYU who
have been dismissed from the university for violating the honor
code. Marriage is encouraged for students who have completed their
missions, and as a result, many students live in impoverished conditions. Laake (author of *Secret Ceremonies*) was very upset when
she became aware of the neglected living conditions that the BYU
community had for the married students.[182]
    One also finds the same impoverished conditions in Utah's
predominately Mormon cities in low income housing areas. The
author recalls one evening, visiting with a young family in a mobile
home section of the city. The mother was trying to handle a baby

and her other two young children while at the same time trying to carry on a conversation. The mobile home itself was in a bad state of repair, with doors hanging open and parts of the inside coverings torn away from the walls. This is but one example of the church's spending millions of dollars of its members' hard earned money to build temples and to pay for radio and television commercials for promoting Mormonism, and not helping to improve the lot of these needy families.

First Presidency and the Twelve Apostles Control Brigham Young University

The General Authorities are in complete control of BYU as nine of the thirteen-member controlling board are members of the First Presidency, his Two Counselors or the Quorum of Twelve. In addition, the head of the church's parochial education system, a member of the Presidency of the Seventy, is also a member of the BYU board. The remaining three seats are filled by women presidents of the women's and young women's auxiliaries "both appointed by the top General Authorities." The thirteenth seat is filled by a secretary. The current president of BYU is a member of the First quorum of Seventy.[183]

While the current (2000-2001) undergraduate student tuition of $1,470 and the graduate fee of $1,730 per semester are extremely low, even when compared with a public state university, the student pays a high price in loss of individual freedom in such areas as religion, lifestyle and academic freedom. If a student becomes indoctrinated into the Mormon faith (as most are), the lifetime cost of spending many hours a week in activities and service to the church in addition to paying the ten percent annual tithing is tremendous payment for receiving (for many students) a lifetime career. An LDS BYU student must attend religious classes and conform to the regulations drawn up by the university administration and approved by the controlling board. In addition, to remain in the university, Mormon students (98.6 percent of the enrollment) must receive an annual recommendation from their bishops. Non-Mormon students must either receive a letter of recommendation from their own church minister or one from a local Mormon Church bishop. No other university in the United States assumes such control over its students.

Academic Freedom at BYU?

Assuring that BYU students will receive a religious (LDS) education, are the 98 percent of the faculty who are Mormon. Some faculty members have attempted to obtain a measure of academic freedom, but have not been successful. D. Michael Quinn who attempted to attain academic freedom in his historical writings and research as a BYU professor, finally gave up his tenured position as a full professor of history and in his resignation letter, wrote: "...academic freedom merely survives at BYU without fundamental support by the institution, exists against tremendous pressure, and is nurtured only through the dedication of individual administrators and faculty members."[184]

Academic freedom is a cherished right of university professors since it permits them to accomplish honest and objective research and to teach without interference and censorship from university administrators or others. Academic freedom also allows a professor or a student to express his/her beliefs (political, economic, religious, etc.) without arbitrary interference. Without academic freedom, points of view on issues within the university could be forced upon them by administrators and other controlling authorities. Academic freedom is especially important in the social science fields such as sociology, history, political science and geography which often deal with controversial areas. This is not to say that academic freedom is not important in other areas such as medicine, business administration, physics, English, foreign languages and the arts. Single political party control of a university, for example, that would prevent professors from being members of opposing parties or cause to be prevented certain research that might be harmful to the political party in control, would be intolerable in a university within a free and open society.

BYU does not have academic freedom as is generally promoted by National Organizations of Professors (such as the American Association of University Professors) and restricts its students and professors from expressing or practicing anything that does not square with the teachings and doctrine of the church. To prevent professors or students on campus from being "contaminated," non-church approved films such as *The Godfather* have been banned from the campus as have such speakers as Senator Edward Kennedy, Betty Ford, Senator George McGovern, Ralph Nader and former Secretary of State Henry Kissinger.[185]

A student newspaper *Seventh East Press* was banned by the university when it published an interview by Dr. Sterling McMurrin, former U. S. Commissioner of Education in which he stated:

"I came to the conclusion at a very early age, earlier than I can remember, that you don't get books from angels and translate them by miracles; it is just that simple. So I simply don't believe the *Book of Mormon* to be authentic. I think that all of the hassling over the authenticity of the *Book of Mormon* is just a waste of time. Many things have been intentionally ignored and sometimes concealed or have been taken to have religious meanings or implications which, in my opinion, have no religious connections whatsoever. I believe that the church has intentionally distorted its own history by dealing fast and loose with historical data and imposing theological and religious interpretations on the data that are entirely unwarranted."[186]

Since the General Authorities still hold that the *Book of Mormon* is an authentic history, any attack on the book as being false is considered to be unfaithful. And there is irony in that BYU claims to be a university that teaches honesty and truth, while at the same time attempts to cover up all of the evidence that shows many of the Mormon Church's doctrines and teachings to be false. As a result, conflicts between honesty and cover-up are constants in the church's administration and leadership at the university, not only among students and faculty but among relationships with outsiders.

While BYU has managed to keep its accreditation by an outside agency in spite of its lack of academic freedom, it failed in 1992 to be approved for a local chapter of the Phi Beta Kappa "the nation's most prestigious academic honors society ... on the grounds that its mission as defined was incompatible with academic freedom."[187]

Several BYU faculty members have run into trouble with the General Authorities and the BYU administration. There was a great deal of opposition to the university rule that faculty members must have an annual "checking-up" letter on file from their bishop saying that they were temple worthy which made all scholarly careers subject to the endorsement of non-academic, off-campus church officials.

David Knowlton and Cecilia Konchar Farr appealed the negative results of their tenure reviews, Knowlton, among other things, for publishing in Dialogue and Sunstone and Farr "for her feminism and support of abortion rights." Another BYU professor was fired in 1995 "over criticism of the violence in his award-winning book of short stories, *Altmanns' Tongue*. Still another faculty member's tenure was saved (he had completed research that "suggested the church's international activity level is considerably lower than convert baptisms suggest") when he convinced one of the Apostles of his sincere testimony.[188] Another BYU professor was fired in 1996, "contrary to her department and college recommendation. The reason for terminating the English teacher was for expressing feminist views off campus. ...In support of this decision, a university spokesman notes that five percent of her student evaluations complain that [her] courses in English literature do not offer 'gospel insights' and are not 'spiritually uplifting,' even though 95 percent of student evaluations rank her highly."[189]

One official connected with the university was so upset with "what the brethren want and what we know is right" that he said: "It still bothers those of us who work here and must constantly juggle what the brethren want and what we ourselves know is right. You really have to wrestle with your conscience sometimes in cases like this because if you don't, you're going to be in deep trouble. There are no accolades for heroes here. You either keep your mouth shut and do what you're told, or take a stand for honesty and find yourself immediately unemployed. Those, I'm afraid, are the hard, cold facts of life when you decide to work up here."[190]

"Academic Freedon" Controlled by General Authorities

Academic freedom and freedom of speech are clearly not included in the goals of the General Authorities. The mission of the General Authorities is to perpetuate and enhance the Mormon Church, and they have the financial resources to do this by having control of all income generated by the church. By offering several attractive, career-building programs such as pre-medicine, law, education, pre-dentistry and pre-optometry, along with low tuition costs, they can attract promising students to their university. The students and faculty have the responsibility to support church leaders and to be faithful to church doctrine and teachings. For most Mormons, these are not difficult responsibilities since they have been so immersed in church teachings all of their lives to be faithful to their church and to believe that the General Authorities are infallible. For others, who feel that freedom of individual thought, honesty and truthfulness, along with the basic American freedoms of speech and press are more important, they remain silent. The attitude often is: "I get a low cost education with a good paying career, and for this I can pretend that I believe in church doctrine even though I know it is false." In other words, it is much easier to accept things as they are than it is to fight for freedom, truth and honesty.

Just as the United States Army has its military academy and the United States Air Force has the Air Force academy, the Mormon Church has BYU for training its future leaders. There are at least 100,000 leadership positions for Mormon priesthood holders to assume including bishops, stake presidents, mission, district and branch presidents and the General Authorities. What better way could be found to provide for the thousands of leaders for the Mormon Church than to give them a low cost education which not only ensures further indoctrination into church teachings and beliefs, but also provides students with a lifetime comfortable income? And ten percent of this income will be funneled back into the church to pay for continued proselytizing and expansion of the church all controlled by a handful of men, the General Authorities. To these Church Authorities, it is a marvelous plan, but to the average American, who values basic freedoms and individual rights it can be disastrous. In reviewing literature on the Mormon Church, the author concludes that the General Authorities are bent on replacing the American free and pluralistic democratic society with a society controlled and governed not by freely elected officials, but by the male hierarchy of the Mormon Church who would control the appointment of all government officials, including the congressional members, governors, state legislators, local officials and even the President of the United States. The ultimate plan of the Mormon Church and its authorities is to take all power to themselves, their President/Prophet becoming the king of the world!

And the Mormon Church hierarchy's indoctrination program which also prepares leaders for the American government is having outstanding success, for according to a BYU survey of its students, 98 percent believe in Joseph Smith as a Prophet and 98 percent believe that the Mormon Church is divine, the "Only True Church on the face of the whole earth." In addition, 88 percent would "place obedience to authority above your own personal preferences." (These statistics have been furnished by Brigham Young University, and their authenticity has not been verified.)[191] This BYU survey is troubling for non-Mormons who have read extensively concerning the doctrines and beliefs and the history of the LDS Church and are convinced that Joseph Smith was a false prophet, that the doctrines of the church are not of a divine nature, and who believe that "obedience to authority above your own personal preferences" is a most undesirable attribute for students in an American society.

More on the Mormon Church "Educational" System

In addition to the religious instruction that students receive at BYU, Ricks College and Hawaii's BYU branch of about 2500 students, an extensive high school religious curriculum has been developed, as mentioned earlier, that is taught for an hour a day, five days a week during the Mormon students' four year high school. According to Ostling and Ostling, "Mormon wards operate weekly Sunday school classes, as most Protestant churches do. But among major U. S. religious denominations there is nothing remotely comparable to the CES (Church Educational System) in scope. It operates a worldwide 'Seminary program,' which does not refer to graduate-level professional theological study but to catechism instruction for high school students... In the 1998-99 school year there were more than 379,000 seminary students enrolled worldwide, including more than 140,000 outside the United States, with some 15,000 each in Brazil and Mexico alone. The 'institute' program offers college level training for Mormons attending non-LDS campuses with 117,000 enrolled in the United States for 1998-99 and 149,000 elsewhere. CES classes, all using identical instructional materials translated into many languages, reach 144 countries. The massive network reports 3,300 full and part-time paid employees, assisted by 34,000 volunteers and missionaries."[192]

And as noted earlier, several western states allow released time for high school students to attend seminars. In addition to the seminars, the church's vast satellite television and radio station network provides additional contact with church leaders. A regular monthly "Fireside" message is given by a church Authority, translated into several languages and beamed to members spread throughout the United States and the world.

To reemphasize, the Mormon program of indoctrination at regular Sunday services, the religious instruction, teacher visitation program in the local wards, the high school Seminary instruction, the college institutes and the BYU religious program encompass total involvement of the Mormon Church member from "cradle to grave." The Church Educational System (CES) of the Mormon Church prepares an identical curriculum for each of various divisions of Mormon education. All curriculum materials are translated into various languages as needed throughout the world. According to Ostling and Ostling, "Curriculum materials for this huge enterprise have become more conservative in the late decades of the twentieth century, with all materials standardized and carefully vetted by the officially constituted screening committee. The Mormon sociologist Armand Mauss, a retired professor at Washington State University, says, 'An in-depth historical and contemporary study of the Church Educational System would almost certainly demonstrate in great detail the gradual (and probably deliberate) transition from a pedagogical philosophy of intellectual articulation and reconciliation to one of indoctrination.'"[193]

As has been discussed in an earlier chapter, there was a period of about sixty years from 1900 to 1960 during which time the General Authorities' counsel to church members was considered as advice only; which counsel the member could accept or disregard. However, after the 1960s, the leadership of the church has increasingly insisted that members accept its counsel and are enforcing the concept that "when the leaders speak, the thinking has been done." In the years 1900 to 1960, there was a hands-off policy by the General Authorities regarding individual political decisions.

Since the 1960s, a hardening of the General Authorities' attitude toward members who deviated in politics and from church doctrine has occurred. This indoctrination has resulted in selecting only teachers for the CES who are loyal to the church. Intellectual inquiry and academic freedom in the eyes of the General Authorities have no place in the Church Education System. As Mauss wrote "CES has become increasingly anti-scientific and anti-intellectual..."[194]

Church Educational Materials Carefully Monitored

CES materials are carefully monitored by committees working under the direction of church leaders to include only faith-promoting materials. Materials that are damaging to the church are left out even though they are true. Incidents in history that promote the church such as the anti-Mormon Haun's Mill Massacre in 1838 are fully presented in CES materials. But the Mountain Meadows

Massacre in which the Mormons used trickery to get the Fancher
train to give up arms and ammunition and then systematically murdered the remaining 120 or more members is treated lightly and
makes no mention of the Mormon responsibility for this tragedy.
*Even Mormon President Gordon B. Hinckley at the September 11,
1999 dedication for the Mountain Meadows monument went so far
as to deny any Mormon Church involvement in the massacre at all.*
And to reiterate, Hinckley said "That which we have done here must
never be construed as an acknowledgment on the part of the church
of any complicity in the occurrences of that fateful and tragic
day."[195]

In the LDS student study materials for the *Book of Mormon* no
mention is made concerning the following:

• That innumerable phrases in it were copied from the Bible.

• That thousands of changes have been made to the original
publication of the *Book of Mormon* under the directions of later
Mormon Church leaders.

• That the inaccuracies in the book show that it is not an
authentic or divine history. It lists several animals and plants that
were not in the Americas as described in the *Book of Mormon*.

• That the author of the *Book of Mormon*, Joseph Smith, was
bound over for trial for fraud by claiming that he could find hidden
treasures by using his "seer stone" and defrauded depositors in his
bank endeavor.

• That Joseph Smith had 27 or more polygamous marriages.

As mentioned above all church-approved publications that are
used for religious instruction, proselytizing and for members' bookshelves always leave out any incidents that reflect poorly upon the
church. One who has read the history of Brigham Young, for example, would be amused that the church (in the book, Teachings of
Presidents of the Church; Brigham Young) presents Young as a
monogamist rather than the polygamist that he was. Indeed, he had
as many as seventy wives "sealed" to him. In addition, in the same
book, there is no mention of his belief in blood atonement, nor of
his controversial teaching that Adam was God and Eve was one of
God's wives.

"Mormon teachers are required to present the currently acceptable, faith-promoting, official view of history, Apostle Boyd Packer
said in a famous speech to the annual Church Educational System
Religious Educators' Symposium in 1981. Packer, giving marching

orders to CES Seminary and institute teachers gave four 'cautions': (1) There is no such thing as an accurate, objective history of the church without consideration of the spiritual powers that attend this work'; (2) 'There is a temptation to want to tell everything, whether it is worthy or faith-promoting or not. Some things that are true are not very useful,' (3) 'In an effort to be objective, impartial, and scholarly, a writer or a teacher may unwittingly be giving time to the adversary. (4) The fact that something is already in print or available from another source is no excuse for using potentially damaging materials in writing, speaking, or teaching: 'Do not spread disease germs!'"[196] Those who are concerned that the church through its indoctrination program is developing an obedient and compliant membership that is willing to believe without question what their church leaders teach, should be very much concerned about the statement by Packer: "...In the Church we are not neutral. We are one-sided. There is a war going on and we are engaged in it." Many would wonder what war is going on, and if the Mormon Church is engaged in it, with whom?

In order to ensure the success of the General Authorities' indoctrination of church members these men often place themselves "above the law." This is illustrated by Apostle Dallin Oaks when he said: "Criticism is particularly objectionable when it is directed toward church authorities. It is one thing to deprecate a person who exercises corporate power or even government power. It is quite another thing to criticize or deprecate a person for the performance of an office to which he or she has been called of God. It does not matter that the criticism is true."[197]

This concept of church leaders' being immune from criticism by church members is also reinforced by the president of BYU and a General Authority himself who says: "Although we want to ensure that every faculty member has the right to discuss and analyze as broadly and widely as possible any topic, including religious topics, including fundamental doctrine of the church, we do not believe they should be able to publicly endorse positions contrary to the doctrine or to attack the doctrine. Secondly, we don't believe they should be able to attack the church deliberately, or its general leaders."[198]

Teachers and faculty members in the Church Educational System and institutions of higher learning such as BYU and Ricks College are expected to conform to church doctrine, and as a result teachers and faculty members exercise self-censorship about what

they teach, write or say about religious matters, even though in some
cases they may be teaching and writing falsehoods. In 1960, one of
the counselors in the First Presidency told the BYU president that
"You have got some members of the faculty who are destroying the
faith of our students. You ought to get rid of them."[199]

While most American teacher education curricula stress freedom of inquiry and adjustment of instruction to meet individual
abilities and needs, the CES curriculum stresses restriction of
inquiry in learning with little attention to individual abilities and
needs. Conformity to church doctrine as defined by the General
Authorities is demanded of CES faculty and Mormon higher education faculty. "The educational system is successfully feeding into the
church the kind of members and leaders it (General Authorities)
wants: bright, dedicated, disciplined, hardworking, intensely loyal,
obedient, fairly homogeneous in outlook, impressively capable of
altruism and personal sacrifice, generally highly submissive to
ecclesiastical authority and committed to official orthodoxy as
defined by the hierarchy."[200]

While these goals may be useful for the General Authorities of
the Mormon Church in maintaining control of their membership and
in expanding membership rolls and continuing expansion of financial resources, it is not helpful to the development of a healthy
democracy which provides for full expression of individual aspira-
tions and for reaching optimum economic success. While these
goals may be necessary for the General Authorities to reach their
aim of establishing a "kingdom of God" on earth, they are detrimental in developing the concept of a pluralistic society which provides for individual equality with political, economic and religious
freedoms. In short, Church Authorities do not want the general
membership of their church to be involved in doctrinal debates or
issues. They wish to continue the autocratic methods of administration of the church that were developed by Joseph Smith and sys-
tematized and reinforced by the iron-fisted rule of Brigham Young's
thirty-year reign over the church. If the Authorities' current autocratic control of the Mormon Church is an example of how they
would control the United States and the world if they had the power
to do so, they would have a monarchy or dictatorship controlled by
these men in the LDS Church hierarchy, with their prophet crowned
as king. The CES and the higher education system which are shaping church members and church leaders to be "obedient, intensely

loyal, disciplined, submissive to ecclesiastical authority, committed to official orthodoxy as defined by the hierarchy," are just what the Church Authorities intend.

Confirming that the General Authorities are committed to the continuation of the shaping of their members by the CES and BYU programs is the statement by Apostle Packer quoting the ultraconservative former President of the Mormon Church, Ezra Taft Benson, warning CES teachers, "not to purchase books or subscribe to periodicals that publish writings of church critics, particularly 'known apostates,' for either Seminary or *personal bookshelves.* ...We are entrusting you to represent the Lord and the First Presidency to your students, not the views of the detractors of the church."[201]

Even non-Mormons are pressured by Church Authorities to prevent promotion of the true history of Mormonism. Juanita Brooks' renown book, *The Mountain Meadows Massacre,* would have made an excellent movie, but the Warner Brothers' plan to make such a movie was killed after intense pressure from the Mormon hierarchy.[202] While D. Michael Quinn and other Mormon historians promote truthful and honest history of the Mormon Church, other Mormon writers of its history are quite willing to acquiesce to church leaders and write history that is often untruthful and which glorifies Mormonism. This is what Quinn calls fraud. In reality, if church members were presented a truthful and honest history of Mormonism, they would question much of the doctrine that is taught by their Authorities through their CES teachers and their BYU professors. That the General Authorities of the Mormon Church have suppressed history that is harmful to the church is clearly illustrated by Counselor Gordon B. Hinckley's involvement (in the 1980's) with Mark Hofmann in arranging for the purchase of documents from Hofmann in order to prevent them from being viewed by the church membership and the public. These documents were later found to be ingeniously crafted forgeries by Hofmann.

According to the mission statement of Brigham Young University, students are encouraged to pursue all truth and be led by the gospel of Jesus Christ since it contains these truths.[203] It also contains an extensive statement on academic freedom for students, faculty and the institution. The academic freedom statement also places limitations on faculty and restricts behavior which is harmful to the church.[204]

BYU's statement on academic freedom makes it clear that the Mormon as well as non-Mormon faculty is expected to be faithful to the church and to BYU's mission. They are expected to be responsible in their academic freedom and to have a commitment to the gospel.[205] According to the academic freedom statement, the university expects students and faculty to be guided by the gospel.[206]

Assuming that the "gospel" in the academic freedom statement includes the *Book of Mormon*, had BYU students and faculty members read research on archaeological discoveries in North and South America concerning the origin of the Native Indians, they could not be believers. Likewise, if BYU students and faculty had reviewed archaeological research of the tools that the Indians had for their use, they could not be believers in the *Book of Mormon* since these discoveries and research clearly show that the tools they used as described therein were not in existence at the time. Furthermore, students and faculty members of BYU who read the *Book of Mormon* would find that it described horses, cows, oxen and asses living in America between 600 B. C. and 421 A. D. (1 Nephi 18:25, Alma 18:9-10). Since archaeological evidence shows that such animals never existed on the American continent before the Spaniards arrived in the 1500s, they could not be believers in Joseph Smith's book. Also, BYU readers of Smith's book should know that more than 3,000 phrases were copied from the KJV Bible. If BYU professors and students are asked to seek and learn the truth, how can they be dismissed from BYU if they believe or teach that the *Book of Mormon* is not authentic or divine, but a product of 1830s thinking as contrived from the minds of Joseph Smith and his scribes. Moreover, many of the other doctrines and writings of Joseph Smith, such as the *Book of Abraham* have also been proven to be false. Are BYU student and faculty members "free indeed?" Or are they pawns of the church leadership coerced into following a false doctrine? The professor, in order to keep his job, must follow the false teachings of the General Authorities. The BYU student, in order to obtain a career, is likewise forced to accept these teachings.

A Study of BYU Academic Freedom

How do faculty members feel about academic freedom at BYU? Paul M. Rose completed a study with the title of "The Zion University Reverie: A Quantitative and Qualitative Assessment of

BYU's Academic Climate" during the 1997-98 academic year. According to Rose, the AAUP (a national organization of college and university professors) upon an investigation by its committee reported: "Much more than an isolated violation of academic freedom, the investigating committee's inquiries into complaints at BYU have revealed a widespread pattern of infringements on academic freedom in a climate of oppression and fear of reprisals."[207] Rose prepared a questionnaire which he distributed randomly to 295 professors of which 221 were returned or 75%. Of these respondents, 10 percent were female.[208] (Seventeen and a half percent of the faculty at BYU are female.) Rose found in his study that the majority of the respondents did not perceive academic freedom as a significant problem at BYU. However, he did find a "notable minority of respondents (23%) disagreed or strongly disagreed that they had the freedom to 'discuss and advocate controversial and unpopular ideas.'" He also found in his study that about one-fourth of the female respondents "perceived a lack of fairness in hiring and advancement decisions on their behalf."[209]

It was interesting to note that in Rose's study almost two-thirds of BYU professor respondents agreed or strongly agreed that they "should not conduct research that calls into question church or university procedures."[210] In his conclusions, Rose indicates that his study implies a strong commitment by the faculty to self-censorship. Self-censorship involves what to teach and what to research. And one's own behavior at BYU is guided by all encompassing involvement by faculty members in church indoctrination. The life-long indoctrination that the Mormon faculty member has received leads to this self-censorship. The total immersion into Mormon Church doctrine and beliefs has made them immune to any questioning of their religion. Therefore, it is not surprising that the majority of BYU faculty members do not perceive academic freedom as a problem at that institution. Faculty members know that they cannot continue on the faculty if they question essential church doctrine and beliefs as defined by the General Authorities. Either they accept this, get fired or resign and go somewhere else.

Undoubtedly a significant number of BYU faculty members do not believe in the authenticity and divinity of Joseph Smith's book, the *Book of Mormon*, and they do not believe in much of the church doctrine. However, they do not consider their non-belief serious enough to break their ties to the university. They may become what

one author has called "Partial Covenant," believers which he
defines as one who "practices the faith, but through a compromised
acceptance of church authority consistent with personal integrity,
and does so silently."[211] Others no doubt believe not at all in the
Mormon religion but remain silent in the interest of maintaining
economic and family tranquility. Others cannot accept the church's
false teachings and are alarmed that so much human and financial
resources are wasted in the proselytizing efforts toward the church's
goal to control the United States and ultimately the world.

In response to the statement, "When our leaders speak, the
thinking has been done," the Mormon Church Leadership replied to
one inquiry from a non-Mormon who complained about this statement writing: "Even to imply that members of the Church are not to
do their own thinking is grossly to misrepresent the true ideal of the
church..." they (the Mormon Church leadership) did not retract this
statement made to the entire LDS membership. The Mormon hierarchy has one message for the general public and another for their
obedient membership.[212]

General Authorities of the church even have control of academic freedom in public institutions of higher learning in Utah. In
April, 1964, Daryl Chase, Mormon president of Utah State
University, confided that "the LDS Church has a greater strangle
hold on the people and institutions of the state now than they had in
Brigham's time (1847-1877). Complete academic freedom is actually non-existent."[213]

Other examples of student and faculty restriction of freedom
by the Mormon hierarchy include:

1. April, 1966, BYU president Ernest L. Wilkinson makes first
reference in his diary to receiving reports from "spy ring" he has
authorized and which become national scandal within ten months.[214]

2. February, 1967, BYU student publicly admits that under
direction of BYU's president, he and ten other undergraduates committed classroom "espionage" on eight professors to document their
liberal "political conviction." All student spies were members of the
John Birch Society and of BYU's on-campus Young Americans for
Freedom.[215]

3. June, 1968, BYU's president receives "confidential draft"
by Terry Warner, professor of philosophy and religion that "freedom
of speech as it is known today is a secular concept and has no place
of any kind at the BYU."[216]

4. February, 1980 Apostle Ezra Taft Benson instructs BYU students in televised address "Fourteen Fundamentals in Following the Prophets," describing: "1. The Prophet is the only man who speaks for the Lord in everything. 2. The living Prophet is more vital to us than the standard works [scripture]. 3. The living Prophet is more important to us than a dead prophet. 4. The Prophet will never lead the church astray. 5. The Prophet is not required to have any particular earthly training or credentials to speak on any subject or act on any matter at any time. 6. The Prophet does not have to say 'Thus saith the Lord.' ...The two groups who have the greatest difficulty in following the Prophet are the proud who are learned and the proud who are rich.[217]

MUNDUS VULT DECIPI !!
ERGO DECIPIATUR !!
The world wants to be deceived !!
So it should be deceived !!

Chapter Six

Missionaries: Proselytizing
and Two More Years
of Indoctrination

The Mormon Church has been in the missionary business for almost 170 years, from the time of Joseph Smith who started the church in 1830 to the present time. John D. Lee, the adopted son of Brigham Young, who was executed in 1877 for his role in the Mountain Meadows Massacre, served as a missionary in 1841, traveling through Illinois, Kentucky, Tennessee and Arkansas. Joseph Smith was well aware of the value of the missionary in the expansion of membership rolls and sent Brigham Young to England in the late 1830s and early 1840s to recruit members, for it was well-known that this was fertile ground for new members. Since so many of these people were living from hand to mouth, they quickly accepted the Mormon religion because it meant the possibility for immigration to the United States and a chance to get away from their miserable lives in England. Joseph Smith also went on a mission to Canada to recruit members to his church.

Guiding Principles of the Missionary System

The century and a half or more of experience in missionary service for the Mormon Church has evolved into several principles which guide the missionary system. These include at least five discernible aspects: appearance, tracting, visitation, referrals and developing trust.

1. Wearing the trade-marks of young missionaries: the white shirt, black nameplate, black tie and black business suit, and neat appearance.

2. Tracting, whereby missionaries leave tracts (religious pamphlets) trying to set up appointments.

3. Visiting of referrals, neighbors and friends of Mormon Church members whose names are given to missionaries.

4. Inviting non-members and the missionaries to meet in homes so the missionaries can present their "canned" memorized speeches.

5. Developing memorized lessons to use in teaching the LDS gospel to non-members. Some of these lessons are described by Scott as "...forty-five minutes and are illustrated by slick flipcharts ...which start with emphasis on the family unit, to prepare for future discussion of temple work and genealogy. The first lesson deals with the story of Joseph Smith's search for truth. Other lessons (presented in the order deemed appropriate by the missionaries) cover eternal progression, continuing revelation, individual responsibility, truth versus error, the baptismal challenge, obedience, our relationship to Christ and membership in the kingdom. These "canned lessons" require much memorization on the part of the missionary...."[218]

6. Developing trust and fellowship between the prospective new member, church members and the missionaries. This is accomplished by giving them copies of the *Book of Mormon*, inviting them to church potlucks and services, and calling good prospects "brother" and "sister," etc.

Gaining a Foothold in Foreign Countries

The Mormon missionaries are supported by a $50 billion corporate church with a well-organized and financed proselytizing campaign. As reported earlier, nearly all of the 60,000 missionaries pay their own expenses, and it is estimated that the church spends nearly one billion additional dollars each year to support their efforts through public relations and advertising campaigns. This estimate is based on a report by *The Arizona Republic* that in 1991 the church spent $550 million in support of 45,000 missionaries.[219] Ten years of inflation, increased income of the church and increased numbers of missionaries could easily double the amount of money spent by the church in 2001.

The Mormon hierarchy is always looking for opportunities to make inroads into foreign countries for their missionary work. One example of the efforts made by the church's hierarchy, was President Abdurrahman Wahid of Indonesia who was befriended by an American Mormon. Wahid (as reported in the January 26, 2000 issue of the St. George, *Spectrum*) was going blind, and the Mormon missionary recommended that he go to Salt Lake City to receive treatment at the University of Utah's Moran Eye Center. When Wahid arrived there, President Gordon B. Hinckley met with him and was invited by Wahid to visit him in Indonesia. Special inroads into Indonesia were needed since its government had banned foreign missionaries. The Mormon Church did not miss the opportunity, and Hinckley traveled to Indonesia to meet with Wahid in January, 2000. In order to impress Wahid, fifteen busloads of Indonesian Mormons (paid for by Mormon Church officials) were on hand to greet Hinckley upon his arrival in Jakarta. The buses and Indonesian Mormons were rounded up by Chad Emmet, a geography professor at Brigham Young University, who had served on a mission there in the 1970s. It was hoped by the Mormons that Hinckley's visit would result in Wahid's opening the door to Indonesia for Mormon missionaries.

The Mormon Church not only uses every opening it can get into foreign countries to proselytize, it also uses its congressional power to insure entry. "In July, 1996, Alekandr Lebed, a security leader and de facto second in command of the Russian Republic publicly apologized for calling Russia's Mormons 'filth and scum.' The LDS Church had only 5000 converts and 300 missionaries there. The apology occurred because LDS members [Republicans] of the Republican-controlled U. S. Senate asked the Democratic Clinton administration to reconsider aid to Russia because of Lebed's stand."[220]

Missionaries, called Elders by the Mormon Church, are always seen in groups of two, pedaling their bicycles, wearing black and white helmets, black suits, black ties, black shoes and white shirts. They carry backpacks that contain their lesson materials for presentations to prospective converts to the Mormon Church. Oftentimes the missionaries are seen outside their temporary foster home waiting for a ride when appointments or duties take them too far to go by bicycle. For a non-Mormon a question might be: What are these young men doing riding around on bicycles in black suits? As you will soon discover there are reasons for the bicycles, the blacksuited young men and the backpacks.

Encounters with Missionaries

I remember my first contact with two missionaries who were present at a Sunday dinner at a Mormon neighbor's home. These missionaries were about nineteen years of age and wearing their uniforms, with name tags identifying them. It was soon evident that this was not to be a friendly dinner with our new neighbors, as had been anticipated, but an attempt to convert my wife and me to Mormonism. The neighbor's use of this to proselytize puzzled me. Furthermore, using two young men barely nineteen years of age to influence two mature adults to join the Mormon church caused indignation. It was a setup all the way and was resented very much. I could barely keep from telling my neighbor how improper I thought it was, but being a proper guest, I ate dinner and listened to the canned speeches about the church being "true" and a few prayers and testimonies. I finally ended the episode by diplomatically telling them that in this country we have freedom to believe in what we want which includes freedom of religion. I wanted to tell them much more, such as Joseph Smith's fabrication of the story of the golden plates, his talking with God and Jesus Christ and the angel Moroni, and his claim that he translated the golden plates by use of a seer stone into the *Book of Mormon.* It was difficult for me not to tell them that Joseph Smith's idea of pre-existing spirits awaiting for their turn to be born into human families was nonsense. And Smith's teachings that every worthy priesthood holder would eventually become God of his own planet would not even qualify as science fiction. (In fact, Joseph Smith had taught that there were men living on the moon.) Only recently has science found evidence of planets in space beyond our own planetary system, and none has been discovered that harbors human life. How would these potential millions of Gods find or travel to these millions of planets when science has not discovered even one such planet other than earth?

Occasionally missionaries become stranded without their bicycles and must beg a ride to their next appointment. Such happened to the author when two young missionaries, ages 20 and 24, knocked on the door. They were invited in so that the author could learn more about their sales pitch for the Mormon Church. The more experienced missionary began his testimony on why he joined the Mormon Church four years ago. He said that he had been a member of the Catholic Church in Mexico but had felt no real relationship with God. However, after he took the six lessons with the Mormon missionaries, and after reading the *Book of Mormon*, he received a "burning of the bosom" and was able to receive messages from God "in his heart." He quit the Catholic Church and joined the Mormon Church. He asked if the author had read the *Book of Mormon* to which the author replied yes, several times. The missionary was asked why he believed in the *Book of Mormon* and the Mormon Church since research clearly shows that much of this book was plagiarized from the Bible and from several other contemporary books of the 1800s, including Ethan Smith's book *View of the Hebrews*. It was explained that the material in Joseph Smith's book reflected the wave of religious fervor that swept through the people living in his area at that time. In addition, it was explained that Joseph Smith's description of the Lamanites and the Nephites in his book as immigrants to the Americas from Israel does not square with archaeological research that shows that the American Indian descended from the Asiatic people who crossed a land bridge that existed between Siberia and Alaska about 12,000 years ago. The missionaries were told that steel objects that were mentioned in the *Book of Mormon* did not exist in the Americas during the time of Smith's Lamanites and Nephites. The author then asked the older one why he believed that the The *Book of Mormon* was true. He replied that God told him it was true.

He was then asked how God told him that it was true. He said through an "inner feeling" that he had.

Several other aspects of the Mormon Church that make the church's doctrines questionable were discussed with the young missionaries. It was found that the two Elders had read very little history of the church. The author asked the senior Elder why he would join a church and make a two-year missionary commitment when he did not really know the background and history of the church. It was surprising to learn that neither one of them knew the history of the church, that which had been assumed every Mormon would know. It was also surprising that these two young men were sent out by their church to promote the Mormon religion and to secure converts without arming them with a rudimentary history of the church.

Finally, the two elders were encouraged to read about the history of the Mormon Church, and they both promised that they would. They were asked if they would leave the Mormon Church if they found in their study of its history that such important documents as the *Book of Mormon* were indeed false? The younger Elder would not answer this question but the senior answered that he would not, since he knew that the book was true. How did he know it is true? "By a feeling in my heart that God has told me it is true."

Missionary System Provides Further Indoctrination into Mormonism

The Mormon Church system of missionary development and service is the keystone of Mormonism. During the training of these young men and women for service as missionaries (all of these assignments are theoretically made by the President/Prophet of the church) the Mormon doctrines are ingrained in their minds. The instruction that these young missionaries receive convinces many of them that the *Book of Mormon* is true. They are taught to memorize the discussions that include the basic principles of the church's belief as well as scriptures from the Bible and the *Book of Mormon* they must use when confronting those they are trying to convert. During the 170-year development of the missionary training system the church has witnessed an increase in membership from just a handful in 1830 to over eleven million as claimed by Mormon Church authorities today. Over one-half of the membership is scattered throughout 192 countries of the world with the rest found primarily in Utah and surrounding states. A few are scattered across the rest of the United States.

The Mormon Church counts as members all who have been baptized, and even those who have not attended for many years. Many of them attend other churches and have denied their belief in Mormonism, but do not bother to take their names off the records because the church has made it so difficult to do. Since church authorities never release statistics on active members, the more than eleven million number as claimed by the church is distorted. This reported membership of the church is also reduced by the low retention rate of converts in many countries, especially in South America where missionary work is concentrated today. These new members often find themselves losing touch with their heritage, friends and even family members as they adopt the Mormon style of living. One missionary reported that he found a recently baptized South American convert clutching his Bible and crying uncontrollably trying to reconcile his breaking away from his former religion. This upset the missionary so much that he eventually left the church because he felt responsible for putting this man under such extreme emotional stress.

What makes these 60,000 current missionaries so devout in their beliefs, so willing to spread false beliefs and "voluntarily" serve two-year missions? Probably the greatest pressure comes from the church itself, which teaches that serving a mission is essential to advancing into leadership positions within the church. And in Utah it is socially and economically advantageous for their futures. Such missionary service is also taught to be essential to reach the highest kingdom of the three degrees of Mormon heaven. Because of this and the great pressure the church puts on parents to make sure that their sons (and a few daughters) serve missions, many simply go just to please everyone in the church and family.

By the constant repetition of the church-furnished propaganda the missionaries become "brain-washed." As Scott writes: "he [the missionary] is called on constantly to 'bear testimony' of his church. Many missionaries will admit frankly that they had no real 'testimony' of their religion before going on a mission. Lewis Price noted, 'Testimonies exercise a kind of thought control, sometimes even a hypnosis over him. He is a victim of his own propaganda.' Even if a missionary were to begin to doubt Mormonism, his companion would surely notice, and duty-bound, report it to his leaders. If such a doubter were being profitably influenced by a Christian, it wouldn't last long. The wavering missionary would be transferred to another district before he knew what was happening to him."[221]

Armed with their knowledge of the *Book of Mormon* and other teachings of Joseph Smith such as the *Pearl of Great Price* and the *Doctrine* and *Covenants*, and schooled in the principles of convincing non-members to join the church, missionaries are ready to begin. As mentioned earlier, some missionaries become very zealous in their work and attempt to remove books from libraries that may be harmful to the Mormon Church. One description of their tactics is to "approach the check-out desk with a number of books in their hands. They [have] told the librarian they would like to take these volumes, which were quite old and not in the best of condition and replace them with newer books. Fortunately, the college librarians are professionals and frequently were more than a little suspicious. A call was made to the Bible Department to confirm that it would be best to keep the books already in the library collection. In fact it was decided that these particular books should be put in a secure position in the library. ...Mormon missionaries are visiting libraries all over the country trying to replace counter LDS Church books with books of their own choosing, especially those early historical books that proved embarrassing to the Latter-Day Saints movement."[222]

Who Serves as Missionaries and Who Pays for Them?

It is likely that some missionaries do not believe in the work they are doing during their missions but continue it because of possible future advantages such as college entrance or to obtain a better vocation. As noted previously, many go on missions due to parental pressures or because their "big brother went on one," and so it is the "thing to do." In addition, some go for the adventure of it. However, there are also those who go because they believe that they will be helping the church by bringing new members into God's kingdom.

Some young men are prohibited by the church from serving on missions. In 1993, the First Presidency of the church excluded the following from serving: "Individuals who have become HIV positive ... Persons 19 to 26 who have been divorced ... Young men who have encouraged, paid for or arranged for an abortion resulting from their immoral conduct. Sisters who submit to abortions growing out of their immoral conduct ... [anyone who] has fathered or given birth to a child out of wedlock ... Persons with 'homosexual activity' would be eligible only on these conditions: 'if there is no current indication of homosexual tendencies' or if 'there is a strong evidence of complete repentance and reformation, with at least one year free of transgression.'"[223]

As discussed in Chapter 5, by the age of nineteen, when young Mormon men go on their missions, they have been thoroughly indoctrinated. They have been through workbooks containing information about the *Book of Mormon* and other religious materials developed and approved by the General Authorities of the church. In addition, life itself has been lived among other Mormons with most of their free time revolving around church-sponsored activities. The Mormon Church is indeed watching over its children, insuring that "once a Mormon, always a Mormon."

The cost of Mormon missionaries is almost nothing to the church since families begin saving money for their children's missions from the day of birth. In the year 2000, the amount that must be saved to support a two-year mission is about $9,000.00 ($375 per month). These financial savings for their son's (and in some cases daughter's) mission are in addition to the family's regular ten percent tithing.[224] According to Scott, "Many Mormon children have little cardboard banks given to them with their first allowance. These banks have three slots, one marked 'tithing,' one marked 'savings,' and the third marked 'mission.' Mormon parents often start saving along with their young children for their future missions.

"...A potential missionary is interviewed by his bishop to see if he is worthy to serve a mission and if he (or his family) can support him for two years. (On rare occasions a needy missionary will be supported by his home ward during his mission.) The bishop forwards the result of this interview to the stake president, who sends it to the President of the church. A 'call' comes by mail, signed by the Prophet himself. It contains encouragement, an area assignment and a date for the missionary to report to the mission home in Salt Lake City."[225]

After arriving in their mission home in Salt Lake City, missionaries are not permitted contact with their families except through letters or phone calls. They assemble their missionary uniform consisting of a white shirt, black tie, black pants and a black jacket with their name printed on a black badge, such as Elder John Doe, or Elder James Jones. During their two-week stay in the mission home, they meet General Authorities, hear lectures and receive their endowments in the temple.[226]

The Missionary Boot Camp

After a two-week orientation in the mission home, the young recruit attends a Missionary Training Center which not only readies him for missionary service but also helps the young trainee to solidify his own faith, cement ties to the church and be trained for future lay leadership roles. One of the main Missionary Training Centers is located in Provo, Utah. (In 1998, 27,000 missionaries were trained there.)[227] This Missionary Training Center was first established in 1925 and was expanded greatly in 1978. Area Missionary Training Centers have been established in such other places as Latin America, Europe, Asia and the Pacific Islands.[228] In this new environment, the missionary's hair is cut short, similar to a Navy or Marine boot camp

style. The new "recruit" is assigned a companion who will be with
him during this "boot camp." For this time and for the next two
years of his missionary assignment, he will not be allowed to date,
have visitors, receive calls from home, have outside reading and
generally has the following schedule:

> 6:00 Arise, shower, dress, personal prayer
> 6:45 Breakfast
> 7:45 Session with all those assigned to the same country
> 8:00 Memorization drills
> 10:00 Scripture study
> 11:00 Memorization drills
> 12:00 Lunch
> 1:00 Language class (if going to a foreign country)
> 4:00 Physical Education/cultural lectures
> 5:00 Dinner
> 5:45 Session with all those assigned to the same country
> 6:00 Language laboratory
> 7:00 Group study
> 10:00 Group prayer and lights out.[229]

If the missionary is assigned to a foreign country whose citizens speak a language other than English, he is sent to a six-week
training program to learn the rudiments of the language so that he
may relay the "canned Mormon message" to these possible foreign
converts. While it is impossible to become fluent in a foreign language in this short program, it is possible for the missionary to learn
enough to make one memorized presentation. The missionary will
gradually become attuned to the new language while on his two-
year mission, and no doubt near the end of the first year, will be able
to communicate with his foreign contacts. When he arrives in his
new country, he is assigned to an experienced missionary who has
been in the country for about a year. This experienced missionary
probably knows the basics of the foreign language and will help the
new missionary in this area. As Scott writes: "This young man (to
whom the new missionary is assigned) will be the one with whom
the new missionary will eat, work and live for the next few months.
A missionary is not allowed to get out of sight or hearing of his
companion for the entire time they are assigned to each other."
(Usually they are together for about three months, after which time

they receive either a new companion or are transferred to another area with a new companion. Weaker missionaries are usually assigned to stronger missionaries.)[230] This constant contact with each other helps insure that one or the other will not stray from the official Mormon Church doctrine. It also insures that neither will violate the rules against having girlfriends or dates during his missionary period. Constant companionship helps protect the church from any deviation from church rules and policy during the mission period, whether it be in the United States or in a foreign country. With supervision by the mission president (an older mature adult, usually residing on location with his wife and family), the young missionary is carefully monitored. These safeguards provide nearly foolproof assurance to the General Authorities that the message which they have approved will be propagated throughout the missions.

Scott writes: "In 1978 there were over 26,000 missionaries serving the Mormon Church. (In 2001, this number had increased to over 60,000.) However, Mormons may boast of such a figure as an indicator of faith, it tarnishes their image somewhat to have it revealed that this represents only about one-fifth of those young Mormons who are eligible, and thus expected to serve in missionary service.

"Mormon elders serving on missions are considered to be ordained ministers who may baptize, confirm, conduct funerals, and later in life as fathers, bless and name their newborns and heal the sick. Their primary duty though, is to teach. But the *Doctrine of Covenants* warns them, 'Ye are not sent forth to be taught, but to teach.'(43:15) They believe that they are the only ones in the world authorized by God to preach the gospel."[231]

As stated above, these young missionaries who are called Elders are closely supervised by older adults (mission presidents) while on their missions. This insures that missionaries will adhere to the official Mormon doctrine and that they are accomplishing their assigned responsibilities. Missionaries are not sent any place in the world, including the United States, without their being a part of the mission president's center. Just as missionaries are assigned to their missions by the President of the church through the church bureaucracy, so are the mission presidents.

Scott writes: "Missionaries serve under a mission president ... ... A missionary who watches over several of his peers is known as a district leader. Several districts are the responsibility of a zone leader, who reports to the mission president. Missionaries have a system in which mission districts compete with each other— a certain number of points are given to an Elder for a baptism, and sometimes points are deducted for such things as sleeping in when there is tracting to be done.

"...Missionaries are expected to rise at [six] o'clock in the morning and study until seven. Typically they eat and dress between seven and eight; then study again until ten. Tracting fills up the two hours before lunch. From one until five they tract and make calls. ...Evenings are spent attending meetings, setting up and teaching cottage meetings with nonmembers.

"...Missionaries are only allowed a certain modest amount of money, out of which they must pay rent, groceries and car rental fees and gasoline.

"...Many (missionaries) see mission life as a challenge of hierarchical offices to be ascended and 'glory sheets' of accumulated points to be boasted about. The pressure of the regimented life has caused many young men, to go 'AWOL,' or to indulge in fornication and has driven others to suicide. Scarcely a missionary alive finished his mission without a sigh of relief that the 'best two years of his life' are finally over.

"..Many R. M's [returned missionaries] put their foreign language to lucrative use and become teachers. Many others, because of their knowledge of a foreign tongue and their unquestioning obedience to authority, have been successfully recruited to CIA work."[232]

Testimony of the Missionary

Hutchinson writes: "If they (missionaries) are challenged by a statement which they have made in a presentation and can't come up with a suitable defense, they are told in their training to give their testimony. An example of a testimony given by a missionary is: "I know by the power of the Holy Ghost, that the *Book of Mormon* is true and was restored by divine revelation to the prophet Joseph Smith ... that Jesus is the Christ ... President Gordon B. Hinckley is a Prophet, seer, and revelator ... and the Church of Jesus Christ of Latter-Day Saints is the only true church upon the face of the earth!"[233]

And according to Hutchinson, Mormons "are taught from toddluihood to memorize this testimony. Church leaders especially encourage it, knowing that the verbalization of one's faith tends to give more meaning to beliefs. As children are growing up, they rattle it off as a conditioned response and as an incentive for acceptance and approval ... Training Mormon children to memorize a testimony eventually produces an inner conviction that it really is true. When this happens, it translates into an emotional experience that becomes personally meaningful. They are told that this emotional 'feeling' is the Holy Ghost confirming their beliefs."[234]

Hutchinson, a former Mormon and missionary writes that "I know" is a very important phrase in the testimony and if used with conviction impresses non-Mormons. Even more importantly would be to use the phrases, *"I know beyond a shadow of doubt"* and "I bear witness."

Marketing the Missionary Program

Hutchinson (a teacher of religion) writes that the Mormon Church's proselytizing "functions at three levels: marketing strategy, missionary lessons and use of friendshipping families... Seventy-five million dollars was earmarked by Bonneville International, the Mormon Church's powerful communications branch, for satellite dishes in Canada and Mexico. The same goal was set for South America, Europe, Asia and the Philippines. One source says the Mormon Church's satellite is the largest video network in the world, having the ability to merge into any cable system in North America ... it spends approximately $550 million a year."[235]

In addition, the Mormon Church has been *cosmitized,* that is; a *sacred canopy* has been developed. According to Hutchinson, the following explains what a cult like the Mormon Church must do to establish this sacred canopy:

"1. Claim contact with heaven or the cosmos.

2. Claim God has chosen a leader as His divinely chosen representative.

3. Give royal or divine status to the leader.

4. Insist their society mirrors the divine structure of heaven.

5. Claim to be God's chosen people.

6. Build temples to practice sacred ordinances.

7. Produce sacred literature.

8. Proclaim a bigger and better canopy than Christianity's."[236]

Purpose of the Missionary Proselytizing System

Hutchinson also claims that "The real purpose behind their proselytizing is based on a conviction promulgated in secret during early Mormon history. ...The Mormon Church plans on gaining a political stronghold in our government. Early Mormon leaders described this goal as a one-world government ruled by their priesthood. ...It's more than a government, as we understand it. Rather it's a government ruled by a *king*. ...So to define it in a nutshell, the *public* facet is the church, the visible structure of the Church of Jesus Christ of Latter-Day Saints and its doctrine. The *private* facet is the political machinery, officially named the kingdom of God, also called the government of God.

"Now to us the two titles, *church and kingdom*, sound synonymous but not to those who understand early Mormon history. Joseph Smith set up his 'restored gospel' in two parts. The public front of the church with beliefs everyone is already familiar with, and the private belief, his political kingdom."[237]

The author believes that the political kingdom is the real motive behind the reason why the General Authorities of the Mormon Church are willing to budget over a billion dollars a year to proselytizing throughout the United States and the world. The model for the Mormon Church governance of the United States and the world after their successful worldwide proselytizing efforts, is already in place. This model, developed by Joseph Smith, has a Council of Fifty, a secret organization that was to govern his *kingdom of God* with, of course, Joseph as the King over it all. Brigham Young *appointed* the Council of Fifty as the Utah territorial legislature shortly after arriving there in 1847. All government officials were nominated and appointed with the approval of the Council of Fifty. It is believed that the Mormon Church even today maintains this Council of Fifty, ready to take control the United States and the world if and when the opportunity arises.

As is the current Mormon tradition (in appointing Church officials) *government officials* in the Mormon kingdom of God would be appointed by the President (Prophet). As Hutchinson writes: "...the Law of Common Consent, raising one's hand to confirm those appointed within the church, is still operative. If a Mormon dares vote contrary, he or she is called in for the dreaded *interview*. If the individual doesn't repent, excommunication is inevitable."[238]

Therefore, the Mormon Church Authorities would destroy democracy as we know it in the United States and replace it with a king (a Prophet of the Mormon Church). The Mormon President using the power which he says he receives from God would serve as a virtual dictator in a Mormon-controlled government. **This is the reason why all citizens of the United States and the world must know and understand the plans of the Mormon Church. History has shown us that sometimes only a handful of men, dedicated to a cause, can gain control of a government. We have witnessed Lenin's gaining control of Russia in 1917 and Hitler's rise to power in Germany in 1933. We must be vigilant in our efforts to keep our freedoms of thought, speech, religion and individualism intact.**

We live in a pluralistic society encompassing many nationalities, religions and cultures. Most of us believe in individualism and free thinking. From this pluralistic society our laws have been developed. That may not be pleasing to all, but our laws have been accepted by the majority. Within this society, we have individuals with the necessary leadership abilities to maintain and improve our freedoms. Hopefully, we have the capability to prevent the control of our society by an organization that would limit our individual freedoms and democracy. Since it is believed that Mormon General Authorities conspire to turn this country into their kingdom, we must expose them and insure that they will not succeed.

Missionary Strategies

Unfortunately, Mormon missionaries and Mormons in general are not taught about the political kingdom or the Council of Fifty. They are taught that their mission is to bring members into the church so that they have the opportunity to be admitted to the highest level of heaven. They are taught that individuals who are not Mormons may not enter the highest level of heaven, but will be restricted to lower levels.

What else are these young missionaries taught to present to potential converts and how are they taught to make these presentations? According to Hutchinson, in their presentations missionaries are told to: "Figure out ahead of time what you can do to make the investigator feel the Holy Spirit. Convince the investigator that when he or she *feels good* about what is being discussed, it is the Holy

Ghost confirming the truth. Use the suggested scriptures to develop spiritual *feelings,* not to demonstrate a point. This will prepare investigators to more easily make commitments which will lead them to convert and be baptized."

"To create a good feeling in investigators, share with them about your home town, schooling, family and personal interests. Also inquire about these same areas in their life. The more you can establish a relationship through personal rapport and trust, the more this same feeling will be carried over and applied to the concepts you teach in the rest of the discussions."[239]

Hutchinson summarizes the five missionary strategies as:

1. Convince one that feeling good is the only confirmation needed to authenticate truth.

2. Falsely prioritize Jesus Christ.

3. Convince one that Mormonism is a continuation of God's plan.

4. Do not tell all beliefs up front.

5. Decrease the use of Bible scripture as lessons progress and replace with Mormon scripture.[240]

The Missionary Lessons

In presenting their first lesson to prospective converts, missionaries often use a "friendshipper" who introduces the missionaries. The "friendshipper" may be a neighbor or some other person known by the prospective convert. "The friendshipper" method used in proselytizing is designed to enhance closer relations between missionaries and their potential converts. According to Hutchinson, in a study by Stark and Bainbridge, one out of every two contacts that "friendshipper" make is successfully converted.[241]

In the first lesson one of the two Elders opened with a prayer followed by, "Many people believe in God, although under various names. Elder Black and I have very strong testimonies about God and would like to share our *feelings about Him with you.*"[242] The Elders continued their first presentation by reading various passages from the Bible that were to lead to the introduction of Joseph Smith as the first Prophet of the church. "In 1820, He (God) chose a Prophet, Joseph Smith, to whom He revealed the fullness of His gospel. I bear you my witness that I know he is a Prophet, for I have received that special feeling and testimony in my heart."[243]

If one reads Fawn Brodie's book, *No Man Knows my History*, it becomes clear that Joseph Smith was not appointed by God to be the Prophet, but rather Joseph Smith appointed himself as a "Prophet."Also you will note that the Elders say that they have a special *feeling* that Smith was chosen by God. This feeling is necessary for Mormons to have in order to believe that what they are taught is true since there is no evidence to prove that the Mormon doctrine or their scriptures are true.

The second presentation of the Elders began with a filmstrip which was an attempt to provide some information that gave a thread of proof to the *Book of Mormon*. This filmstrip shows excavations of Indian cities built in Central and South America. The Indians presented in the missionaries' film were South and Central American Indians living over three thousand miles away. It is true that these South and Central American Indians had built cities and developed a civilization. However, none of this evidence relates to the *Book of Mormon* as written by Joseph Smith or the time period it describes.

This second presentation continued with one of the Elders explaining that the *Book of Mormon* tells of three migrations from the Middle East, one led by Lehi in 600 B. C., the Mulekites about 589 B.C. and another by the Jaredites about 2000 B. C. The story of people from these three migrations and after their arrival in America constitutes much of the writings of the *Book of Mormon*. The Elders had no archeological evidence to show that the *Book of Mormon* was true, saying: "It is the witness of the Holy Ghost. Both Elder Black and I have received that witness. We know that the *Book of Mormon* is true and that it contains the Word of God even in the face of evidence that appears contradictory."[244]

During their presentation, Hutchinson raised questions with the two Elders in an attempt to show that the *Book of Mormon* was true. "Elder Black, I understand that both of you revere the testimony of those men (witnesses who said they saw the golden plates that Smith claimed he used to translate the *Book of Mormon*) with all your heart. However, since your own Dr. Hugh Nibley at BYU stated that the *Book of Mormon* should be tested, I'm sure you won't mind some questions.

"Do you believe that viewing an object in real life is the same as seeing it in a vision?"

"No," Elder Black replied. "Naturally there's a difference. However, the vision might indeed be from God."

"Well, what if I were to tell you that I had a vision where an angel showed me the rod Moses used. What if I described it as having the shape of the bull's head at the top, with the rest of the staff carved in Greek letters? Could you say to me that you believe my vision without any reservation? Could you testify with certainty that you know Moses' rod looked exactly like that?"

"No, of course not," Elder Barret said. "How would I know but what you conjured the vision up out of your own head? I might believe it, but there would be no real proof unless the rod was actually found. That is..." he hesitated, "unless the Holy Ghost witnessed the truth to me."

"But if archaeologists did indeed find Moses' rod, then which would you say would carry more weight — my vision or seeing the actual rod?"

"Obviously seeing the real thing. But," he added, suspecting where I was headed, "concerning the *Book of Mormon* plates, the three witnesses actually saw the plates in broad daylight."

"Are you sure?"

"Why, of course," he puzzled, pointing to the page. "It says so right here."

"In the LDS *Church Almanac*," Hutchinson continued, "it states that the three witnesses 'viewed the plates in a vision.' That means it was similar to my vision of Moses' rod.

"Pulling a small piece of paper from my purse, I said, 'Martin Harris, after being asked 'Did you see those plates with your naked eyes?" told John Gilbert, the printer of the *Book of Mormon*, 'No, I saw them with a *spiritual eye*.' Harris later answered the same question of an attorney who came to Palmyra. He said, 'Why, I did not see them as I do that pencil case, yet I saw them with the *eye of faith*. I saw them just as distinctly as I saw anything about me — though at the time they were *covered over with a cloth*.'"

"Now Elders, if they were covered with a cloth, there's no way he or the other witnesses could actually see them. The only alternative is a vision. and if it was a vision, how can I be sure it wasn't conjured up out of their own mind because they wanted so desperately to obtain a witness?"

"But," Elder Barrett said firmly, "the other eight witnesses actually hefted the plates."

"Well now, they could have been hefting something else. It would have been an easy thing, especially since Oliver Cowdery had been a blacksmith, to make a set of metal plates. And since they were covered with a cloth, the makeshift plates wouldn't have needed much detail — only the necessary weight.

"Elders, I guess my main question is this. If Martin Harris admitted it was really a vision and all indications seem to point to this, why isn't this made clear in the published statement printed in the *Book of Mormon?*"

As Hutchinson watched the Elders' confusion, she suddenly felt sorry for them. Here she was destroying two young men's faith.

Elder Black spoke up. "While we understand that it's normal for you to have questions, it's well to remember that many enemies of the church have made statements about the witnesses to the *Book of Mormon* that aren't true — even going so far as to sign affidavits slandering the Prophet, Joseph Smith."

"But Elders, I didn't quote enemies of your church. I quoted Martin Harris himself, Brigham Young University, and the LDS Church's own *Almanac.*"

"Then we feel," Elder Barrett insisted, "that you have taken isolated statements which, if quoted in full context, would probably clarify the matter. This is why a testimony of the gospel is so important. If, for example, the Holy Ghost gave you a special testimony of your vision of Moses' rod, then that would settle it."

"Even if the vision portrayed *Greek* letters on his rod?"

"Both Elder Black and myself have received a special testimony that the gospel is true. We know that Joseph Smith translated the plates by the power of God. Further, God went beyond His requirement of two or three witnesses and provided eleven! Yes, a testimony given by the Holy Ghost is the *surest* witness."[245]

It is clear from this conversation between Hutchinson and the Elders that the Mormon religion has no logical basis. Only the testimony that one supposedly receives from the "Holy Ghost" in the individual's heart is the thread that holds the religion together. Mormons have only faith that the General Authorities of the Mormon Church (who *claim* to be representatives of God) are providing them with information that is true. But documentation in this book shows that the General Authorities *are not* providing truthful information to their members, but are using members' hard earned dollars to develop dishonest and untruthful literature which in the opinion of the author is to promote their own interests and receive power and their own glory. Since the General Authorities provide no accounting of the ways in which they spend the tithes received by their followers, they spend it in ways that satisfy their own self interests. The result is a flood of inaccurate and distorted publications to promote the Mormon Church. This flood of publications is produced by highly skilled writers, illustrators and public media personnel and is designed to attract and hold members.

The third presentation by the Elders was a continuation of the reading of the scriptures giving reasons why Joseph Smith became Prophet of the church. The Elders also discussed the apostasy that they say occurred after the apostles of Christ died and which continued on through the Dark Ages. This apostasy, according to Mormonism, resulted in the restoration of the church by Joseph Smith in 1830. However Hutchinson explained that in reality "God began His restoration through Martin Luther and the Reformers." She wrote: "I believe that the Reformation, started by Martin Luther, was the restoration of Christ's true church. It started that memorable day, October 31, 1517, when Martin Luther walked up to the Wittenberg Cathedral and nailed his ninety-five theses to the door."[246]

The fourth presentation of the Elders was the Mormon doctrine of pre-existence and the plan of salvation. In this presentation, the Elders first showed a chart containing two globes, one representing a place where pre-mortal spirit children of God lived, the second a globe representing earth and life here. After these, the Elders put up a poster with four more globes. "A grayish one, directly above earth, was entitled 'Spirit World.'" The three other globes were placed in a row above the 'Spirit World' globe and represented the Telestial, Terrestrial, and Celestial heavens. The 'Spirit World' was explained by the Elders as, "After death, our spirits go to the 'Spirit World,' which is divided into two sections. One section is Paradise, for those who accept the *truth* while on earth. The other is Spirit Prison, for those who did not." The Elders further explained that since spirit children, before they are born to human parents, have no bodies, they cannot be baptized, which is necessary for salvation. Those who accept Mormonism while in this mortal state, are baptized, and they can enter the Mormon temples and perform baptism for those who have lived and died without knowing or accepting Mormonism. This is known as "baptism for the dead," which assures that those who did not have an opportunity as living humans to become Mormons, can have an opportunity through proxy baptism, to enter the kingdom of God.[247]

Is it strange that none of the above is mentioned in the *Book of Mormon* which is supposed to be the basis for the Mormon Church and is said to contain "the fullness of the (Mormon) gospel?" The truth is that these ideas, as described above, were conjured up years later in the highly imaginative mind of Joseph Smith and introduced into the church *after* his *Book of Mormon* was written and published. We must also remember that this is the same Joseph Smith who was charged by a court of law of being a disorderly person and an imposter for "money digging" and using a peep stone to find buried treasure. His Mother, Lucy, described young Joseph as often telling the family many fantastic and magical stories that he made up. This and plenty of other evidence shows that Joseph Smith was not bashful about inventing stories to reach his objectives. His story of the golden plates and his translating them by the use of the same "seer stone" was just another example of his deception.

And now back to the young missionaries who leave family and friends to serve on two-year missions which take them to mission fields throughout the United States and to many countries of the world. They often live in austere conditions, with only the bare necessities without the normal comforts of home they have been used to, such as televisions, computers or radios. Nor are they allowed to listen to the radio. Missionaries are limited in the amount of contact they may have with their parents, and all telephone calls must be approved by the mission presidents. Calls home are limited to twice yearly, on Mother's Day and Christmas, and missionaries are expected to remain at their missions even in times of emergencies such as death of a family member.

How Successful are the Missionaries?

How successful is the missionary program in converting people to Mormonism? According to Ostling and Ostling, in 1997, 317,798 persons worldwide were converted by being baptized into the Mormon Church. Considering that many of these converts were first invited to hear the Mormon "gospel" by local Mormons rather than by the missionaries, this probably amounts to one or two baptisms per year per missionary, which is a very low success rate. But it must be remembered that one of the primary objectives of the Mormon missionary program is to indoctrinate their own youth *so they will become committed members* of the church. Missionaries are even told, "The most important person you will convert while on your missions is yourself!" While conversion numbers are important to General Authorities, equally important is the missionary's return to the church after the mission as a fully indoctrinated and committed member. (A few leave after a mission, disillusioned with the church, but most of those who do remain do so as fully committed members.)

Ostling and Ostling report: "Ordination to the Melchizedek priesthood among adult converts provides a better picture of the retention rate. A male growing up in a Mormon family normally reaches that rank at about age nineteen, and an adult convert about a year after joining the church." According to a study by Lawrence A. Young of BYU in 1994, about 70 percent of baptized males reached the Melchizedek priesthood in Utah, 59 percent reached it in the United States, 52 percent in Canada, and only 19 percent in Mexico and 17 percent in Japan.[248]

While the Church Authorities claim a worldwide membership of nearly eleven million, (April 2, 2000 St. George Spectrum) with over one-half living outside the United States, these figures are inflated when one considers that reaching the Melchizedek priesthood defines active male membership. Probably not more than 30 percent of those claimed by the church hierarchy in foreign countries are active members. In the United States, no more than 60 percent of those baptized in the church are participating members. If only participating members were counted, then the Mormon Church in the United States could count fewer than 3,300,000 members and outside the United States, 1,650,000 reducing the total membership to around 5,000,000. However, we must remember, as mentioned earlier, that the Mormon Church counts all who have been baptized, even if they never attended church after that. They keep them on their records regardless of their attendance or belief, and make it very difficult to have their names removed, even when asked by these members to have their names taken off. Many Christian denominations, however, delete the names of those from their records who no longer attend or are attending elsewhere. Even though the Mormon Church membership totals claimed by church authorities are inflated, many of the inactive members support church goals through their voting and other activities. In addition, the priesthood keeps in touch with inactive members through home visitation and teaching programs, insuring that inactive members do not stray too far away.

Stories of Missionaries Who Have Left the Mormon Church

The following are the stories of former Mormon missionaries who have left the Mormon Church (Summarized from *Recovery From Mormonism* Internet Website):

* * * *

One man begins his story which tells why he left the Mormon Church by presenting a model which he calls the "Investment Paradigm." The more that a Mormon has invested in the church (such as being a member of the Mormon Boy Scout program, being involved in church athletic leagues, serving in various church callings, getting married in the temple and eventually being "called" to leadership positions as bishop and or president), the more difficult it is for him to leave the church. Some become so heavily brainwashed that they refuse to read anything but officially approved Mormon literature. If they accidentally come across non-faith promoting literature or books contrary to church teaching, they automatically regard them as without credence, a model that explains the behavior and belief patterns of most Mormons. In its simplest form the "Investment Paradigm" predicts the typical Mormon's reaction to "real world facts" based on his/her emotional investment in Mormon theology. So it follows that if one is heavily invested in Mormonism, that individual will be reluctant to give credence to anything that is critical of the Mormon Church. In fact, most will actively avoid anything that will rock the theological boat. He says his brother is a perfect example. In a recent discussion about the *Book of Abraham*, his brother rejected his offer to send him a copy of *By His Own Hand upon Papyrus* (that describes the *Book of Abraham* as not authentic, a product of Joseph Smith's imagination) stating that he was too busy trying to fulfill his church duties to read anything else. He added that there were already too many LDS books that he would rather read first. His brother is perhaps one of the most heavily invested Mormons he knows. Instead of blindly rejecting books that expose Mormonism as false, he feels that his brother and all Mormons ought to consider information from all sources. After all, since the church is bold enough to declare itself the sole provider of truth on the planet, he thinks a claim of this magnitude should be able to withstand all assaults and asks why are Mormons so afraid. Truth need not fear any investigation.

Why does the Mormon hierarchy want their Mormon men to marry almost immediately after their missions? — to increase the membership, of course, and to keep them busy raising children and working in the church, having less and less time to investigate what the real truth is!

He believes that the true meaning and essence of the mission is to make a person go through two years of living hell. The worse the experience is, the more that person believes he has sacrificed, therefore solidifying the investment value of a completed mission. When the Elder finally returns to the flock, what else is there to do but protect the investment? After all, he paid for it with two years of blood, sweat and tears and his parents' hard-earned money. He purchased the investment with his youth. You're twenty only once. The idea that the best part of your youth was squandered by knocking on doors and hassling people with false religion is unbearable. Returning missionaries are all too willing to adopt the company line, close ranks with other returned missionaries and protect their precious investment. At least this was his experience. When he returned, he took rank and file with the dullards, spouting scripture and assuring everyone that his mission experience was priceless.

Eventually he began to question the church doctrines and as a result began reading church history, including reading into areas forbidden by the "Mormon Patriarchy." He found out from these readings that *the church claims were misguided at best, and downright falsehoods at worst.* He felt horrible to have his world view stripped from him so completely. It was one thing to question the church as he had done all his life; it was quite another to come to the conclusion that the church is built on a foundation of lies.

He says that three books that really convinced him to leave the Mormon Church were: *By His Own Hand upon Papyrus* by Charles M. Larson, *Studies of the Book of Mormon* By B. H. Roberts and *No Man Knows my History* by Fawn M. Brodie.

* * * *

This missionary found that serving 18 months as a missionary was difficult for her. She hated doing the door approaches though at the time she believed in what she was teaching. She often cringed at wondering how people would ever believe what she was telling them. She now realizes that the church's taking people and controlling their lives twenty-four hours a day as the church does with its missionaries, is a great way to keep their "testimonies" in line. She had a "companion" twenty-four hours a day. She studied Mormon scriptures and taught and testified of them every day. She attended weekly district meetings with other missionaries during which discussions were held of scriptures and testifying to each other of their truthfulness. She had "periodic zone meetings where several districts got together going over discussions, studying scriptures, practicing door approaches and teaching techniques and testifying again." She made weekly reports to the President, accounting for her hours for each day of the past week. She even had a space to report the number of hours wasted. She could report any uplifting experiences and confess if she or her companion broke any rules. She said "Yep, we were expected to keep each other in line and dutifully report any infractions."

She was married in the Salt Lake City Temple, and although her father was a very good, decent and kind man, he was deemed "unworthy" of entering that building. At the time of her wedding, she was so immersed in the Mormon Church that she did not let this bother her, but now she regrets it deeply as he has since passed away. This is the church that so lovingly extols the values of its family-centered teachings in countless television commercials. This same church denied her father access to her wedding simply because he was not a card-carrying, tithe-paying member of their organization.

She began reading literature about the church that was not published by the Mormon Church, which caused her to have doubts about the truthfulness of its doctrine. She read the book, *Mormon Murders,* about the Hofmann document forgeries. She was appalled by the involvement of the General Authorities, especially Gordon B. Hinckley. If these men were so inspired and had direct communication with the Lord, why did they not know that the documents Hofmann made were fake? How could they meet so often with Mr. Hofmann and then deny knowing him? Innocent people even died as a result of all the document dealings with Hofmann. The church leaders did not kill those people, but they did everything they could to hinder the investigation so they could protect the church. Hinckley had covered up the church's involvement in the deals, and look at where he's now and he was not the only one. After reading about the Hofmann murders, her mind was made up; she must leave the church.

She knows now why we were constantly reminded to "follow

the Prophet" or "when the Prophet speaks, the thinking has been
done." Church leaders know full well that there is a wealth of
information available that proves the fallacies behind their doctrines. What's even more amazing is that there is enough information within the church's own books and writings to condemn the
religion. New versions of books are revised to reflect the new
improved look that the church wants to show the world. She won-
ders: What are they trying to hide?

Once she started thinking on her own again rather than following the group mindset, she started facing the reality that what
she had been devoting her time, energies and money to for so long,
was a lie. "Follow the Prophet" simply meant don't think, don't
question, don't read material negative to the church's image, just
do what we tell you to do or else you will never be able to dwell in
the presence of God after this life, and your family will be lost to
you forever.

* * * *

This ex-Mormon felt that even his marriage that ended in
divorce wasn't as bad as being a Mormon missionary. Adding to
his misery, during his two-year stint of proselytizing for the
Mormon Church, was the lack of privacy in the Mission Home
with the constant scrutinizing of his behavior, even having his
room wired with microphones. One night in particular he felt that
he was a robot when during a pillow fight in one of the mission
rooms, every guilty missionary raised his hand when the Dorm
Master barged in and asked: "Who was pillow fighting?" He was
further belittled for his participation in the fight by being fined five
dollars. During his mission, he described himself as being naive
and embarrassed that his hair was cropped short when the only
acceptable style for young men at that time was long hair.

When traveling through the streets in his proselytizing efforts,
he was subjected to stares and such indecencies as being "given the
finger." Others assumed that he was a store clerk or from the CIA.
The missionary uniform of white shirt, black tie, black shoes and a
pack of proselytizing materials made him conspicuous, exactly the
opposite of what he wanted. He longed for the time when he could
walk the streets in clothes that would allow him anonymity. He
couldn't remember a time when he hoped that someone would
answer the door when he knocked.

His mission president required that he and his companion prayerfully select a home, knock on the door and tell the residents that "We are messengers of the Lord Jesus Christ, and He has directed us to YOU and YOUR HOME to teach you His gospel and baptize you into HIS CHURCH." He tried it one time and was never so scared in his life. He feels today that this "Spiritual Contacting" program was a huge mission failure.

The best two years of his life, which he describes as prime years, were wasted: no girls, no music, no movies and no phone calls home. Although looking prosperous in a business suit and tie, he lived in dumps, ate lousy food, and in spite of these poor living conditions, worked diligently to achieve numbers, baptism numbers, even though he felt his life threatened every time he knocked on a door,

And twenty-two years later, in a return visit to his mission area, he rode his bike up and down the streets remembering houses and sidewalks and the fear he felt when knocking on doors and walking in the neighborhood. When knocking on every door at least five times, some of them were opened by African- Americans whose men were not admitted to the Mormon priesthood before 1978, the year the Mormon Church hierarchy decided, after a lot of pressure, to allow black men into the priesthood. At this time, young missionaries were instructed not to try to convert African-Americans and were not allowed to present missionary lessons to them unless they specifically were asked to do so. He thought "good for them" since they never asked him to teach them. And if they had, they would have had to ask him each and every time they desired another lesson. They would also have had to request being baptized because he could not offer it to them. Having been indoctrinated in the Mormon teachings that men of black skin were inferior, he was confused when upon returning home from his mission to learn of the "revelation" that permitted worthy black males to hold the priesthood.

He feels today that the Mormon Church's teaching of love and family togetherness is in opposition to its actual practice of tossing a young missionary overboard to see if he will sink or swim. And if he sinks, he doesn't get to die, he goes home as a failure, an embarrassment to his family and Mormon friends. He said: "They told us in the Mission Home give two years ... gain ten. Ten years of what???"

"... learn to do as you are told, both old and young; learn to do as you are told ... none of your business whether it is right or wrong." *Journal of Discourses* 6:32, November 8, 1857, Heber C. Kimball

Chapter Seven
Authority, Obedience and Political Activities

As we have seen from the very beginning, the Mormon Church has been administered from the President on down. At the age of 23, through the use of the authority that he claimed he received from God, Joseph Smith was able to coerce Martin Harris into selling his farm to finance the printing of 5,000 copies of the *Book of Mormon*. Smith learned early that by claiming authority from God, he could make people accede to his wishes. Smith used this scare tactic not only for religious purposes but to obtain such personal pleasures as sex with attractive women. He often told young women, "God commands you to marry me."

Brigham Young claimed this same authority after he assumed the leadership of the Mormon Church and became President in 1847, three years after Smith's death. During his reign as President of the church from 1847 until his death in 1877, Young exercised this authority to be sealed to seventy wives (although he cohabited with only about twenty-seven) and amassed vast amounts of property and wealth in Utah. When he wished to have something accomplished, such as developing a new settlement in another part of his Deseret State, he sent a call out to a church member whom he felt was qualified to do it. If the member wished to remain in good standing in the church, he accepted the call.

While Young faced some restrictions placed upon him by federal authorities, generally he had control over his followers especially from 1847 to 1870, or until the federal government again turned its attention from the Civil War to problems in Utah. "In his [Young's]

time, the President of the church was virtually a law unto himself in Utah both in religious and worldly matters, for it was hard to find the line that divided them. Today the President is still completely powerful in religious matters, but his authority over the greatly expanded church is shared with his colleagues at the top.

"...For many years it has been the custom of the Mormons to hold semi-annual conferences. At each of these it is the practice for the audience — once representing the majority of the Saints right there present in the Tabernacle, but now just a relative few who manage to get to Salt Lake City and find a seat — to vote to sustain the General Authorities. The hands shoot up automatically when the question is asked.

"...In fact, as the years have passed, it has become the most serious of religious crimes to question the integrity or good faith or power of the General Authorities. Illustrative of this increasing reliance on control by the General Authorities is the prominence given to one question among the ten that a bishop is told to ask an applicant for a permit to visit the temple. The first question is:

'Are you morally clean and worthy to enter the temple?'

The second question:

'Will you and do you sustain the General Authorities of the Church, and will you live in accordance with the accepted rules and doctrines of the church?"[249]

U.S. Government: A Temporary Convenience for the Mormon Church Hierarchy

The church supports the Constitution of the United States and has described it as of divine origin, even though the writers of the Constitution did not know that they were being divinely guided. As we have read in previous chapters, the Mormon Church leaders have probably ordained their President as the king of the new government to be established in the United States and eventually throughout the world. It is believed that the General Authorities have also established the framework for this new government by secretly continuing the Council of Fifty originally established by Joseph Smith and continued on by Brigham Young. The Council of Fifty is prepared to assume top governmental positions necessary to administer the affairs of the country. As we have also discussed in previous chapters, the control of the Council of Fifty would be in the hands of the king, (the President of the Mormon Church), his two Counselors and the Twelve Apostles. Common consent rules the governing of this group. That is, the President consults with his counselors and apostles and the "king," then puts his proposals to his Counselor and Apostles for unanimous approval.

In this type of government, there would be no opposition party. The General Authorities of the Mormon Church would rule nations in the same way that they govern the church today, making decisions and passing these down to their members. Church authority is absolute in the relationship between the General Authorities, lower echelon administrators and the church membership.

Following is a summary of the work done by Joseph Smith and Brigham Young who controlled the church and its membership from 1830 to 1877. Their policies and activities have formed the basic framework of authority, control and administration of the church today.

Joseph Smith and Authority

Smith claimed that his authority over his flock was granted to him by God, and he used this "God given" authority to demand obedience from his followers. He used the threat of God's wrath to control them. This fear of God's and Joseph's wrath caused his followers to endure great suffering and anguish during his short fourteen-year reign as head of the Mormon Church. Because Smith's appetite for authority and glory was so strong, he made many blunders that led the "children of Israel" into crisis after crisis. In addition, Smith used his keen imagination to form extravagant religious inventions, many of which he claimed were revelations from God. These inventions were of a religious nature and were the cornerstone of his ability to control his followers. Smith's imagination and ability to conjure up religious inventions were reinforced by his magnetic influence over his friends. Cowdery, Smith's scribe in writing the *Book of Mormon*, described Smith as having "mysterious power, which even now I fail to fathom."[250] Not only did Smith's imagination allow him to invent fantastic stories, he quickly learned that his "mysterious power and magnetic influence" could control people. He used these attributes to gain and wield power in building his church.

Lucy Smith, Joseph's mother, described her son's imagination as follows: "During our evening conversations, Joseph would occasionally give us some of the most amusing recitals that could be imagined. He would describe the ancient inhabitants of this continent, their dress, mode of traveling, and the animals upon which they rode; their cities, their buildings, with every particular; their mode of warfare; and also their religious worship. This he would do with as much ease, seemingly, as if he had spent his whole life with them."[251] These evening conversations occurred almost three years before Joseph Smith claimed that he had received the golden plates from the angel Moroni. God had, according to Smith, empowered him to translate these plates through the use of Urim and Thummin, magical stones, but this claim is refuted by his mother's description of her son's "recitals" at family gatherings years before the golden plates were even received. These same recitals appeared later in Smith's *Book of Mormon*.

Mormon Church authorities maintain that Joseph Smith's *Book of Mormon* is of divine origin and was translated by Smith by the power of God given to Smith through the use of seer stones or Urim and Thummim as Joseph Smith had claimed. They claim that only by this God-given power was Smith able to translate from the golden plates and write the *Book of Mormon*. If this were true, how was Joseph Smith able to describe the central theme of his book more than three years before he had even received the plates? One can assume that it was because his vivid imagination was fueled by the book, *View of the Hebrews*, and other similar books written and circulating in the area where he lived. But because the *Book of Mormon* is the cornerstone of the Mormon Church and because Lucy Smith's autobiography of her son Joseph Smith's life had put the church's claim of divineness of his book in jeopardy, Brigham Young ordered Lucy's book destroyed in 1865. However, a copy was kept and "corrected" by a "committee of revision."[252]

Several other attempts at suppressing material by General Authorities that could be damaging to church doctrine or the Mormon religion have been described in prior chapters of this book. The most bizarre of these attempts was (as written previously) the Mark Hofmann forgeries described in a book by Linda Sillitoe and Allen Roberts, *Salamander, the Story of the Mormon Forgery Murders.*

Joseph Smith was not shy about assuming power over the members of his church. From the very onset in developing his religion and church, Smith claimed himself to be the exclusive communicator with God in order to obtain what he wanted. One example of his self-proclaimed God-given powers included the revelation of polygamy that he falsely claimed was received from God. This allowed women and girls to be married to him in order to satisfy his sexual appetite.

Smith used these powers to expand his authority and personal wealth. For example, he established a fraudulent bank in Kirtland, Ohio, with worthless bank notes. He was also successful in obtaining a charter from the State of Illinois that gave him far reaching authority. This authority granted from the state gave him almost complete autonomy in the development of the city of Nauvoo, Illinois. Smith was not satisfied with being just the Prophet, but had to assume all leadership positions, including Mayor, Lieutenant General of the Nauvoo Legion (militia) and President of "Nauvoo University."

Smith's power over his Mormon clan was absolute; he controlled with an iron fist. Any member of the Mormon Church who dared question his authority was charged with questioning the authority of God. After all, Smith represented God, and acting as God's appointed servant and official communicator, he could do no wrong.

Following is a description of the actions of a man, who had thirst for power and glory and had the ability to induce and force people to give him such power. Listed are some of the many mistakes that occurred during Joseph Smith's fourteen year reign (1830-1844) as head of the Mormon Church.

1. Smith made several blunders in writing his book, including plagiarizing from several parts of the Bible; writing that the Jaredites (about 2000 B. C.) brought horses, swine, sheep, cattle and asses from Israel (when it was known even in his own day that Columbus had found the land devoid of these species) and writing that the American Indians (Lamanites) were Jewish descendants.

Even today, church approved writers are attempting to satisfy or make excuses, regardless of the lack of proof, why they still must hold onto the *Book of Mormon* as truth. Many pages in the Mormon Church *Ensign* periodical are devoted to trying to show that the *Book of Mormon* is true and that the designation of Smith as a Prophet of God is authentic. One example of these faith-promoting books includes Christ in America by Delbert W. Curtiss. This book attempts to show that the *Book of Mormon* is true by using historical evidence gathered by the Mormon Church instead of independent sources of genuine archaeological research.

2. As has been discussed previously, Joseph Smith used revelations he said he had received from God to maintain his authority. One of these "revelations" which was the key to his authority, gave him and only him the power to receive revelations from God. When others in his church claimed that they too could receive revelations, Joseph quickly reported that he had received a revelation from God which said: "...no one shall be appointed to receive commandments and revelations in this Church, excepting my servant Joseph Smith, Jun." This "revelation" was very important for Smith in establishing his sole authority to lead the church.[253] Smith was always able to come up with a "revelation from God" when something was threatening his control of his church or his subjects.

3. Smith's church was autocratic from the beginning, and the Prophet of the church would never allow any semblance of democracy to emerge. He was God's appointed Prophet, and he made decisions about the proper worship of God and who should be the leaders of such worship. "...he forbade the preaching of Mormonism by anyone except elders 'regularly ordained by the heads of the church'." While every man in the Mormon Church could be a member of the priesthood, the final authority rested with the self-proclaimed Prophet of God. Smith also established priesthood offices within the church such as deacon, priest, elder, "seventy" and high priest. "Each title carried a certain rank, progression from lower to higher being dependent upon a man's faith, his zeal for the church, and the good will of his superiors in the hierarchy." In this way, Smith encouraged his followers not only to have faith in his teachings but to strive for rewards of higher offices in the church, working hard to promote the success of the church.[254]

4. Joseph Smith made another major blunder in 1834 when he had gathered together a small army of 205 men in Kirtland, Ohio, which included a new convert, Brigham Young. At this time in the history of the Mormon Church, two settlements of Mormons had been established, one in Kirtland, Ohio, and one in Jackson County, Missouri. At first the settlement in Jackson County flourished, but in their endeavor to acquire land and more economic and political influence, non-Mormon settlers in that area became alarmed. They were fearful that the Mormons who voted as a bloc would take over the Jackson County government and their land. As a result the non-

Mormon settlers began to harass the Mormons, and increased friction between the two groups resulted in fighting which caused deaths on both sides. Hearing of this, Smith, who was in Ohio at this time, assembled a small army.

The purpose of Smith's "army" was to relieve the Mormon settlers in Jackson County, Missouri, of non-Mormon harassment and to protect the Mormons from suffering further abuse. While Smith attempted to march the eight hundred miles from Kirtland, Ohio, to Jackson County in secret, the word leaked to the Missourians that his army was coming. In the meantime, it appeared that the troubles between the Mormons and non-Mormons were being worked out. "...several influential citizens in Jackson County had been working feverishly for a peace settlement." But when the Missourians heard of his "army" labeled as "Zion's Camp" was on its way to Missouri, they became infuriated and ransacked and burned many Mormon homes. "The Governor (of Missouri) had said explicitly that it would bring the state militia down upon the heads of the invaders."[255]

Smith's blunder, as described by Brodie, was caused by his failure to "gauge the repercussions of his policies upon the opposition. Strategically, the whole concept of Zion's Camp had been a mistake." Smith had ventured outside the natural protection which he had within his own community of faithful followers. He was always able to control uncomfortable situations within his Mormon community through his claim of "God-given authority" as Prophet of his church.[256] However, his "God-given authority" was not recognized by non-Mormons. Smith had overestimated his power and authority outside the boundaries of his own territory. His inability to foresee what his actions meant to non-Mormons lost him the opportunity to save his settlement in Missouri. As we shall see later, his over estimation of his power and authority probably cost him his life and led to the Mormon exodus from Smith's greatest achievement, the city of Nauvoo.

Upon returning to Kirtland, Ohio, Smith resumed his autocratic control of his Mormon followers. All "elections" to church offices were made from a list prepared by him and his two Counselors. Once a candidate was selected and put to a vote by the church members rarely did any member vote not to approve Smith's choice. "Dissenting votes quickly became so rare that the elections came to be called — and the irony was unconscious — 'sustaining of the authorities'."[257] During the next three years, Smith's Mormon colony in Missouri languished in isolation and poverty while he concentrated his efforts on his followers in Kirtland, Ohio.

Joseph Smith's Bank

5. The self proclaimed Prophet of God was not satisfied with the peace and prosperity of his faithful, but ventured into a new calling, banking. Smith had borrowed heavily to finance his new temple and several purchases of surrounding land. He became worried about how he would pay off the huge debt that he had accumulated. In 1836 after consulting with the brethren, he organized the Kirtland Safety Society Bank Company, with a capitalization of not less than four million dollars. Smith's bank vault was filled with boxes each marked "$1,000." Each box contained a top layer of fifty cent silver coins and the rest filled with sand. If any one doubted the safety of the bank, the box was opened, and it appeared that the box was full of silver coins. Patrons could lift the box if they wished to insure that it was "filled with coins." Smith had used similar methods to fool his followers into believing that he had the golden plates when he asked them to heft the wrapped metal plates. (As mentioned before, the plates were probably fashioned by his scribe, Oliver Cowdery, a skilled iron maker.) Smith knew that he had fooled his faithful, so why not do the same with his bank patrons?

Smith's bank printed a large number of notes to pay off his debts and to speculate in land purchases. However, it wasn't long before people with the notes began redeeming them, and Smith, realizing that he would be ruined, closed his bank less than one month after it had been opened. Several lawsuits were brought against Smith who was "terribly in debt." Smith "...was arrested seven times in four months, and his followers managed heroically to raise the $38,428 required for bail." His total debt at the time was estimated at $150,000. The Mormon Church was in turmoil, as "At least six of the twelve apostles were in open rebellion." One of the apostles, Parley Pratt wrote a letter to Smith on May 23, 1837 saying in part: 'And now my dear brother, if you are still determined to pursue this wicked course until yourself and the church shall sink down to hell, I beseech you at least to have mercy on me and my...for those three lots...which you sold to me at the extraordinary price of $2,000, which never cost you $100. For it stands against me it will ruin me and my helpless family ... will you take the advantage of your neighbor because he is in your power...If not I shall be under the painful necessity of preferring charges against you for extortion, covetousness, and taking advantage of your brother by an undue religious influence...Such as saying it was the will of God that lands should bear with such a price; and many other prophesyings, [sic] preachings, and statements of a like nature.'"[258]

Things were very bad for Joseph Smith. Brodie writes that "Heber Kimball was probably not exaggerating much when he said that at this time 'there were not twenty persons on earth that would declare that Joseph Smith was a Prophet of God.' But as he had done many times before in evading the law, Smith was able once again to extricate himself from a bad situation. Sometimes he extricated himself by talking his way out, or using his faithful to get him free, or simply getting on a horse and riding out of town. In this situation, after Smith learned that Grandison Newell, a prominent anti-Mormon, "had secured a warrant for his arrest on a charge of banking fraud, Joseph knew that this was the finish, he fled on his horse toward his Missouri Mormon settlement."[259] This time Smith underestimated his flummoxed investors.

His Mormon settlement in Kirtland, Ohio, was in shambles; dissenters seized the temple and many left the Mormon Church, their financial condition being ruined. Smith had been driven from his Kirtland temple by his own disciples. One would believe that this would be the end of Mormonism, but Smith was to be given another chance. He was welcomed with open arms when he arrived in his new settlement, Far West, Missouri. In spite of poverty and without Joseph, Far West, with its fifteen hundred Saints was making a remarkable recovery. And 600 Saints from Kirtland later followed Joseph to Missouri.

6. Joseph returned to his Missouri colony of Mormons in 1837 after being threatened by his creditors with huge fines and possible jail sentences for his activities connected with the failed Kirtland Safety Society Bank. And as he did in 1834 when he attempted to rescue the Mormons in Missouri from non-Mormon's abuse by using his "Zion's Camp" of armed men, he misjudged the power of his "enemy" in Missouri, the old settlers. His blunder was the failure to integrate the Mormons into the regular economy of the New Frontier. Instead, as Smith had done in Kirtland, he organized a theocracy in the middle of state, local and national goverment. In addition, he organized the "Danites," a secret armed group of

Mormons designed to enforce the doctrine of the church and absolute obedience to Joseph Smith and his rule, as well as protect the Mormons from the local settlers.

One example of how the Danites enforced the church's control over members is as follows: Three dissenters, Oliver Cowdery (Smith's scribe for the *Book of Mormon* and his early close associate) and John and David Whitmer were in opposition to some of the policies of the church. John Whitmer was told by Joseph Smith "— if you will put your property into the hands of the bishop and high council and let it be disposed of according to the laws of the church, perhaps after a little while the church might have confidence in you."

To that, John Whitmer replied that he wished to control his own land and wanted to be governed "by the laws of the land and not the laws of the church."

Since John Whitmer, his brother David and Cowdery were not willing to cooperate with the church edict, they were given three days to depart from the county, and if they did not, "we" "...will cause you to depart." Upon receiving the ultimatum the above three with Lyman Johnson traveled to Liberty in Clay County to hire a lawyer. In returning, they were met by their families who told them that the Danites forced them to leave with only their clothing and blankets. They had been forced to leave everything else behind and were threatened with death if they returned.[260]

Not only did Smith have his own police force, he called upon the Saints "to deed their property to the church and promised in return that every man would receive a tract of land for his 'everlasting inheritance,' the number of acres being determined by the size of his family. The 'surplus property' was to remain in the hands of the bishop, to be used for building the temple, supporting the church presidency, and 'laying the foundation of Zion.'"[261]

From Palmyra, New York to Kirtland, Ohio, to Far West, Missouri, the Mormons attracted dislike and aggression from their non-Mormon neighbors. This dislike was not only a result of the close association which Mormons had with one another, but within the communities they created, which always seemed to distance themselves from their non-Mormon neighbors. In Missouri, for example, the *old* settlers were used to living in their households often five miles away from other settlers. The Mormons came in and accumulated land, but lived together in villages, not on separate farms. Not only that, their bloc voting caused the non-Mormons to fear that they would lose all political power to the Mormons. As dozens of Mormon immigrants came to Missouri and gobbled up a large portion of the land, the intense antagonism of non-Mormons increased. Smith's blunder was his inability to gauge the hostility that he was creating by attempting to organize his **Mormon** kingdom of God *separate* from the regular flow of surrounding community life. The non-Mormons promoted independent thinking in their frontier life, while independent thinking among Mormons was discouraged by the organizational structure of the church and its practices in community living, community property and church doctrine. These were foreign and considered to be a threat by the non-Mormon community.

Once again Smith's and his Mormon colony's forced removal from Missouri was due to his inability to gauge the reaction of non-Mormons to his attempts to organize his own police force, his attempts to organize his Mormon colony into a self-sufficient community separate from the non-Mormon community, and his illegal and cruel treatment of dissenters.

Joseph Smith and his Mormons Forced to Move from Missouri

7. Thus, the stage was set for another Joseph Smith retreat with his colony from a major Mormon settlement. Smith, in failing to incorporate his Mormon Church members into the mainstream of community life, and by attempting to develop his own "kingdom of God," had stirred the already boiling pot into full eruption.

At that time, there was an election at an outlying Mormon settlement of Adam-ondi-Ahman when a non-Mormon and a Mormon got into a fight at the polling place. This fight spread to about thirty Mormons and two hundred non-Mormons and resulted in a small riot. Rumor was that two Mormons had been killed although actually no one was killed. Smith, upon learning of the rumor, marched a small army to Adam-ondi-Ahman and learned that the riot report was exaggerated. However, upon returning he stopped at the home of the Justice of Peace, Adam Black, and demanded that he sign an agreement of peace. This was felt by the authorities to be intimidation on Smith's part, and he was arrested and put in Liberty jail.

Upon hearing about Smith's intimidation of the Justice of Peace, Missourians abused Mormon farmers by whipping them, and it became evident that they were hell bent to drive the Mormons out. These and other incidents infuriated the Mormons and as a result, they went on the offensive, set fire to several non-Mormon cabins and took wagon loads of possessions from the Missourians which they called "consecrated property." Several other skirmishes occurred between the Mormons and non-Mormons, some resulting in deaths, which caused Governor Boggs to call out the state militia to end the fighting.

The fighting ended when Joseph Smith and other church leaders were arrested and charged with treason, murder, arson, burglary, robbery, larceny and perjury. Fawn Brodie provides a comprehensive description of the Missouri-Far West confrontation between the Missourians and the Mormons, including reported atrocities committed by the Missouri State militia against the Mormon citizens. Had Smith been able to foresee the consequences of his and Sidney Rigdon's attempt to organize a theocracy in Missouri separate from the government of the United States and Missouri, which included Smith's own militia and police force, the disastrous confrontation could have been avoided. Yet, as we shall see, Joseph Smith was still not to see his errors, as the same blunder was repeated in Nauvoo, Illinois.[262]

Joseph Smith and his Followers Move to Nauvoo, Illinois

Joseph Smith remained in the Liberty jail for four months after being put there on November 30, 1838. In the meantime, at least 8,000 Mormons began their exodus from Missouri, with Brigham Young making some of the plans for their departure before he himself fled because of the possibility of his arrest. Smith was able to escape from his Missouri captors by offering $800 to the sheriff in bribery money, and the sheriff furnished him and Smith's fellow prisoners with several horses. "Joseph mounted a fine dark chestnut stallion and with the other prisoners close behind him pounded up the road toward his old settlement, where he joined the last remnant of the Mormons who were headed for the Mississippi."[263]

Smith, a fugitive from justice, fled away in the night on his horse as he had done before when he left his pursuers in Kirtland, Ohio. He lasted a little more than a year as the leader of the Missouri "kingdom of God" before his followers were again forced to leave. Palmyra, New York; Kirtland, Ohio; and Far West, Missouri had been the home of his followers during the short time of eight years. Each time his Saints had been forced to leave because of the pressures exerted by non-Mormons against Joseph Smith's religion. Each time Joseph and his flock moved to a new territory, the intensity of the antagonism by non-Mormons increased. Had Joseph learned anything from the mistakes he had made in his relations with non-Mormons? To learn the answer to this question, one must follow Smith to his new destination, Nauvoo, Illinois.

8. Nauvoo, a name which Joseph took from Hebrew, meaning beautiful plantation, was situated in Illinois on a bend in the Mississippi River across from Keokuk, Iowa. Here was to be the site of Joseph's new "kingdom of God" which flourished from 1839 until Joseph's death in 1844. In this city, the second largest in Illinois after Chicago, Smith had complete control of all land sales to his Saints and reserved the best lots in Nauvoo for his most trusted and faithful "servants of the Lord." Smith controlled all the activities of the city of Nauvoo, including permits for industry, the police force and ordinances passed by the "city council." To illustrate his power, Smith claimed that he received a revelation from God that his Saints were to build a hotel in his "beautiful plantation," which was to include a "suite of rooms for himself and his posterity for...ever and ever."[264] The hotel was completed shortly thereafter.

Taking advantage of the destitute people and the poverty which Smith's Mormon missionaries found in England, the Mormons were able to bring hundreds of converts from there to Nauvoo. The missionaries advertised America as "...millions on millions of acres of land lie before them unoccupied, with a soil as rich as Eden"...Nauvoo soon became a city of over ten thousand residents as the impoverished Englishmen streamed into the "beautiful plantation." Smith's city was enhanced by the special charter that was given to the Prophet, empowering him to 'make, ordain, establish and execute all such ordinances not repugnant to the Constitution of the United States or of this State.' The charter also gave Smith the power to organize his Nauvoo Legion which was a part of the state militia, but "answerable only to the Governor. Typical of Smith's mania for power and glory, he made himself Lieutenant General (after receiving a commission of lieutenant-general from state Governor Carlin) of his Nauvoo Legion. The Nauvoo Legion often had parades within the city, led by General Smith in his colorful uniform consisting of "a blue coat with a plentiful supply of gold braid,

buff trousers, high military boots, and a handsome chapeau topped
with ostrich feathers. On his hip he carried a sword and two big
horse-pistols. Delighting in the pomp and splendor of parades, he
called on the Legion on every possible occasion, marching at the
head on his magnificent black stallion, Charlie." This had to be
heady for the poor farm boy who had suffered the indignity of
spending time in a dingy jail in Missouri. This was a time for him to
repay the Missourians who had put him into so much embarrassment
only a few years before.[265]

The Mormons were given guns and cannon by the state of
Illinois to arm Smith's Nauvoo Legion, a force of 2000 men (all men
between the ages of 18 and 45 were required by Smith to join the
Legion). Since Smith was a fugitive from justice from the state of
Missouri, his Legion gave him protection from attempts by Missouri
officials to arrest him. Such an attempt was made, but upon learning
of this attempt, Smith went into hiding. Fleeing and hiding from his
enemies occurred many times during Smith's leadership of the
church. Fearing that he might be arrested, Smith also formed an elite
bodyguard of twelve men, his toughest fighters and most devoted
friends.

Joseph Smith Introduces Polygamy to Nauvoo

As noted earlier, Smith introduced polygamy in Nauvoo, which
he and several of his apostles practiced secretly. It was easy for a
woman to be enticed into a polygamous marriage since so many of
the wives in "beautiful plantation" were alone while their husbands
were away serving on missions. In addition, many women converts,
mostly from England, some of whom had left their husbands to
make the long journey to America's heartland, were anxious to be
"married." Brodie lists 48 women who were plural wives of Joseph
Smith.[266] Brigham Young was among the apostles who were married
to more than one woman while in Nauvoo. He also married several
of Joseph Smith's wives after Smith was killed in 1844.

Joseph Smith Runs for President of the United States

Smith's never ending lust for power is illustrated when he made
himself a candidate for president of the United States in the spring
of 1844. His platform for the presidency included:

(1) Reducing of the number of congressman by two-thirds.

(2) Cutting down of the pay of the remaining two-thirds to two dollars a day.

(3) Prison-reform legislation to facilitate the granting of pardons.

(4) Abolishing capital punishment and life imprisonment.

(5) Greater economy in government.

(6) Less distinction among the classes.

(7) Abolition of slavery by 1850.

(8) Establishing a national bank with state branches.

(9) Giving the president authority to send the army into any state to put down a mob.

(10) Inviting Oregon, Texas, Canada and Mexico into the Union.[267]

The establishment of the Mormon kingdom of God on earth has always been the goal of the Mormon Church, with America targeted to become the first country of the world to be controlled by the Mormons. Joseph Smith was heady about his achievements in founding the city of Nauvoo and building it into one of the larger cities in the United States with twenty thousand inhabitants. Running for president of the United States was a continuation of the great confidence that he had developed in his ability to control men in building his kingdom of God in Nauvoo.

While Smith sent his "missionaries" to all parts of the United States to campaign for his presidency, his real goal was to establish his kingdom of God on earth in Oregon. He knew that further expansion of his kingdom around Nauvoo was impractical for he was "living in constant fear of mobbing or assassination, hiding the apprehension in his heart, the doubts, the misgivings, seeking consolation in the thrills of fresh seductions."[268]

Joseph Smith's Misuse of Authority

That he was seeking an escape from this fear is evident, as is shown in one of his speeches to his Mormon audiences, he said: "Our enemies, the mobocrats, may seem to have the upper hand; but there is light in the west!" Within his Nauvoo, however, Smith was in complete control, and he pursued his interests in young women with heedless abandonment. "The recklessness and the egotism of Joseph Smith was never more strikingly displayed than by his

attempt to seduce the wives of Wilson Law and Dr. Foster. Joe knew
Foster and the Law brothers, William and Wilson are able men,
above the average in wealth, culture, ability and force. His conduct
toward them had been what it was toward all able men who had been
attracted to Mormonism. He recognized their talents and put them to
work, utilizing them for the benefit of the church. No matter how
clever the individual might be, Joe believed himself more than a
match for him. He put him at the job for which he seemed best fitted, feeling confident that if he showed signs of ambition or dissen-
sion, a word from the Prophet would be sufficient to put him in his
place. Thus, he dominated many men of greater ability than himself,
used their talent for his aggrandizement and cast them aside when
their usefulness was past or they rebelled against him.

"Martin Harris had money. Joe needed it. He got it, and thereafter had no use for Harris. Sidney Rigdon had learning in theology,
unusual oratorical ability, and prestige as a churchman. The new
church needed these qualities. Joe elevated Rigdon to a seat at the
right hand of the throne; but when his eloquence and prestige were
no longer essential, Sidney was demoted. Isaac Morley had money,
lands and ability as an organizer. Joe put him to work as he did
Brigham Young.

"...Give them power, give them honors, they can never become
rivals. With one word I can ruin them, the egotist said. But his egotism carried him too far. It convinced him that he was irresistible to
women; no woman could for long repulse his advances. Sooner or
later, if he persisted, she must yield to his overwhelming attraction."[269]

"Up and down the river from Rock Island to St. Louis, stories
of the Prophet's amours were bandied about. The roustabouts on the
steamboats related them to loafers at the boat-landings at each city
and hamlet along the river, and the loafers put them into circulation
in town. ...From Carthage and Quincy, enemies of the Prophet spread
stories of his infamy throughout the state.

"Joe's own words formed the basis of many of these yarns. He
was free in discussing his conquests in what he assumed to be con-
genial circles, even to the extent of comparing the degree of pas-
sionate satisfaction afforded by each of his favorites. Some of these
remarks achieved a national circulation such as: 'God doesn't care if
we have a good time here in Nauvoo, if only other people don't
know about it. And whenever I see a pretty woman, I have to pray
for grace.'" [270]

One of Joseph's Smith's messages to Emiline White, whose house along the river was known to all the men along the river, was intercepted and broadcast throughout the area:

"My Sweet Emeline,
You know that my love for you as David said to Jonathan is wonderful, surpassing the love of women. If you need anything while I am gone, call upon either of the Bishops, Vinson Knight, or Alanson Ripley and show them the signature of 'Old White Hat' and they will provide for you. Do not be afraid to receive anything of me, as these men are confidential. You need not fear to write me, and I do assure you that a few lines would be very consoling on a journey. Sign it 'Rosanna.'

Your humble servant,
Old White Hat"[271]

Joseph Smith was called Old White Hat because he often wore white beaver hats.

"Other stories they told up and down the river concerned the isolated brick house of the flats a mile and a half out of Nauvoo, fitted up by Bennett as an abortion hospital; the eight girls in the Nauvoo Mansion House, whom Joe called his 'daughters,' Emma always referred to as 'nieces' and the steamboat men as 'the harem.'"[272]

The evidence is clear that Joseph Smith had sexual encounters with several women, a trail which extended from Kirtland, Ohio to Nauvoo, Illinois. Beardsley lists twenty-eight women who were married or "sealed" to Smith and contends that there were several others who served as common law wives. While Emma denied to her deathbed that Smith had sexual encounters with other women, this is discounted since Emma was trying to protect her family from the embarrassment which such encounters would entail.[273] There is also the question of the offspring from these encounters of Smith with other women, since not one of their children has been identified as an offspring of Smith. This too is partially explained by Beardsley who contends that: "Many of the members of Joseph's Celestial harem were married women, and offspring of such unions might easily be credited to the legal husbands in the official records, regardless of what entry might be made in the book of Celestial glory. Then there was the hospital in the isolated house on the flats."[274]

In the spring of 1844, presidential candidate, Joseph Smith, while his leading loyal Mormon followers were stumping for him around the country, was enjoying the fruits of his fourteen years of labor in building his kingdom of God. His unusual sexual appetite for beautiful women was being satisfied, his ego as the Prophet of his church was being fulfilled. His demands on his church members were being met by them without question. He was certainly at the high point of his short career as the total and despotic leader of his flock.

Polygamy Taught and Practiced by Joseph Smith

Smith taught that a man who took ten wives with him to heaven had ten times as much chance of becoming God of his own planet than a man who took only one wife. It is said that Joseph's own adventure with plural marriage began with Fannie Alger. Oliver Cowdery who, at one time was second in command of the Mormon Church, called Joseph's relation with Fannie Alger, at that time about eighteen, "a dirty, nasty, filthy affair."[275] Joseph's polygamist marriages did not stop with unmarried women, as he also "married" Priescindia Huntington Buell, who was the wife of Norman Buell who had left the Mormon Church. Priescindia had stated that she did not know whether her husband or Joseph was the father of her child. A picture of her son Oliver Buell in Fawn Brodie's book, *No Man Knows my History*, shows a resemblance to Joseph Smith. Brodie also states that Oliver Buell was "sealed or adopted" to Smith in the Mormon temple in Salt Lake City.[276]

Smith was "married" to several other married women, including Zina Huntington Jacobs, whom he married in 1841, while her husband Henry B. Jacobs was away on a mission with John D. Lee.[277] Maintaining fidelity to one's own husband was difficult while the husband was away from home serving on a mission in a far off country, or for a long length of time in parts of the United States. In addition, as stated earlier, many of the women converts had left their husbands in foreign countries to come to Nauvoo to live. Therefore, Joseph Smith and other leaders of the church found a fertile field in which to practice polygamy. Some might even say that Smith may have purposely sent husbands of attractive women away on long missions so that he could secretly "marry" their wives.

Probably the most embarrassing account of attempted polygamous "marriage" in Nauvoo by Brigham Young and Joseph Smith was the following account as described by Brodie: "...a self possessed eighteen-year-old English girl, Martha Brotherton, chose to speak her mind. Brigham Young, who had not been bashful in following his prophet's lead, had set his heart on the high-spirited English lass. He took her to the famous rendezvous over Joseph's store, locked the door and proceeded with the curious, bobtailed, hortatory courtship that was becoming so common in the city:

"Brother Joseph has had a revelation from God that it is lawful and right for a man to have two wives...If you will accept of me I will take you straight to the Celestial kingdom, and if you will have me in this world, I will have you in that which is to come, and Brother Joseph will marry us here today, and you can go home this evening, and your parents will not know anything about it.

"When the girl demurred and begged for time, Brigham called to Joseph, who also urged her to make an immediate decision. 'Just go ahead, and do as Brigham wants you to,' he said and added with a laugh: 'He is the best man in the world, except me.' Then he went on more seriously: 'If you will accept of Brigham, you will be blessed — God will bless you, and my blessing shall rest upon you...and if you do not like it in a month or two, come to me, and I will make you free again; and if he turns you off, I will take you on.

"'Sir, it will be too late to think in a month or two after,' Martha answered wryly. 'I want time to think first.'

"...Finally and reluctantly they (Smith and Young) let her go home, where she promised to pray in secret for guidance. The moment she arrived, however, she wrote down the whole episode while it was still fresh in her memory and showed it to her parents. The Brothertons in high dudgeon took a steamboat to St. Louis, but not before they had given Martha's recital enough circulation so that everyone in Nauvoo knew it within a week. Eventually Martha published her account in a St. Louis paper"[278] (The account of Martha's recital appeared in the *St. Louis Bulletin,* July 15, 1842.) Joseph Smith never replied to her charges, but Brigham Young and Heber Kimball called her a liar, and her two sisters and a brother-in-law who remained in the church called Martha a liar and a harlot.[279] The truth is most likely that the story occurred exactly as Martha described it, for throughout his history Joseph Smith acted in the name of God for many other favors that he wanted from his converts and followers. Some of these actions included: telling his Saints that

he received a revelation from God that they (Saints) were to build
him a hotel in Nauvoo, and providing the Smith family a suite of
rooms for their use in this hotel, and in his revelation from God,
Smith "received" a complete description of how the hotel was to be
built. In addition Smith received a "revelation from God" giving
his first wife Emma (who had been fighting her husband's attempt
to introduce polygamy into his family) a commandment 'to receive
all those that have been given unto my servant Joseph' and to
'cleave unto my servant Joseph, and to none else...and if you
(Emma) do not, you will be destroyed ..."[280]

Joseph Smith's history clearly shows that he was a man with
a great passion for power and fame. He also knew that he must
share liaison opportunities of the "principle of polygamy" with his
appointed leaders of the church since he needed their leadership
skills to maintain control of his Saints. The self-proclaimed Prophet
of God was never reluctant to use the power that "God gave him"
to enhance his authority, glory, comfort and personal pleasures. The
great trauma, the shattering of human lives, especially women's
who Smith's introduction of polygamy caused, can never be meas-
ured. The Saints had been taught that the Prophet (Smith), as God's
personal representative on earth, could not and would not make a
mistake. If God's representative told them that it was God's plan
that they have sex with him (through a pretentious polygamous
marriage), most of the faithful would accept even though they
abhorred the proposal.

Joseph Smith: General, Prophet, Mayor of Nauvoo and
Polygamist, had made great progress in fulfilling his ambitions and
pleasures in the three years since he had left Missouri as a fugitive
from justice in April, 1839. When he arrived at a bend on the
Mississippi River to establish his new "Kingdom of God" at
Nauvoo, he also had with him twelve thousand voters, who delivered their votes in the way that the Prophet desired. Smith used this
bloc of votes to enable him to receive a special charter from the
Illinois Governor and the state legislature. With such powers he
was able to establish his theocracy in Nauvoo with little interference from the state and national governments. However, in 1842,
Illinois legislators and Governor Ford were beginning to become
disenchanted with Smith and his Mormons. Smith's improprieties
such as using "God-given authority" to fulfill his lust for women
(polygamy), his use of his secret police organization (Danites) to

enforce his doctrine and overall authoritarian control of his "Saints" were beginning to leak out to the surrounding non-Mormon community. This leaking was being enhanced by his number two man in his church, John Bennett.

John Bennett's Excommunication Opens up Pandora's Box

Bennett was pursuing Smith's introduction of polygamy in Nauvoo with such a passion it was becoming a great embarrassment to Smith, especially when his Nauvoo community of Saints became acquainted with some of Bennett's sexual conquests. Included in Bennett's sexual promiscuity was his seducing of innocent women by telling them that he had the Prophet's approval. Bennett had been attracted to the Mormon Church because he had heard that they encouraged and practiced polygamy. Finally Smith excommunicated Bennett from the church, hoping that this would save himself further embarrassment. However, Bennett wrote letters to the editor of the *Sangamo Journal* of Springfield, Illinois, accusing Joseph Smith of threatening him "...with death by the Holy Joe, and his Danite band of murderers." He also accused Smith of plotting to establish an empire with himself as king of the western states, which was to be accomplished with his Nauvoo Legion. Bennett also wrote that all Nauvoo Legion members had taken the Danite oath to defend Smith "whether he was right or wrong." Bennett also wrote to the editors of several papers that Smith had set up "an elaborate system of prostitution for the special benefit of the church hierarchy.[281]

Even though Bennett's letters to the editors and his book, *The History of the Saints,* were considered as overly sensationalized and as a result many were eventually rejected by newspaper editors, Bennett had succeeded in opening "Pandora's box and the most frantic efforts could not recapture all the furies that he loosed."[282] Joseph Smith was able to survive the embarrassment by what Brodie called "The Bennett Explosion" within his own theocracy, Nauvoo. But non-Mormons generally accepted that Smith not only had been sexually promiscuous but was also attempting to build his own theocracy independent of the state and national governments. Because of the Bennett letters, the non-Mormon community's antagonism against Nauvoo increased, setting the stage for violent reactions to Smith's kingdom of God. Once again Smith's inability to gauge non-Mormon's reactions to his leadership of his Saints was in danger of exploding into violence.

In the meantime, Smith was facing more trouble and more problems since he had been a fugitive from justice in Missouri. As discussed earlier in this chapter, Smith had been charged in 1838, with treason and other associated crimes when he led a group of armed men from Far West to supervise elections in a neighboring county in Missouri. This group of armed men was not connected with any government authority in Missouri, but rather was Smith's own private army. For this and his intimidation of a Justice of Peace, Smith and other leaders of the Mormon Church were charged with treason. After remaining in jail for four months, Smith and other church leaders were able to arrange for their escape in the spring of 1839.

Smith had never forgiven Missouri Governor Boggs for what he considered to be a great injustice toward him. A rumor was that Smith, the Nauvoo Mayor, General and Prophet of the church, had predicted that Boggs would meet a violent death, and this is just what almost happened in May, 1842 when Boggs was shot. Although shot three times, Boggs managed to survive the shooting. Since Smith's bodyguard, Porter Rockwell, was absent from Nauvoo at the time of the shooting, Boggs assumed that Porter Rockwell was responsible, and Boggs "swore out an affidavit charging Joseph with being 'an accessory before the fact of the intended murder.'"[283]

Joseph Smith on the Run Again

On August 8, 1842, Joseph Smith was on the run again, trying to avoid Missouri Governor Carlin's issue of a writ and warrant for Joseph's and Porter Rockwell's arrest. For a period of about four months, Joseph hid in many places, including islands on the Mississippi River, in a secret hiding place in his own house and on various farms away from Nauvoo. His church had been in existence for fewer than twelve years, but in this short time, Joseph had been forced to flee from Palmyra, New York; Kirtland, Ohio; Far West, Missouri; and now from Nauvoo, Illinois. In fewer than sixteen years, he had been charged by a court of Law of being a disorderly person and an impostor (1826), was arrested seven times in connection with suits against him for failure to redeem worthless bank notes (1837), was arrested and charged with treason in 1838, and now in his "kingdom of God" in Nauvoo, Illinois, he was charged with accessory before the foot for attempted murder (1842).[284]

Joseph Smith escaped the noose that surrounded him, put there by frequent visits of sheriffs from Missouri to Nauvoo. After Ford took over as Governor of Illinois late in 1842, he supported the invalidity of Smith's Missouri warrant for his arrest. This was later confirmed by an Illinois judge in January of 1843, after which Smith returned to Nauvoo, Illinois as a free man again.[285] Even so, the rumor that he was involved in planning the shooting of Boggs still persisted, and his second counselor in Nauvoo, William Law, in his declining years, swore out an affidavit that "Joseph told me that he sent a man to kill Governor Boggs of Missouri. The fellow shot the governor in his own house."[286]

Nauvoo Expositor is Born

Although Smith had avoided the noose put around him by the state of Missouri, he was not to escape from the most serious blunder of his short career as a church leader, the destruction of the *Nauvoo Expositor* printing press. This destruction came after its first issue (Vol. 1 No.1) was printed on June 7, 1844. William Law and six other Mormons started the *Nauvoo Expositor* after they became disenchanted with Joseph Smith for his economic policies and even more so for his infidelities. Robert Foster, one of the initial five Mormon writers of the *Nauvoo Expositor*, also became violently opposed to the Prophet when he found him dining with his wife after returning from a business trip. Mrs. Foster confessed after a violent confrontation with her husband that Joseph had preached "...the spiritual-wife doctrine and had endeavored to seduce her." This infuriated Law, and he found later that several other Mormons were furious as well with Smith and other Mormon leaders for practicing promiscuous sex with unmarried as well as married women in the name of God who they said had sanctioned polygamy. One of these men, disaffected, Chauncey Higbee, claimed that "...leading elders had as many as ten or twelve wives apiece and described how they recorded the names of all the women they wished to marry in a large book called the Book of Law of the Lord, kept at the home of Hyrum Smith. After the names were inscribed, the book was sealed, and the seals were broken in the presence of the unsuspecting women, who were thereby convinced that the doctrine was true and that they must submit."[287]

Soon William Law found several Mormons within the city of Nauvoo who wished not to destroy the Mormon Church, but to reform it and especially to get rid of the debauchery of "God-sanctioned polygamy." This led to the birth of the *Nauvoo Expositor* which was to lead to the death of Joseph Smith and the eventual Mormon exodus from Nauvoo to Salt Lake City, Utah. Law's newspaper was written with care in order to avoid any sensationalism and to protect any of the polygamist wives from undue exposure or embarrassment. He wished to use the newspaper as a means to turn the church away from the adulterous and sexual misbehavior which he felt was destroying the church. In Vol. 1 No. 1 of his newspaper, dated June 7, 1844, he proposed that Joseph Smith's pretensions to righteousness should be scanned by church members. "...How shall he, who has drank [sic] of the poisonous draft teach virtue? ...We are earnestly seeking to explode the vicious principles of Joseph Smith and those who practice the same abominations and whoredoms.." Law and his six other writers wrote that "many females in foreign climes have been induced to forsake friends to embark on a long journey overseas only to be requested upon their arrival to meet with Brother Joseph or some of the Twelve at some insulated point, or at some particularly described place on the bank of the Mississippi, or at some room which wears upon its front: *Positively no Admittance.* The harmless, inoffensive and unsuspecting creatures are so devoted to the Prophet and the cause of Jesus Christ that they do not dream of the deep laid and fatal scheme which prostrates happiness and renders death itself desirable, but they meet him... and they are told... never to divulge what is revealed to them with a penalty of death ...that God Almighty has revealed it to him that she should be his (Joseph's) spiritual wife...but we must keep those pleasures and blessings from the world, for until there is a change in the government, we will endanger ourselves by practicing it — but we can enjoy the blessings of Jacob, David and others as well as to be deprived of them, if we do not expose ourselves to the law of the land. She is thunder-struck, faints, recovers and refuses. The Prophet damns her if she rejects. She thinks of the great sacrifice and of the many thousand miles she has traveled over sea and land that she might save her soul from pending ruin and replies God's will be done, and not mine. The Prophet and his devotees in this way are gratified. The next step is to avoid public exposition from the common course of things; they are sent away for a time, until all is well; after which they return from a long visit."[288]

The *Nauvoo Expositor* also contained several resolutions which Law's group had made including:

(1) Declared the secret acts of excommunicating William and Wilson Law, Mrs. William Law and R. D. Foster "as being unjust and unauthorized by the laws of the church and consequently null and void.

(2) "That we disapprobiate [sic] and discountenance every attempt to unite church and state;

(3) "That we consider the religious influence exercised in financial concerns by Joseph Smith, as unjust as it is unwarranted...

(4) "... we look upon sending of special agents abroad to collect funds for the temple and other purposes as a humbug practiced upon the Saints by Joseph and others, to aggrandize themselves, as we do not believe that money and property so collected, have been applied as the donors expected, but have been used for speculative purposes, by Joseph, to gull the Saints the better on their arrival at Nauvoo, by buying the lands in the vicinity and selling again to them at tenfold advance,

(5) "That we consider all secret societies, and combinations, under penal oaths and obligations, (professing to be organized for religious purposes), to be anti-Christian, hypocritical and corrupt."[289]

The first (and only) issue of the *Nauvoo Expositor* also contained the following affidavits:

One by William Law certified "Hyrum Smith did (in his office) read to me a certain written document, which he said was a revelation from God. He said that he was with Joseph when it was received. He afterwards gave me the document to read, and I took it to my house and read it, and showed it to my wife and returned it next day. The revelation (so called) authorized certain men to have more wives than one at a time in this world and in the world to come. He said this was the *law* and commanded Joseph to enter into the *law*. — And also that he should administer to others. Several other items were in the revelation, supporting the above doctrines."

Jane Law certified: "that I read the revelation referred to in the above affidavit of my husband. It sustained in strong terms the doctrine of more wives than one at a time in this world and in the next. It authorized some to have to the number of ten and set forth that these women who would not allow their husbands to have more wives than one should be under condemnation before God."[290]

The *Nauvoo Expositor* also included an announcement that the circuit court "...Grand Jury found two bills against Smith (Joseph), one for perjury and another for fornications and adultery; on the first of which Smith delivered himself up for trial, but the State not being ready, material witnesses being absent, the case was deferred to the October term."[291]

Also reported in the *Nauvoo Expositor* was an article taken from the Quincy Whig in which it was stated: "We think these Mormon missionaries are laboring under a mistake in one particular. It is not so much the particular doctrines, which Smith [Joseph] upholds and practices, however abominable they may be in themselves, that our citizens care about — as it is the anti-republican nature of the organization over which he has almost supreme control— and which is trained and disciplined to act in accordance with his selfish will. The spectacle presented in Smith's case of a civil, ecclesiastical and military leader, united in one and the same person, with power over life and liberty, can never find favor in the minds of sound and thinking republicans. The day has gone by when the precepts of Divine Truth, could be propagated at the point of the sword — or the Bible made the medium of corrupt men to gratify their lustful appetites and sordid desires."[292]

Smith, upon reading the June 7, 1844 issue written by Mormon dissidents, realized that he had a major crisis on his hands. Here in the center of his "kingdom of God" were traitors of his theocracy who had respect, financial means and journalistic skills that could seriously threaten and weaken the power of the "king over Israel on earth." (Joseph Smith was secretly anointed king over Israel on earth by the Mormon theocratic Council of Fifty in 1844.)[293] William Law ran a housing construction business that had been very prosperous in Nauvoo in which he employed a large number of men. Law also was respected, intelligent and was not interested in tearing down the Mormon Church but wished to reform it in such ways as getting rid of polygamy, cooperating more with the surrounding non-Mormon community and maintaining a separation of church and state. Separation of church and state was in direct contrast to Joseph Smith who saw the church and state governments as one and the same. Had Smith permitted Law's printing press to remain in Nauvoo, it is probable that his autocratic rule of his theocracy would have ended, and the violent and tragic events which followed would never have occurred.

Smith's presidential campaign was in full swing, with his

Twelve Apostles and nearly five hundred other leaders of the church away trying to convince the voters that their candidate was indeed the best one for their country. As Beardsley writes: "...It was a disastrous move. They left Nauvoo when affairs were in a critical state. It is possible that had some of them remained, their counsel might have deterred the Prophet from his headstrong course and averted the tragedies that ensued."[294]

Smith convened the Nauvoo City Council at which a resolution was passed ..."denouncing the paper as a public nuisance." It was "Resolved by the City Council of Nauvoo that the printing-office from whence issues the *Nauvoo Expositor* is a public nuisance and also all of said N*auvoo Expositors* which may be or exist in said establishment, and the Mayor is instructed to cause said printing establishment and papers to be removed without delay, in such a manner as he shall direct, passed June 10th, 1844."[295]

Nauvoo Expository Printing Press Destroyed by Joseph Smith

Once again Smith was not able to gauge the true measure of non-Mormon feelings and opinions about his "kingdom of God," and he made a final blunder. Joseph Smith immediately ordered that the printing press be destroyed after which he assisted the city marshal and his deputies in their fulfillment of his orders. The press was hammered into pieces, piled in the street, soaked with kerosene and burned. These actions set the stage for the end of Smith and the end of his leadership of "God's kingdom" of Nauvoo. While he knew that he could fool his followers all of the time, he also knew that the non-Mormons surrounding his city needed a lot more convincing. Many of the surrounding non-Mormons were already antagonistic toward his kingdom, and the destruction of the press was like pouring gasoline on the fire.

Soon the word spread that Law's opposition newspaper was destroyed by Joseph Smith. This unleashed the fury of the surrounding non-Mormon community that had already been fuming with the rumors of Smith's adultery, his autocratic rule of his city of Nauvoo and his shady land dealings. While destroying the *Nauvoo Expositor's* printing press provided the fuse for the bomb which was later to explode on the Mississippi River plain, Brodie writes that there were other underlying issues: "...the political exploitation of Mormon numbers, made doubly repugnant by the presence of immigrant converts from monarchist England, was perhaps the most volatile fuel feeding the anti-Mormon fires. Those who lived closest to the Mormon mass were desperately afraid of being crushed. They hated Joseph Smith because thousands followed him blindly and slavishly. ...To them the Nauvoo theocracy was a malignant tyranny that was spreading as swiftly and dangerously as a Mississippi flood and that might eventually engulf the very government of the United States."[296]

The Fosters, Laws and Higbees charged Joseph Smith with interfering with their rights of freedom of speech and destroying private property. And Smith fearing retaliation from surrounding non-Mormons, declared martial law in the city of Nauvoo. He assembled his Nauvoo Legion, and before a large crowd in his Lieutenant-General's uniform denounced the owners of the printing press as apostates and mobbers. Arms and equipment were issued to his Legion, and he told them that they must fight in defense of their lives, their families and homes.

"It is thought by some," Smith said "that our enemies would be satisfied by my destruction, but I tell you, as soon as they have shed my blood, they will thirst for the blood of every man in whose heart dwells a single spark of the spirit, of the fullness of gospel. The opposition of these men is moved by the spirit of the adversary of all righteousness. It is not only to destroy me, but every man and woman who dares believe the doctrines that God hath inspired me to teach to this generation."[297]

Smith's speech also included references to the American citizenships held by Mormon followers and the rights and liberties which they held. "Those rights, so dearly purchased, shall not be disgracefully trodden under foot by lawless marauders without at least a noble effort on our part to sustain our liberties," said Smith.[298] Apparently Smith felt that destroying an opposition printing press **was not a violation** of the rights and liberties held by other Americans.

Fifteen thousand followers answered yes when Joseph Smith asked them: "Will you stand by me to the death and sustain at the peril of our lives, the laws of our country and the liberties and privileges which our fathers have transmitted unto us sealed with their sacred blood?" These laws of our country, liberties and privileges were often interpreted and defined by Smith quite differently from those of the non-Mormons. Smith's "liberties and privileges" were those he chose for his people using his self-proclaimed "God's Prophet and official communicator" powers. As the number one servant of God, the Prophet's words and actions were those of God. Only God could allow a printing press to be set up and operated in Smith's kingdom of God, and God gave his orders only through his prophet, Joseph Smith. Since the printing press was operating in Nauvoo without God's orders, in the eyes of Smith and his followers it should be destroyed.

Joseph Smith's actions in mustering his militia, and fortifying the city of Nauvoo was in the eyes of state government, an outright defiance of state authority. This, as well as the destruction of the printing press, was a clear violation of the law and forced Governor Ford to intervene, especially since the surrounding non-Mormons were buying arms and ammunition to deal with what the non-Mormons felt was treason. It was the responsibility of the governor to avoid a bloody confrontation between the two sides.

Joseph Smith Flees from Nauvoo

After stirring up his people against the non-Mormons, Joseph and his brother, Hyram Smith, left for the Iowa side of the Mississippi River at night and prepared to flee to the West into that vast unknown where lay the Rocky Mountains, the Oregon Country and the site of the "City of Joseph."

"Three wagons were procured and loaded with supplies from the Mormon store at Montrose. (Porter) Rockwell was to return on the 'Maid of Iowa' with horses and mules, a few cattle, arms and ammunition.

"Joe for the first time in months was care-free. He was leaving his troubles behind, starting out on a new adventure. He would have no political ecclesiastic problems to burden him, he reflected; no marital discord, no spies, no enemies, no intrigue. He would live in the open, sleep beneath the stars, live on the country. Hyrum and Rockwell were ideal companions for such a trip, and Rockwell had promised to bring along two or three hardy Danites to act as teamsters and do the heavy work of the camp.

"...That night Rockwell and a few others crossed the river on the 'Maid of Iowa' with the equipment for the Western expedition. They found Joe and Hyrum still at work in a shed supervising the loading of the wagons. The shed and barn were filled with provisions; a few hours and all arrangements would be complete."[299]

Rockwell carried a message for Joseph Smith that the people of Nauvoo felt that Joseph Smith was a coward. "They were hurt and angry that their Prophet, Seer and Revelator should run away and leave them to work out their own salvation. Rockwell handed him a letter from some of the leaders, expressing these sentiments, also one from Emma, reproaching him for running away."[300] Little did Emma realize that encouraging Smith to return would result in his death.

In the meantime, Governor Ford had organized a state militia to preserve the peace and urged representatives of Joseph Smith to send all the Mormons who were issued arrest warrants to Carthage for trial. The governor argued that tensions would be reduced by showing non-Mormons that Mormons were law abiding citizens.

Smith would have liked to have invented another revelation that he could send back to his flock in Nauvoo, telling them that God had demanded that he leave Nauvoo to set up another kingdom of God in the West, bringing his people there after he had made preparations for them. But this was a revelation that would be hard for his church members to understand. Shouldn't the Prophet be with the people in their time of crisis? Hyrum Smith, who was planning to flee west convinced his brother that they must return and face trial under the protection of Governor Ford. So after talking things over, Joseph and Hyrum decided to return to Nauvoo to face the charges.

"The next day, Joe, Hyrum and members of the Nauvoo City Council were brought before R. F. Smith, Justice of the Peace, on charges arising from the destruction of the *Expositor*. Smith (R. F.) was one of the leaders in the anti-Mormon movement in Hancock County and Captain of the Carthage Grays [state militia]. All of the defendants were bound over to the next term of the Circuit Court and released on bonds. Immediately after the hearing, however, Constable Bettisworth served Joe and Hyrum with new warrants charging them with treason and open rebellion against the State of Illinois, in that they had illegally called out the Nauvoo Legion to make war against the citizens of the county and had placed Nauvoo under martial law."[301]

Smith and his brother Hyrum were arrested and taken to the jail in Carthage, Illinois. Joseph Smith's presidential campaign was in shambles. He had recalled his Twelve Apostles and nearly five hundred of his church leaders to handle the crisis that was now facing him and his kingdom of God in Nauvoo. His Twelve Apostles were now responsible for the governing of his city since he had traveled to Carthage to face trial.

Joseph Smith hired two Iowa lawyers, Wood of Burlington and Reed of Fort Madison, since he felt that Illinois lawyers would be biased against him. Smith and his party were taken to the county jail since the charge for treason "did not permit bail." Governor Ford met with Smith the next morning. "Here in the bare quarters of the debtors' room of Carthage jail, the "Prophet of God" and the Governor of Illinois faced each other for the last time. They had met before in the State House at Springfield in the Executive mansion, across the dinner-table. Life had played capricious tricks on each of them and had further caprices in store. The former boy water-witch had achieved pomp and power. The country judge, who at forty-two looked forward to passing the remainder of his life on the bench, had been unexpectedly elevated to the post of chief executive of the State. The passions of one had brought him a culprit to the bar of justice; the passions of the other were to drag him down to degradation and poverty. The culprit was to achieve infamy and immortality; the memory of the chief executive was to be saved from extinction largely because he included in his history of his administration an account of the troubles of the culprit."[302]

In a letter to Emma, Joseph Smith wrote that Governor Ford was coming to Nauvoo and that he, (Smith), was going to accompany the Governor, and that he, along with the other prisoners, would receive bail. However, the Governor did not take the prisoners with him to Nauvoo, but left them under the guard of the Carthage Grays, who were bitterly opposed to Joseph Smith and his followers. Ford defended his action to leave Smith and the other prisoners guarded by the Carthage Grays saying: "...since that unit was composed of neighbors of the Mormons, he supposed they would realize that they would be the first to suffer reprisals in case harm should come to the prisoners, and would, therefore, refrain from violence. But the fact that the Nauvoo Legion had been deprived of its arms was well-known, as was the fact that the citizens of the vicinity of Carthage were well-armed and capable of defending themselves. In view of these conditions, the probability of any serious retaliation by the Mormons seemed slight. Also the Governor had ample opportunity to observe the hatred of the Grays toward the Mormons and the lack of discipline in their ranks."[303]

This feeling by non-Mormons of being engulfed by Smith's autocratic control of his Saints and the loss of political and economic control brought on a wave of violent protest against Smith and the Mormons. So much so, that Illinois Governor Ford was forced to take decisive action to bring a very explosive situation under control. After completing an investigation in Carthage, Ford decided that Smith and other leaders of the Mormons must be brought to trial for destroying the *Expositor* and for other possible criminal acts. Ford must have thought that his support of Smith in January, 1843 (a short year and one-half earlier) which prevented him from being arrested as accessory to the shooting of former Missouri Governor Lilburn Boggs was a stupid mistake. By this time, the tide had turned against Smith in the state legislature and with state leaders. Whereas before, the political leaders of Illinois had scrambled to receive Joseph Smith's controlled Mormon votes, they now did not want them since they were tainted with rumors of promiscuous sex, profiteering on land deals and a stifling of democracy by church leaders. And of course much of this was done with "revelations," or other approvals given directly to Joseph Smith by God. When Smith first came to Nauvoo, Illinois in 1839, politicians bent over backwards in awarding him a city charter with "liberal" autonomy and even allowed him to develop his militia, the Nauvoo Legion which grew into the second largest army in the United States. Smith had shifted his Mormon bloc vote between the Whig and Democratic Party in whichever way would increase his power and influence within his "kingdom of God." With the crushing of the *Expositor* press Smith had effectively destroyed any political control that he still maintained in Illinois. Furthermore, he unleashed the hatred that non-Mormons had for his economic philosophy and the community cohesiveness which did not square with their general beliefs in American pluralism. It also unleashed the fear that non-Mormons would be crushed economically, politically, culturally and socially by the Nauvoo theocracy.

Ford demanded that Joseph Smith and other leaders of the Mormon Church submit immediately to the Carthage constable and come to that city for trial. Smith wanted the protection of his Nauvoo Legion in traveling from Nauvoo to Carthage, but was refused since Ford feared that a civil war might result between the Nauvoo Legion and the state militia which was already camped in the area. Smith at first decided to run and hide, even considering to leave Nauvoo completely and go west, but after he was accused of abandoning his people, he decided to come out of hiding and face his accusers. Joseph Smith, along with other leaders of the Mormon Church, was taken to Carthage jail to await trial. While there, Smith received a six shooter and some ammunition that were smuggled to him. His brother Hyrum, who was in jail with him, also received a single shot pistol.

Joseph Smith, fearing the Carthage Grays, sent a note back with one of the officers instructing him to have the Nauvoo Legion mobilized with private arms to proceed to Carthage and camp at the edge of the city "ready to enter at. any moment, should the occasion require." The note was never delivered by the Nauvoo Legion officer and ...months later, when his dereliction was discovered, Brigham Young sent him on a 'mission' to the West, and shortly thereafter, the report came back that he had 'died of dysentery.' Apparently he was executed by the Danites for his negligence.[304]

Joseph Smith Killed by a Mob in a Gun Fight

A Warsaw crowd and a group from the Grays made plans to attack the jail where Smith and the Mormon prisoners were held. "They broke into a run, flourishing sticks and guns in the air and whooping and shouting. The guard of the Carthage Grays fired a few shots in the direction of the mob, but they fired into the air. Then they retreated en masse, leaving the jail unprotected. Joe stepped back and pulled out his six-shooter. Richards and Taylor had armed themselves with clubs. There was a rush of feet up the stairs, a few scattering shots, then a concerted volley of fire and the patter of bullets against the door. At the same time, fire was directed against the occupants from without through the open windows.

"Hyrum and Richards leaped back from the door, but a bullet, boring a neat hole through the panel, struck Hyrum in the nose. As he fell, another bullet coming through the window hit him in the back, passing through his body and smashing the watch in his vest-pocket. He sank to the floor with a moan. Joe dropped to his knees beside his brother and lifted his head. Hyrum was dead.

"The Prophet leaped to his feet and to the doorway, [.] It was partially open. Taylor and Richards standing [stood] on either side and knocking [knocked] down with their clubs the muzzles of the weapons as they were thrust in through the opening. Joe pushed his revolver through the crack and fired blindly into the crowd. Six times he snapped the trigger, but three of the cartridges missed fire [misfired]. The remaining three took toll, [hitting three attackers] and momentarily the firing from the hallway ceased, as the wounded men were dragged to the rear."[305] Joseph Smith was killed by bullets from the crowd as he leaped from the window of the jail to the ground. Both Smith and his brother Hyrum were killed in the barrage, only a little more than two weeks after he had ordered the *Expositor* printing press destroyed.[306]

Born on December 23, 1805, Joseph Smith lived to be only thirty-eight years old, but had managed to experience and survive many violent crises. The crises into which he had led his obedient and devout followers too often were of such serious nature that it forced them to flee in order to survive. They had been forced to flee Kirtland, Ohio, after Joseph had angered non-Mormons with his failed bank. They had no choice but to flee Far West, Missouri, when Smith failed to integrate his Saints into local communities and instead of cooperating with non-Mormons, organized a separate community with his own army. This caused local citizens to fear that his followers would take their lives as well as their land. Once again in Nauvoo, Smith organized an autonomous theocracy that non-Mormons feared. They felt that the complete autocratic control that Smith had over his Saints, including the practice of polygamy and the devotion and blind obedience of his followers might be forced upon them as well. Most of all they feared that they were in danger of losing their own freedoms of individual ownership of land, property, individualism and independent thinking. These fears caused the great outburst of negative feelings and in some cases violence against their Mormon neighbors. These negative feelings and violence against the Mormons by the non-Mormons caused the leaders of the Mormon Church to conclude that their church, as they envisioned it, could never succeed unless it continued in a place without interference and influence from non-Mormon neighbors. They needed complete autonomy to build their "kingdom of God." The Salt Lake Basin provided the leaders great distance between them and their unfriendly neighbors. It also gave the Saints the autonomy necessary for Brigham Young to establish a Deseret State theocracy that lasted for almost fifty years.

Brigham Young Takes Over

With the charges against Joseph and Hyrum Smith of treason

and open rebellion against the State of Illinois, the counterfeiting of money, the antagonism of surrounding non-Mormons and deteriorating control of the population within the city of Nauvoo, it became apparent to Brigham Young and his Twelve Apostles that continuing the Mormon kingdom of God in Nauvoo was impossible. Therefore, they made plans to move west to find a place that was out of reach of their "enemies" where they could practice their theocracy without interference. This mass exodus began in February 1846, which finally ended in Salt Lake, Utah. The exodus took them across Iowa to their winter quarters at Council Bluffs, with Iowa City, Iowa, serving as a staging area for the movement of the Saints. One can only imagine the great hardships that were endured from lack of food, exhaustion and exposure during the three-month trek from Council Bluffs to Salt Lake.

The kingdom of God was now in the hands of Brigham Young although several groups broke away and formed their own churches. The most important of these churches was the Reorganized LDS Church which was developed under the influence of Emma, the widowed wife of Joseph Smith. This church later named Joseph Smith III to be its Prophet and became centered in Independence, Missouri. However, Brigham Young was able to keep the majority of the members with him in the move from Nauvoo to Salt Lake, Utah.

Brigham Young became the Prophet in 1847, almost three years after the death of Joseph Smith, even though Sidney Rigdon should have been the leader as he was only one of two counselors remaining since Hyrum had been killed. Rigdon was later excommunicated from the church.

Without Brigham Young's desperate zeal to save Smith's "kingdom of God" by moving the Mormon flock to the Salt Lake Basin, it is doubtful that the Mormon religion would have survived. In the Missouri and Nauvoo exoduses of Smith's Mormon followers, we have seen that the Mormon religious leaders were incompatible with their non-Mormon neighbors. It seems that without total separation from the more numerous non-Mormons, the religion could not succeed. Beadle, the editor of *Brigham's Destroying Angel: Being the Life, Confession and Startling Disclosures of the Notorious Bill Hickman,* wrote: "Nor is their social system other than organized selfishness. The Saint must marry many wives. Why? Because he will thus 'build up his kingdom for eternity.' But the numbers of the sexes being equal, even in Utah, he must build it at somebody else's expense: if he marries ten wives, nine other men must do without one apiece. ...Will those who hold such low and imperfect notions of their neighbor's rights have regard for that neighbor's life, or liberty, or property, if he 'stands in the way of the kingdom of God'?" "...If the Mormons are truly that peaceful, quiet, and industrious people we sometimes hear of, fitted for good citizens, why have they come into violent conflict with the people in all their seven places of settlement? For they have tried every different kind of people from New York through Ohio, Illinois, and Missouri, to Salt Lake. ...the facts are patent, and sound reason points to but one conclusion: the organization of the Mormon Church is such that it cannot exist under a republican government or in a civilized country without constant collision." [307]

Brigham Young and Authority

Brigham Young served as the leader of the Mormon Church from 1847 to 1877. As did Joseph Smith, Young claimed that his authority was given to him by God. Like Smith, Young used his "God-given authority" to control his flock relentlessly. He often threatened those who resisted his plans or orders with excommunication or other serious consequences.

While his predecessor, Joseph Smith, was the master of imagination, Young, the former carpenter, was a master of organization and getting things done. The master organizer was also a devout believer in Joseph Smith and the Mormon religion. (Whether Young really believed in Joseph Smith and the Mormon Church or pretended this belief in order to achieve power will never be known.) He supervised the dismantling of Nauvoo, Illinois' largest city of 10,000 people in 1845 and designed and administered the mass exodus of thousands of these people crossing the Mississippi River, the Missouri River, the plains of Nebraska and the plateau of Wyoming into the "promised land" of the Salt Lake Basin. In doing this, Young appointed leaders to organize the building of wagons, leaders to obtain provisions and supplies and leaders to supervise the building of temporary shelters on the shores of the Missouri River, both on the Iowa and Nebraska sides. This exodus from Nauvoo to Salt Lake City was fraught with many dangers for his followers, who often suffered from malnutrition, freezing temperatures and disease. They followed Young to where they could build their kingdom of God without interference from the "gentile" Americans, who had so vigorously pushed them out of Ohio, Missouri and now Illinois. Young organized this exodus strictly along military lines, using the priesthood leadership of the church to maintain military discipline while gathering "the children of Israel" to Zion. The core of Young's leaders in the Mormon Church were the Twelve Apostles, assisted by the Council of Fifty who later became the government officials in the State of Deseret.

The aim of the Mormon leaders was to establish an independent state in the Salt Lake Basin for their kingdom of God with neither affiliation with the United States or Mexico. (Mexico ceded the Pacific Southwest which included the states of Utah, Nevada, California, Arizona, Colorado and New Mexico to the United States shortly after the first group of Mormons reached the Salt Lake Basin in 1847.) The Deseret State, established in 1849 included not only Utah, but most of Nevada and Arizona and parts of Idaho, Wyoming, Colorado, New Mexico, California and Oregon. As Young had learned from Joseph Smith when he organized the government in the theocracy of Nauvoo, democracy was not a part of God's plan for his kingdom in the State of Deseret. Brigham Young was approved as Governor of Deseret without opposition, and other officers of the state were unanimously elected.[308]

All of the candidates who won election in the territory of Utah were selected by Church Authorities. Of the 96,107 votes cast from 1852 to 1870, 96 percent went to the Mormon Church ticket . And from 1847 to 1875, not one candidate chosen in advance by Mormon leaders failed to win elections."[309] As stated earlier, Brigham Young was in total control of the territorial government during his reign as President and Prophet of the Mormon Church.

To illustrate further that Brigham Young was not only in control of the territorial government, but was also in complete control of the people, consider the following:

1. From the beginning of Young's "kingdom of God" in his State of Deseret, he insured that his followers would elect government officials who had his approval. "Fundamental to the operation of Young's theocratic government that existed in Utah was the election law, which remained in force in the territory for more than a quarter of a century."[310] This election law contained the following: "Each elector shall provide himself with a vote containing the names of the persons he wishes elected and the offices he would have them

fill, and present it neatly folded to the judge of election, who shall number and deposit it in the ballot box; the clerk shall then write the name of the elector, and opposite it the number of his vote."[311] One can see that with the elector writing the names on the ballot with the positions to be filled beside the voter's name and the ballot numbered by the clerk next to the voter's name, it was easy for the "judge of the election" to know how everyone voted. This insured that the slate of officers pre-announced by Young won the election.

During Young's reign, the election law was essential to the continuance of his theocracy. Although there was great opposition to one-sided elections by non-Mormons, a theocracy was guaranteed due to the loyalty and obedience of Deseret's overwhelming Mormon population and the isolation from the United States.

2. Young's theocracy forced male settlers between the ages of 18 and 45 to train in the Nauvoo Legion or the Militia of Utah Territory which eventually totaled some 7,500 men and was more that half the size of the United States Army at the time.[312]

3. "June 2, 1857, Brigham Young says, 'I feel to sustain him,' when informed that Local Bishop Warren S. Snow has castrated twenty-four-year-old Welchman for undisclosed sex crimes. 'Just let the matter drop and say no more about it.' Young writes to Snow."[313]

4. Land to new settlers was assigned as long as they remained faithful to the church and were good stewards. In other words, the church owned all the land and when anyone who left the church was excommunicated, or left Utah, the land was automatically returned to the church. This was in contrast to the liberal laws of the federal government such as the Homestead Act, which allowed settlers to have up to 160 acres of land free, if they would live on and work the land.[314]

5. When the United States planned to send in a territorial governor, Brigham Young said: "Though I may not be Governor here, my power will not be diminished. No man they can send here will have much influence with this community, unless he be the man of their choice. Let them send whom they will, and it does not diminish my influence one particle."[315]

Brigham Young Introduces Concept of Blood Atonement

6. In 1856 Brigham Young introduced the concept of blood atonement in which he said "...the blood of Heifers lambs Doves &c

would again be offered for certain sins but for some sins no blood would be acceptable except the life & blood of the individual." This as apostle Woodruff wrote "...made the H[e]arts of many tremble."[316] Young said "Will you love your brothers or sisters likewise, when they have committed a sin that cannot be atoned for without the she[d]ding of their blood? Will you love that man or woman well enough to shed their blood? That is what Jesus Christ meant."[317] The fear of blood atonement was Young's way of insuring complete obedience from the people to those placed in authority over them.[318]

Can you imagine the feelings of the Mormon people whose lives depended on complete obedience to the "Lion of the Lord?" And can one imagine the terrible feeling of the converts from European countries who traveled for a month or longer on the high seas, transferring to a train to Iowa City, Iowa and then walking and pulling a hand cart for nearly three months before arriving in Salt Lake City? They must have been fearful when they found the terrible conditions with which they were confronted. They no doubt heard Young's sermons on "blood atonement" and his threats of being cast away from sources of food and shelter unless they were faithful to the Mormon doctrine as taught by Young and other church leaders. Where were they to go? Further into the wilderness? Return to Europe? By what financial means? There is no doubt that they felt the full weight of the authority of the Mormon Church upon their lives. Conforming to and accepting the doctrine of the church were the only real choices they had. Rebel against the church? Walk back the 1,400 miles to Iowa City? Move on to the Pacific coast? These were the only alternatives if one were to leave the Mormon environment.

It should be said, however, that Europeans were accustomed to living under authoritarian rule, and they were able to adjust to being obedient and subservient to Brigham Young's church, so blood atonement was easier for them to accept. For Young, these compliant people were just the kind he was looking for in his kingdom of God. Without Young's European converts, the many skills that they brought to his kingdom, and with the isolation of the State of Deseret, it is doubtful that the Mormon Church would have survived without them, let alone to have developed to the degree it has today.

The actual number of how many were killed or bloodatoned, is not known, but records show that many who tried to leave Mormonism, were brutally murdered. Brigham Young's preaching of blood atonement encouraged other leaders to push vigorously for avenging Joseph Smith's death and, if necessary, to let the blood of anti-Mormons spill upon the ground. Orrin Porter Rockwell, according to Quinn, could kill with "impunity and immunity." Porter was believed to be the one who attempted to kill Missouri former Governor Boggs to avenge his imprisonment of Joseph Smith. Porter also killed Martin Oaks in 1860, "an unarmed loudmouth who dared to insult a Mormon enforcer." Porter also killed "an anti-Mormon militiaman in Illinois in 1845."[319]

According to Quinn, crimes that resulted in murder included: "adultery, apostasy, 'convenant breaking,' counterfeiting, 'many men who left this church,' murder, not being 'heartily on the Lord's side,' profaning 'the name of the Lord,' sexual intercourse between a 'white' person and an African-American, stealing and telling lies. Brigham Young's Danites had the blessings of the church to murder in the name of the church, and in fact, they were expected to 'kill various persons who violated religious obligations.'"[320] Is it any wonder that Young had complete control of his followers since they were in constant fear for their lives if they violated any of his laws? Blood atonement sermons were the weapons that Young used to continue the building of the "kingdom of God" after Smith's death. With his Danites to enforce subjugation of followers, what chance of staying alive would an individual have if he wished to leave the autocratic control of the church leaders with the isolation of Salt Lake City from the United States and the fear of blood atonement?

In the 1850s the constant sermons by many of the church leaders about blood atonement contained cruel warnings to all. For example, "time is at hand when those who commit sins worthy of death will have to be slain by the Priesthood (leadership) that is directly over them." "If you should find your father or your mother, your sister or your brother dead by the wayside, say nothing about it, but pass on about your business." "If you see a dead man laying on your wood pile, you must not tell but go about your business."[321]

William H. Dame and Philip Klingensmith, Mormon participants in the Mountain Meadows Massacre (September, 1857) were given blessings by church leaders to avenge the blood of the prophets and in the blessing of Klingensmith, to avenge the blood of Brother Joseph.[322] Isaac C. Haight was among the Mormons who took the blood atonement sermons of Brigham Young seriously, as he ordered the Mountain Meadows Massacre in September of 1857.

Other examples of blood atonement and brutality include: "October, 1857 Cedar City's bishop ordered the blood atonement execution of a Mormon who had sexual intercourse with his step-daughter."[323] "...In April, 1858 the bishop of Payson (with several others) shot to death a twenty-two year-old Mormon and his mother for committing incest."[324] "...young Mormon males in the 1850s were also castrated for the accusation of bestiality. ...the 'handsome young Dane' had been courting a girl whom an LDS bishop wanted. To dispose of his rival, the bishop claimed the young man 'had committed bestiality and had him castrated.'"[325] "For Mormon females who were regarded as immoral, decapitation was the publicly advocated form of blood atonement, and there are two examples that this actually occurred."[326]

The organization and social control of the Mormon Utah community was much greater than it was in other western states and territories, where violent acts against individuals were very high. Quinn says that since the Mormon leaders had a high degree of control over the settlers, it was not necessary to impose such a cruel practice as blood atonement. Regardless, "LDS leaders publicly and privately encouraged Mormons to consider it their religious right to kill antagonistic outsiders, common criminals, LDS apostates, and even faithful Mormons who committed sins 'worthy of death.' Mormon theocracy created such a unique context for Utah violence that it will always be impossible to determine how many violent deaths occurred for theocratic reasons and how many merely reflected the American West's pattern of violence."[327]

7. Concerning polygamy, many women hated it, so much that Brigham Young felt it necessary to silence the women "once and for all," announcing in 1856 that "he would give Mormon women two weeks 'to make up their minds whether they would stay with their husbands or be liberated at the General Conference.' After that period, 'if they decided to stay with their husbands, they should keep the law of God & not murmur or complain.' Otherwise, 'I will set all at liberty." Apparently many women wanted to take Young up on his offer, as he modified it and set up 'certain conditions' before he would release women from unwanted marriages. They must first 'appear forthwith at my office & give good & sufficient reasons' for him to grant divorces from their husbands. After that, he said, they must 'marry men that will not have but one wife.'[328]

8. There were several feeble and unsuccessful attempts by

President Buchanan and later President Lincoln, during 1857-1861, to bring Brigham Young's kingdom of God under federal control and to insure that federal laws were enforced in the territory. Several different governors of the territory were appointed after Young's four-year term had expired. President Buchanan's attempt to enforce federal control of the territory by sending an army in 1857 to protect his newly appointed governor was generally a failure. Young was successful in maintaining complete control of the government from the time that he arrived in the Salt Lake Basin in 1847 until his death in 1877. This control remained even after territorial governors were appointed to take his place, as the population of largely Mormon faithful continued their support of the "Lion of the Lord." The Mormon faithful at Young's urging refused to be subservient to federal government appointees and continued to follow the "ghost government of Deseret" of the Mormon Church.[329]

9. Young's legislative assembly for the State of Deseret continued to make laws, even though they were not officially sanctioned by the United States federal government. This "ghost government" continued for eight years until 1870, after which it disappeared.[330] During this eight year-period, the Civil War brewed between the North and the South, for which Young thought was a blessing for his "kingdom of God." He had prayed that the Civil War would so weaken both the North and South that they would not be able to interfere with his "ghost government of the State of Deseret." Young said: "The United States had persecuted the people of God, and they will not get their pay for it."[331]

United States begins to Assume Control of the Mormon Theocracy

Before the Civil War, the United States was not organized sufficiently to deal with Deseret, which was clearly violating the United States laws and Constitution. It was not until the 1870s when the United States had fully recovered from the Civil War that it began to assume control over Young's "kingdom of God." Fortunately, Young and his apostles realized that the "independence" which they had enjoyed for more than a quarter of a century was about to end. The only way that church leaders could continue to have some control over their state of Deseret was to become a state of the United States. Several states surrounding Utah, including Nevada, California and Colorado, had already been admitted as new states. Congress was reluctant to admit Utah as a new state until it met such constitutional requirements as individual rights and made a greater effort to conform to the laws of the land.

As history has shown, the United States came out of the Civil War stronger rather than weaker, and as a result the government turned its attention to its frontiers. In the meantime, during the Civil War between the states another problem faced Brigham Young in the name of General P. Edward Conner who had been assigned to Utah to protect the overland mail route through Utah, but ostensibly his mission was to watch over the "kingdom of God" ambitions of Young. Young had thought the Civil War would allow him to establish an independent State of Deseret, but Conner thought otherwise and developed a "new crusade aimed at the heart of the kingdom of God as a theocratic form of government and was intended to revolutionize Utah's culture from within."[332] It was an "ingenious scheme to water down Utah's population with a flood of 'hardy, industrious, and enterprising outsiders who found silver ore in Bingham Canyon."[333]

Since the gold and silver were not in stream beds, as in California, it was more expensive to mine, and it was not until the completion of the transcontinental railroad in 1869 that mining became profitable. General Conner's goal of diluting the power of Young's theology gained little ground with his opening of the mines to non-Mormons. Every time that an attempt was made to open federal lands to outsiders, the Mormons had a counter scheme to keep the lands in their control. For example, the federal laws exempted lands within municipalities from claim. To take advantage of this federal law and to prevent outsiders from obtaining land, they expanded city boundaries to "encompass available farm land and to control access by outside homesteaders. County recorders were instructed not to transfer land to anyone unless 'a certificate of survey has been approved and countersigned by one of more of the Selectmen of the county.'"[334]

Some progress was made in privatizing property when Utah title offices were established to permit individuals to obtain title to their homes and land. Still "the authority to decide who obtained land titles and those who did not was covertly exercised by an organization known as the School of Prophets." Whenever there was a leak in the "kingdom of God's" dike, it seemed that it would always be plugged in some way to overcome federal laws. The School of Prophets was established by Brigham Young in 1867 "to instruct Israel's elders not only in the theology of religious communism, but in 'all matters which pertain to the temporal and spiritual lives of the Saints.'"[335]

"In practical operation the organization served to implement a variety of policies, decided by the Council of Fifty and handed down to local groups on a number of subjects, ranging from land claims to elections. At the grassroots level it would function as a town hall or legislature in resolving strictly local problems or disputes. Its larger purpose was to change the hearts of its members and make them willing subjects of a millennial economic and social order And its business was to be kept strictly secret."[336] "All members of the priesthood who were clean, honest and obedient were members of the School of Prophets."[337]

10. The School of Prophets was not the only means that Brigham Young had to maintain his kingdom of God or "ghost government." Young had control of his followers through the church members' faith that when he spoke, he was speaking the word of God. Therefore when he wanted his faithful to buy only from Mormon merchants, he had only to say so in the name of God. His crusade to "establish a closed, communal economy" was done when he was asked: "How tight are you going to draw the reins?" His answer was: "We are going to draw the reins so tight, as not to let a Latter-Day Saint trade with an outsider."[338] And if Mormon women did not stop buying from them, he said, "we are going to cut you off from the church."[339]

11. Brigham Young had learned in 1844, that control of the printing press could prevent material unfavorable to the church from being printed for his followers to read, just burn them.[340] Such controls as assignment and control of land and living quarters and deciding where members could buy their goods and services were not enough for Brigham Young. He and his Twelve also controlled what people could read. A example of this control as mentioned earlier, was Young's displeasure with a book written by Lucy Smith, (Joseph Smith's mother). The book, titled *Biographical Sketches of Joseph Smith the Prophet and his Progenitors for many Generations*, was ordered suppressed and destroyed by Young and his First Presidency on October 21, 1865.[341]

However, as cited previously, a copy of Lucy Smith's book was retained by the Mormon Church and was rewritten by "approved" writers who would insure it was "correct." Lucy Smith's book was dictated to her friend, Mrs. Martha Jane Knowlton Coray. The new "approved" version of Lucy's book was later published in 1902 as the *History of Joseph Smith*. Jerald and Sandra Tanner have published the original book with an introduction. The introduction to this book shows the many changes that were made in the original manuscript to make it "acceptable" to Mormon readers.

Why would the Mormon Church that claims that the Constitution of the United States is of divine origin and why would Brigham Young who supported the divine origin of this Constitution, violate a fundamental right granted to Americans: freedom of the press? This fundamental right is the right of Americans under the Constitution to read anything that is written. This is so, even though a publication may be offensive to certain groups of people. Again the Mormon Church was unwilling to give basic American rights to its members. Apparently Brigham Young and his Apostles perceived that something Lucy Smith dictated to her friend, Mrs. Coray, would harm the church and cause members to leave.

The theocracy of the Utah territory continued after the death of Brigham Young in 1877. Young was succeeded by John Taylor who had been president of the Quorum of the Twelve Apostles. Taylor was head of the theocracy at a time when the federal government was increasingly becoming more involved in the political structure of the territory. For example, on the threat that if the Utah territorial legislature did not change the "marked ballot" system of election to a secret ballot election, Congress would do it for them. Heeding this federal warning, the territorial legislature changed the election procedures to include a secret ballot in 1878. However, the new election law contained residency provisions and continued Mormon Church control over elections through their appointment of election officials.[342]

Edmunds-Tucker Act passed by U. S. Congress

The third President and Prophet of the Mormon Church, John Taylor, died in 1887 at the age of 78 and was followed by Wilford Woodruff who was 80 years of age and had been President of the Quorum of the Twelve Apostles. To limit the powers of the theocracy of the Utah territory further, Congress passed in 1887 the Edmunds-Tucker Act. Some of its provisions were:

* It disincorporated the Mormon Church "in so far as it may now have or pretend to have, any legal existence" and ordered the U.S. Attorney General to "wind up" its affairs.

* It prohibited secret marriages and required all weddings to be certified in probate courts by a license "subject to inspection as other public records."

* It gave to the U. S. marshal and deputies the power possessed by sheriffs, constables and other local peace officers to enforce all federal and territorial laws.

* It abolished the right of females in Utah to vote.

* It dissolved territorial laws providing for the election of probate or county judges and authorized the U. S. President to appoint such local magistrates.[343]

As was usual the Mormon Church authorities again weakened federal mandates which limited federal authority and influence by making the mandates ineffective. For example, in anticipation of an attempted takeover of church property, church holdings were given as "secret trusts to chosen members to keep them out of federal reach."[344] While it was evident that the theocracy of the Utah territory was being diluted with non-Mormon elected officials because of the Edmunds-Tucker Act and other federal mandates to the Utah territory, it was also clear that with these temporary setbacks, the Mormon General Authorities would continue to hold the political control of the territory. The Mormon Authorities also realized that they would have greater political control over Utah after it became a state. But in order for Congress to approve Utah as a state, further action must be taken.

President Wilford Woodruff knew that the most distasteful Mormon practice to non-Mormons throughout the United States was polygamy. However, he also knew that polygamy had been practiced by most of the leaders of the Mormon Church and that abandoning plural marriage must be done with a carefully worded statement. In order to insure that abandoning polygamy would result in Utah's being admitted as a state to the Union, Woodruff and his Counselor, George Q. Cannon, went to San Francisco in 1890 to meet "with prominent Republican leaders including Morris M. Estee. Estee was a California judge who had chaired the Republican National Convention during the successful candidacy of the current U. S. President."[345] Estee told Woodruff and Cannon that he would encourage the Republicans to support the admission of Utah to the Union.

But first, before Utah could be admitted to the Union, it would be necessary for the Mormon Church to make an announcement to end polygamy. Still Cannon believed that there would be much difficulty in writing such a document because of the "danger there would be that we would either say too much or too little."[346]

Utah Admitted to the Union in 1896 after Polygamy is no Longer Sanctioned by the Mormon Church

Woodruff, in order to save his church, made the announcement as suggested by his Republican friend in California saying: "Inasmuch as laws have been enacted by Congress forbidding plural marriages which laws have been pronounced constitutional by the court of the last resort, I hereby declare my intention to submit to those and to use my influence with the members of the church over which I preside to have them do likewise and I now publicly declair [sic] that my advice to the Latter-Day Saints is to refrain from contracting any marriage forbidden by the law of the land."[347]

Finally Utah was admitted to the Union in 1896, forty-five years after Brigham Young's theocracy had first attempted to join the United States. Although Utah had been one of the first states in the West to be settled, because of the "kingdom of God's" failure to follow federal law in generally accepted United States political procedures, it was the last to be admitted. Although the Mormon Church controlled much of the political structure in 1896, it was not absolute control as it had been through most of this forty-five year period following Brigham Young and his followers' arrival in the Salt Lake Basin in 1847. Even today the Mormon Church controls much of the political structure within Utah. All of the U. S. Congressmen from Utah were Republicans before the November 2000 national election and were members of and have been active in the Mormon Church. The state legislature and executive branches of Utah are controlled by Republicans and are members of the Mormon Church. As in the past in Utah, the Mormon hierarchy is firmly in control of the political process, as has been shown by D. Michael Quinn in his laborious and comprehensive research on partisan politics in Utah. While Quinn notes that the church's theocracy in Utah was diminished during the period after its admission as a state in 1896, and continued until after World War 11, since that time the influence of the Mormon Church leadership has increased. Quinn writes: "...infallibility claimed by current general authorities further reduces the likelihood that faithful Mormons will ever privately dissent from the political 'counsel' of LDS headquarters." [348]

Quinn reports that in 1993, 86 percent of Utah's legislators were LDS and that "House and Senate leaders on both sides of the aisle routinely meet before general session with the church's Public Affairs Committee, composed of four members of the Council of the Twelve Apostles." Quinn also reports an instance whereby the Mormon Republican Governor, upon hearing a simple statement from LDS headquarters opposing firearms in chapels, quickly endorsed making that limitation a legal requirement. [349]

According to Quinn, it is a myth "...that Mormons are 'free' to accept, reject or modify the political counsel of General Authorities." Quinn quotes J. Reuben Clark, a Mormon Higher Authority, on the theocratic limits of individual freedom in Mormonism: "I hope Brother (Mark E.) Petersen will pardon me— but this is not a democracy; this is not a republic; this is a kingdom of God. The President of the Church is His premier, if you will, His agent, His possessor of the keys. Our free agency which we have does not make us any more nor less than subjects of the kingdom and subjects we are, — not citizens, Brother Mark." [350]

As reported earlier, the kingdom of God, which Joseph Smith created in Nauvoo, Illinois was transferred to the Great Basin by Brigham Young and his followers. This kingdom of God continued in Young's State of Deseret, although weakened, until about the time that Utah was admitted to the United States in 1896. The kingdom of God waned in Utah between 1896 and 1960 as members of the Mormon Church exercised considerable independence from Mormon General Authorities. During most of this 64-year period all but the most faithful Mormons considered statements by the First Presidency as "merely advice or opinion and not as direction. However, since that time the General Authorities have increasingly claimed infallibility by making such statements as: "We will not lead you astray. We cannot." and "The LDS President will never mislead the Saints." These statements have caused the faithful to follow carefully the political "counsel" of the General Authorities. [351]

Since many Mormons have served in foreign countries during their two-year missions, they are actively recruited by such organizations as the Central Intelligence Agency, United States foreign embassies and the military. Since many of the offices of these branches are located in Washington D.C., Mormons form a disproportionate population there.

Do Mormon United States representatives, senators, federal officials and employees promote the agenda of Mormon Church leaders? Mormon representatives and senators were active in the Republican effort to impeach President Clinton. They were vigorous in their support of the Articles of Impeachment, especially the Articles concerned with obstruction of justice and committing of perjury. They were anxious to remove the President from office because, many believe, he was interfering with their conservative agenda. Concerning the anti-abortion movement, all have been unanimous in their support of it. Also, they have supported many of the aims of the Christian Far Right movement such as permitting prayer in the schools and anti-gay rights. All of these actions are supported by Mormon Church leaders.

Equal Rights Amendment Defeated by the Mormon Church

Senator Orrin Hatch of Utah, from a state that claims that over 70 percent of its population is Mormon, has long promoted the conservative agenda of the General Authorities of the church. Included in his legislative action has been his leadership with the General Authorities in killing the Equal Rights Amendment. (The Equal Rights Amendment included: Section 1. Equality of rights under the law shall not be denied or abridged by the United States or by any State on account of sex. Section 2. The Congress shall have the power to enforce by appropriate legislation the provisions of this article. Section 3. This amendment shall take effect two years after the date of ratification.)[352] The Mormon Church hierarchy publically said that it opposed the Equal Rights Amendment as a moral issue rather than as a political issue and said that it would not dignify women but would put them down.[353] The author believes that the real reason for its opposition was that they thought this would destroy the church doctrine that gives men the exclusive authority in the church and the family. Men hold the priesthood, which women are not permitted to have, and the church hierarchy feared that the ERA would threaten this established practice.

Thirty-five states had ratified the ERA amendment by January 24, 1977. The ERA amendment to the Constitution had smooth sailing from the time of its introduction in the United States House of

Representatives and the United States Senate. The House approved the amendment by a vote of 354 to 24, and the Senate by a vote of 84-8. Hawaii, the first state to approve the proposed amendment, did so without a dissenting vote in the state legislature. Delaware also approved the amendment shortly afterwards without a dissenting vote. Other states followed, approving the amendment by large margins in the state legislature.[354] It seemed that the amendment would quickly be ratified by three-fourths of the states.

However, this simple amendment, equality of rights for men and women, something that clearly was accepted by the overwhelming majority of the American people, something that a large majority of Americans thought was already guaranteed in our Constitution, brought out a bitter and vigorous campaign by the Mormon Church Authorities to have it defeated. The Mormon Church's practice that only men could be members of the priesthood, plus the complete domination in leadership positions in the church by men, would be threatened by the ERA amendment. It is the opinion of the author that this is the primary reason that the church spent large amounts of money and organizational effort in the campaign to defeat the amendment.

Following are several concerns that were expressed about the ERA 27th Amendment by the church:

* Churches that treat men and women differently would lose their tax exempt status.

* Laws prohibiting homosexual conduct and marriages would be unconstitutional.

* Joint male-female restrooms would be mandated.

* ERA would be destructive of the family.

* It would eliminate laws that require a husband to support his wife.

* Local school boards would be prevented from:
— expelling girls who are pregnant.
— separating sex education courses by gender.
— allowing separate athletic contests for boys and girls.

* ERA would eliminate the presumption that married women take their husband's surname.

* Such activities and institutions as Boy Scouts, Girl Scouts, single sex schools and single sex colleges would be eliminated.

* Laws which are protective of women such as domestic abuse, etc. would be eliminated.

* ERA would cause problems for the military which would weaken national security. [355]

Some of these concerns about the ERA have already been implemented in the two decades since the defeat of this amendment such as same-sex marriages in Vermont and special arrangement for girls in public schools who become pregnant during their school career. It has been established that women in the military are performing equally as well as men in what were formerly considered roles for men only. While some attention in congressional debate over ERA was given to such concerns as mandating joint male-female restrooms, being destructive of the family, eliminating laws that require a husband to support his wife, eliminating protective laws for women and prohibiting single sex colleges, schools, and scout programs, there is no reason to believe that any of these concerns would occur by passing the ERA. Surely, a democracy such as the United States has room for an amendment to the Constitution that guarantees equality of rights under the law, regardless of sex.

The Mormon Church has a Special Affairs Committee, which monitors and researches proposed legislation "that affects the Church or its mission." This committee in its beginning was chaired by the present President of the LDS Church, Gordon B. Hinckley, who played a major role in creating it. The author believes that there is no question that Mormon representatives and senators will follow the guidance and suggestions of General Authorities in opposing any legislation that would be harmful to the church and its mission. The Equal Rights Amendment proposal in the late 1970s illustrates the cohesiveness of the Mormon constituency when important LDS Church doctrine is threatened, in this case the submissive role of women in the Mormon Church. Hinckley was also active in organizing the Mormon effort against the ERA. The church must have been alarmed at the quick acceptance of the ERA by an overwhelming vote of approval in the United States Congress and thereafter by overwhelming votes of approval in state legislatures. Hinckley at the time (1970s) was one of the Twelve Apostles of the church and had organized Mormon women to work against the amendment in Las Vegas, Nevada, and several other states. He also organized the effort in Virginia, which was Sonia Johnson's residence at the time she took over the leadership of Mormon Women for ERA.

According to Johnson, Hinckley ordered two regional representatives in the Washington, D. C. area, Julian Lowe and Don Ladd,

to organize the Mormon women into an anti-ERA lobbying coalition. "Elder Lowe sent the message on down the hierarchical ladder
to the bishops to have their Relief Society presidencies find two
women from each ward to attend a special organizational meeting.
The date and place of this meeting were announced just the night
before so...pro-ERA people would not find out about it and picket,
or cause a disturbance, or infiltrate.

"...Regional representative Lowe addressed the gathering first,
telling them that Gordon Hinckley had instructed him and Don Ladd
to organize 'as has been done in other states, that the services of the
Sisters might be appropriately focused, and Brother Ladd and I
decided to organize in the way the church has suggested.' He
announced that this new group, which originally called itself the
Potomac LDS Women's Coalition and later the Virginia LDS
Citizen's Coalition was to be a coalition, as its name implied, and
work with other anti-ERA groups, and that it should submit a budget which it was Brother Lowe's job to get funds to cover. Then he
said, 'Let me say one more thing. I have been given counsel in this.
In other areas, we have found that it is not so good for the men to be
vociferous. It works against the cause. Experience is that if the
Brethren are out beating the bushes it looks like, in the eyes of some,
that we are trying to keep the women subservient (his exact words!).
If we let them talk long enough, they say it all and it is far from that.
This is the exact opposite of what we are trying to do, but is always
interpreted that way.'

Johnson continues:

"...a flame of anger leaped up in my breast as he asked those
good faithful women, my sisters—who are me—to misrepresent the
facts, not to tell that men are behind the scenes pulling their strings.
In short to lie. And I subsequently did hear them lie about this, first
in Virginia, then in one state after another, states in which Mormons
for ERA knew exactly what was going on and relayed it to us. The
magnitude of the moral crisis in this church cannot be overstated."[356]

Johnson describes the way the Mormon men have controlled
International Women's Year conferences "all over the country. ...at
which Mormon men with megaphones, whistles, walkie-talkies and
signs shepherded Mormon women about, body and soul, telling
them when to sit and when to stand, when to come and when to go,
what to say and when to say it and especially how to vote on every
single issue. ...the total subservience of the Mormon women to the

men horrified non-Mormon participants and opened their eyes to the condition of women in the church." Johnson compared the way Mormon women are controlled by men at national and world conferences to the way Arab and Iranian women puppets performed (their masters never far away) at the Copenhagen World Conference on Women in the summer of 1980.[357]

Sonia Johnson was asked to speak to the Senate subcommittee in Washington, D. C. in 1978. The subcommittee was having a hearing on legislation to extend the time for states to vote on ratification of the amendment, which had been passed by the House. Johnson read a statement to the subcommittee, part of which stated: "We (Mormons for ERA) believe that what our early sisters would have wanted, what they would be working for if they were here today, what constitutes the whole loaf with which they would be contented, is ratification of the Equal Rights Amendment."[358]

"When Senator Hatch (a member of the committee) spoke to me, his voice changed. He put on his churchman's voice for me unctuous, condescending, I was not alone in hearing it. Several people asked me afterward whether I had noticed. Indeed, I had, and said to myself incredulously at the time, 'For heaven's sake, Sonia. Do you mean to say that men in the church have been speaking to you like that for forty-two years and *you've never noticed it?* It is incredible how we blind and deafen ourselves so we will not see the truth of how men really feel about us and really treat us. I suppose the only reason I heard it that day was that such a tone was wildly inappropriate in the marble chambers of the Senate Office Building, so out of place that even I, whose ears had become inured to that insufferably patronizing tone from hearing it since birth, was shocked into awareness. This was not church, he was not my spiritual superior in this room, and he was not supposed to be functioning as if he were — that is as if he were a Mormon male.

"...While the revelation of the churchman's voice was maddening, it also gave me unique power. The senator became a known quantity. I understood at once with whom I had to deal, and that recognition calmed and sharpened me. Hatch, on the other hand, being the sort of patriarchal male who tends to view women as so much alike that one approach will work for all, prepared to assert in his usually successful ways his innate male superiority.

"This faulty judgment always gives women the upper hand when dealing with patriarchs, because such men usually have not developed alternative strategies, and are left defenseless and foolish when their stereotypes fail them — as they are increasingly failing them.

"'Mrs. Johnson' he (Senator Hatch) intoned down his shiny Boy Scout nose, 'you must admit that nearly one hundred percent of Mormon women oppose the Equal Rights Amendment.'" (Here's where Bayh allowed the Relief Society sisters from Hatch's ward and stake to applaud and stamp.)

"When the tumult subsided, I replied, (Johnson) 'Oh my goodness, I don't have to admit that. It simply isn't true.'"

"When one has just spoken in one's churchman's voice, one does not expect to be answered back like that and Hatch, chagrined, began his serious work of intimidation and humiliation. Ironically, however, the harder he worked, the more ruffled he himself became and the calmer I felt. We began to have a delightfully brisk dialogue — at least, I enjoyed it:

Hatch: "I notice in your letter to the legislature that you had twenty women listed."

Johnson: "There were not just women on that list...The point here is that numbers of adherents have never proved an issue true or false. You yourself belong to a church of only three million members which purports to be the only true church in the world. That is a pretty precarious position. I am accustomed to being one of few and right."

Hatch: "I notice you are very self-confident that you are right and everybody else is wrong. I would have to admit that the majority can be wrong, but on the other hand I have also seen the minority wrong many times. You may well be wrong here as confident as you are."

Johnson: "You may well be wrong as confident as you are."

Hatch: "That is true, and I am very confident. As a matter of fact, I am very confident that I am right."

Johnson: "And so am I.""

"During the exchange, Hatch began to show signs of ego wear. Repeatedly pulling at his tie, tugging at his sleeves, leaning across the table as if he were preparing to spring at me, he had fended off pleas from his aides who knelt at either side of him (imagine taking oneself so seriously as to have an aide kneeling at one's either side!) and paid no heed to a note from Senator Bayh who was becoming progressively more alarmed as the Utah senator's control visibly and swiftly disintegrated.

"Finally, the struggling senator lost his composure altogether. It was wonderful. I wish everyone who has worked long hours and years for human rights for women could have been there to see it.

"He began innocuously enough. You couldn't have foreseen that he was about to found Mormons for ERA on a national scale. In my journal, I have it recorded like this.

"'It's implied by your testimony that you're more intelligent than other Mormon women, and that if they were all as intelligent as you, they would all support the Equal Rights Amendment.' And then he banged his fist on the table in angry emphasis and shouted. 'Now that's an insult to my wife!'"[359]

In the opinion of the author, this exchange between Johnson and Hatch shows the attitude that Mormon men have toward women, one in which they feel that women will not challenge their priesthood superiority. Clearly, as was reported by newspaper reporters and others present at the hearings, Hatch lost his control and as a result showed that if any state needed the Equal Rights Amendment, surely his State of Utah did. Johnson answers the question that was posed earlier in this chapter: *Do Mormon senators, representatives and federal officials promote the Mormon Church agenda?* as follows:

"From the outset, I (Johnson) have known it is fruitless to try to convince members of my church of the correctness of the Equal Rights Amendment, fruitless because Mormons who are anti-ERA are anti-ERA not because of the demerits of the amendment, but primarily because the President of the church — who, good members believe, is a Prophet as Moses and Isaiah were — has taken a very firm anti-ERA stance. And though Mormons are repulsed by the word 'infallible,' its being such a papist concept, they nevertheless believe that God will not allow the Prophet and President of the Mormon Church to make a mistake. They, therefore, believe in the infallibility of the Prophet, while strongly denying belief in infallibility. It is all very compartmentalized, this thinking; all very morally and intellectually dishonest."[360] Johnson's words of the infallibility of the President of the church were reinforced by a Mormon author who defended the infallibility of the Prophet in his statement against the ERA.[361]

Because the Presidency and the Quorum of the Twelve Apostles were against the ERA and because of their efforts in organizing the Mormon Church membership to lobby for its defeat, the ERA failed to be a part of the United States Constitution. "...sociologist O.

Kendall White wrote that 'small Mormon minorities exerted disproportionate influence over the fate of the ERA in Virgina, Missouri,
Florida, Illinois and North Carolina.' White, a Mormon who had
favored ratification, concluded that Mormons had tipped the scales
for the entire nation." This effort by the General Authorities shows
clearly the influence which a well-organized tiny minority can have
upon an unorganized majority. There is no question that a large
majority of the American people wished to have the ERA passed. It
is unfortunate that a group of fifteen men was able to usurp the vast
majority opinion who had not the interests of what was best for the
nation, but only what was best for them.[362]

Church Hierarchy Political Control

If Mormon Church members do believe that the word of the
President (Prophet) is infallible and that the Mormon God will not
allow the President to make a mistake, does this not make Mormon
Church members follow Mormon doctrine blindly, unable to think
for themselves? Does not belief in the infallibility of the Mormon
Prophet require that Mormons in all walks of life, including United
States representatives and senators, support legislation that their
church officials want? Would not the Mormon voters remove any
Mormon federal official including a senator or representative for not
supporting the Prophet's wishes? The author believes that the
answer to these questions is a resounding yes, and therefore,
Mormon federal officials are marching under the orders of the
Mormon Church. They are not performing their duties concerning
what is in the best interests of the American people, but rather what
are the wishes of the General Authorities of the Mormon Church.

Sonia Johnson, who led the Mormon Women for ERA was
excommunicated from the church for her activities with this organization. However, even though she fought the excommunication, she
did express her happiness at being relieved of the oppression which
she had felt while being a member of the church. She received a
notice from church officials on December 5, 1979: "...the decision
of this court is that you are excommunicated from the Church of
Jesus Christ of Latter-Day Saints. I must remind you that all privileges of membership are hereby denied by this action... I strongly
encourage you to repent..." Johnson wondered why she should
repent since she is happier now than ever before.[363]

The excommunication list includes many other brave souls, former Mormon Church members who value honesty, freedom and truth rather than serving as puppets to the leaders of the church. Excommunication from the church may serve the General Authorities today as a way to preserve their control of members who would deviate from the current doctrine of the church. But as enlightened members choose honesty, freedom and truth over false doctrine and authority, excommunication may prove to become less and less effective. Such bright, talented and exceptional people as Sonia Johnson, Fawn Brodie, Deborah Laake and D. Michael Quinn are but a few of the writers who have been excommunicated from the church for supporting causes or for writing books of which General Authorities disapprove or are embarrassed by what the books contain. Boyd K. Packer, a General Authority may have hit the nail on the head when he declared: "Feminists and 'so-called scholars' and gays were the three primary 'dangers' facing the church."[364] One of these "so-called scholars," D. Michael Quinn, was unwilling to give in to this attitude of the Church Authorities and as a result resigned from his "tenured position as a full professor of history at Brigham Young University." As had been mentioned before, he wrote that "academic freedom merely survives at BYU without fundamental support by the institution, exists against tremendous pressure, and is nurtured only through the dedication of individual administrators and faculty members."[365]

The activities of the General Authorities in the removal of members who question their authority is clearly shown in Packer's "three primary dangers facing the church" (scholars, feminists and gays). The church has been involved in striking down state legislation to improve gay rights. Feminists such as Sonia Johnson and Deborah Laake have been quickly removed from the church. Packer's "so-called scholars" have not fared any better as eminent scholars like Fawn Brodie and D. Michael Quinn typify. The author believes that the General Authorities realize that the doctrine of the church created by the fanciful mind of Joseph Smith, does not hold up under careful and scholarly scrutiny by renowned scholars. Excommunication of distinguished scholars who dare to question church doctrine, who use careful analysis and in depth research, keep other members in line since they don't want to face the embarrassment of excommunication.

Deborah Laake's book, *Secret Ceremonies* (described in an ear-

lier chapter), brought down the wrath of the General Authorities and
resulted in her excommunication. Since Laake has written her book,
she has been able to view Mormonism more objectively. She writes:
"...I believe that Church Authorities have organized to punish their
dissenters and that the purge is only beginning. During my months
on the road, I got a close look at the actions of Mormon Church
Authorities and their champions when they perceived that their control was threatened—that is, the control defined by their possession
of the one proper answer to each of life's most pressing questions,
which they believe is the birthright of their membership in what they
describe as 'the one true church.' (It is these precise answers that
allow church authorities to so exactly guide their members' lives.) I
got a look at a brittle, condemning defensiveness from Church
Authorities that I don't remember from my childhood, and learned
that the range of acceptable behavior for Mormons had narrowed
considerably during my lifetime. Where once church members
could disagree with their leaders and received little censure beyond
a few raised eyebrows, the contemporary church is more and more
creating an environment of fear. Today the issue is the role of
women, but there will be innumerable others issues perceived by the
elderly men inside the blank-faced church office building in downtown Salt Lake City.

"For free thinkers who value their church membership, it's
unfortunate that these old men believe themselves to be besieged: I
do not understand the strength drawn from Mormonism by the men
and women who revere it, but I see it and know that it is real. I see
the grief in these more liberal believers who are afraid for their
church memberships — afraid of being severed from their spiritual
source."[366]

Old Boys' System

The present system of authoritarian control of the Mormon
Church by old men could aptly be described as an "Old Boys'
System." This ranking system of authority based on seniority promotes a hierarchy composed of elderly men. Appointments from the
membership to the higher leadership positions of the church, including the First and Second Quorums of the Seventy, Twelve Apostles
and the Counselors to the First Presidency are made by the aging
leader of the church: the President. Naturally, the President of the

Church (currently Gordon B. Hinckley, age 94) is going to appoint men to the First and Second Quorums of the Seventy and the Twelve Apostles who will continue to preserve the present seniority succession system. Traditionally the Quorums of Seventy serve as recruiting grounds for the Council of the Twelve, and the President will appoint those who are well-known by him and whose views coincide with his. This then insures that the Mormon Church will continue with the same policies that it has held almost from its inception, primarily the policies of its first two dominant authoritarian leaders: Joseph Smith and Brigham Young.

This process insures the continuation of the unconventional ideas of the church that resulted in so much violence in the Mormon Church's early history. The author believes that church leaders still carry the phobia that if they allow dissenters to remain members, its image will be so badly tarnished that the membership will decline, the worst thing that could happen to a church that claims that it is "the only true church." As premised earlier in these pages the primary mission of the church is to increase membership throughout the United States and the world so that the General Authorities can establish "the kingdom of God" upon the earth. These Authorities must punish dissenters, especially if those dissenters are accomplished writers whose books become best sellers. Excommunication is the only effective punishment that the church leadership can utilize against dissenters. And the threat of excommunication provides a very effective deterrent to members who may be considering making the public aware of their disagreement with the church. It is effective because excommunication is considered by Mormons to be disastrous and embarrassing and must be avoided at all costs. Excommunication from the church often ends their association with friends and family, making them social outcasts in the community, especially in areas where there are large numbers of Mormons. So the usual route of one who no longer believes in the church doctrine is to remain silent and become a Jack Mormon (one who is no longer actively involved in the church).

Freedom in Politics in the First Half of the 20th Century

As written previously, Democrats succeeded in carrying some of the elections in the first half of the 20th century in Mormon country. In November, 1932, they overwhelmingly voted for Franklin D. Roosevelt for President of the United States. They also voted for all other New Deal candidates, which resulted in Apostle Reed Smoot, a Republican, being defeated as U. S. senator after almost 30 years in the Senate. He was resentful that Mormon President Heber J. Grant did not ask Mormons at the October conference to re-elect him.[367] In November, 1936, although the First Presidency published an unsigned editorial in Deseret News which argued against the re-election of Democratic President Franklin D. Roosevelt, 69.3 percent of Utah's voters helped re-elect him. Utah's electorate re-elected FDR again (1940 and 1944) despite the First Presidency's opposition.

Church Hierarchy Assumes Greater Control of Political Process in Second Half of the 20th Century

As the following review of national elections shows, the second half of the century showed Republicans dominating Utah's elections. This is consistent with the General Authorities' campaign of infallibility (since General Authorities are led by and speak only God's word, they can't be mistaken in what they say). Because Mormons believe in their infallibility, they are expected to be obedient to the church hierarchy and follow its lead, not only in religious, but also in temporal matters. Clearly in the last half of the 20th century, General Authorities have changed their hands-off policy in politics to one of greater control in the political arena. Some examples of this are:

1. Even though the Congress of the United States overwhelmingly approved the Equal Rights Amendment and it appeared that state legislatures would easily approve the amendment, the Mormon Church in 1982 after an intense campaign, was successful in its defeat.

2. In October, 1973, a First Presidency letter urged 78,800 Mormons in Washington state to vote against a referendum to allow nineteen-year-olds to purchase and consume alcoholic beverages.[368]

3. "In a July, 1994, *Church News* story, "Members Help Defeat Lottery Initiative," tells how two General Authorities coordinated political campaigns in Oklahoma where Mormons make up less that one percent of the state's population. LDS Public Affairs officials and their Protestant allies achieved overwhelming defeat of the lot-

tery proposal even though "public opinion polls show 75 percent were for the initiative" before this Mormon-directed campaign."[369]

4. In 2000, the Mormon Church was active in defeating western states' Equal Rights laws for gays.

The Republican party has been the torch bearer for the Mormon Church in Utah for the past fifty years as shown by the following elections in that state:

In the 1976 national presidential election between Democrat Jimmy Carter and Republican Gerald Ford, Ford received 331,900 (62.4 percent) and Jimmy Carter 179,400 (or 33.7 percent). In the same election, Republican Orrin Hatch received 284,890 (53.7 percent) votes and Democrat Frank Moss received 237,588 (44.8 percent) votes. A Democrat, Gunn McKay, won one of two congressional seats, with Republican Don Marriott winning the second seat with 53.5 percent of the vote.[370]

In the 1980 national presidential election Republican Ronald Reagan won by 74 percent of the Utah vote, while Jimmy Carter received only 21 percent. The only Democrat in the Utah congressional delegation was defeated. In 1984, Reagan won re-election by a wide margin of three to one over the Democrat, Walter Mondale. Two Republicans won congressional seats by margins of three to one. In 1988, George Bush, Reagan's Vice President, won by 54 percent of the vote, compared to Michael Dukakis who received only 38 percent. In the 1988 congressional elections, Republican Orrin Hatch easily defeated his Democratic opponent, Brian Moss, by a 2 to 1 margin. All incumbent national representatives retained their seats. Republicans Howard Nielson and James Hansen won by 3 to 1 margins, while Democrat Wayne Owens won by a 58 to 42 percent margin.[371]

The landslide support for the Republican candidates continued on into the 1992 election with the winning candidate, Democrat Bill Clinton, receiving only 182,590 Utah votes as compared to George Bush's 320,858. Ross Perot, the Reform Party candidate, received more votes than Bill Clinton with 202,796 votes. Republican Bob Bennett defeated his Democratic opponent in the U.S. Senate election by a margin of 4 to 3.[372] In the presidential election of 2000, George W. Bush received 512,161 votes from Utah voters, compared to 202,732 for Gore.[373]

The increasing margins for victory for Utah Republican Mormon candidates in the latter part of the 20th century is the result of the change by the church hierarchy from a hands-off policy in politics in the first half to a more active role in politics for the second half of the century. Although General Authorities no longer serve in state and national elected offices, they are active in maintaining regular consultations with state and national representatives and senators. As reported earlier in this chapter, a Public affairs Committee of four apostles meets regularly with elected Utah state and national officials on both sides of the aisle.

History shows us that sometimes a handful of men, dedicated to a cause, can gain control of government. (Witness Lenin's gaining control of Russia in 1917 and Hitler's rise to power in Germany in 1932.) We must be vigilant in our efforts to protect our freedoms of thought, speech, religion and individualism.

Chapter Eight
The Conspiracy

In the opinion of the author, there are many practices of the Mormon Church that defy logical reasoning, that mold minds into obedience to Mormon doctrine and the teachings of the church's General Authorities. These include: the baptism for the dead, the temple ceremonies, the authoritarianism of the religious leaders, the demand that women be subservient to their husbands, the sacred garments and the general "big brother" control of Mormon Church members by the priesthood to insure obedience to church doctrine that prevents the creation of freedom-loving and open-minded people who are needed in a vibrant, dynamic and democratic society. The indoctrination process that the church hierarchy has developed, over its 170-year history, is a controlled and sophisticated system, which floods members' homes and minds with church propaganda. This propaganda is designed to convince them that the church provides the avenue to a glorious everlasting life after death. Missionaries and most of the general membership of the Mormon Church members are not aware of what the author believes to be the church's conspiracy to deluge the United States and the world with Mormonism. It is also thought that the church hierarchy is so indoctrinated into church beliefs that perhaps they too may believe in the propaganda that they are promoting.

Laundering of Faith-Promoting Materials

The author has presented information in previous chapters that shows Mormon-sponsored publications are carefully laundered to remove any information, although true, that could be harmful to the church. The apostles and other General Authorities of the church often write articles in the *Ensign* (a periodical and the official organ of the Mormon Church) glorifying Joseph Smith and describing the Mormon Church as the only true church in the world. The articles include attractive artwork that emphasizes key points in the apostles' sermons. The *Ensign* periodicals contain eyecatching illustrations that depict Jesus Christ, surrounded by bright light, appearing before Joseph Smith. Accompanying the stories of Joseph Smith and the golden plates are stunning, often handdrawn, pictures showing these glittering plates.

In many *Ensign* articles, information is presented that shows the progress of gaining new members to the church, especially those from foreign countries. Beautiful pictures of temples, new and old, often appear in this magazine. Smiling faces are numerous, including those of happy missionaries going about their work, happy converts on their way to church, happy seniors working in food processing plants and happy General Authorities meeting with national and foreign leaders.

Glorifying Mormonism

In the opinion of the author the *Ensign* is a slick public relations instrument that hides the dark history of the Mormon Church, makes the *Book of Mormon* story and other writings created from the imagination and fantasies of Joseph Smith sound as though they are true. It ignores the dictatorial nature of Brigham Young's leadership, his many wives, his promotion of blood atonement and his self-aggrandizement. Also the First Presidency and the Quorum of Twelve are made to appear as holy representatives of God. This periodical glorifies the fifteen top leaders, all apostles of the church, by publishing their photos, usually with the President having the largest picture, next to his two Counselors with the medium-sized photos and the remaining Twelve Apostles in even smaller photos. This glorification of the apostles appears in lead articles that the apostles write and by an occasional biography such as the one on apostle James E. Faust entitled "Pure Gold." (Ensign August, 1995, Volume 25 Number 8)

Building Temples to Increase Tithing

The Mormon Church hierarchy has been on a temple building binge in recent years in the United States and throughout the world. In the Mormon tradition, the temple is not a church to which members go for regular church services, but a special place for secret ordinances, marriage and sealing ceremonies and baptisms for the dead rituals. The admittance to Mormon temples, as described earlier, requires a temple recommend from the bishop, received only after a strict interview with him that demands, among other things, full ten percent tithing. Building additional new temples easily accessible to members enriches the Mormon Church hierarchy's treasury. If members have a temple close by, they are more likely to pay full tithing and be actively involved in the church in order to gain entrance to it. As mentioned earlier it is also considered socially desirable by most Mormons to have their offspring married in the temple, and this naturally adds to the tithing income of the church. Many pay up in order to remain in good standing in the church and to be respected among their friends and families.

It is believed that the church hierarchy, realizing the status symbol attraction of the Mormon temple for members, sees it as a money making proposition. The more money that is collected by the church, the greater opportunity they will have to build the Mormon kingdom of God on earth. More money means that better satellite communication systems can be purchased for media advertising to be used in promoting the church and for attracting new members. With more members, the church can expand its missionary system, its publications systems, its church educational systems and other forms of propagandizing. The temples are advantageous to the church hierarchy since by controlling entry into the temples, these men force members who wish admittance to be obedient, follow their rules and pay full tithing.

Evidence has been presented that the Mormon Church controls the state government in Utah, that is for all practical purposes, a one-party system — the Republican party. This control stifles individual and group involvement in the political process and contributes to an unhealthy political system. And without allegiance to the Mormon Church, one generally does not stand a chance of winning any election, at least outside of Salt Lake City. Diversity in religions, cultures and economics in Utah is limited.

Most Mormons would deny that the General Authorities have as their goal: to gain dominion of the world. While the Authorities may actually have this as their goal, it is kept secret from members, and many members may think that it is foolish to believe that such a conspiracy of the church hierarchy exists. However, several practices of the church pointing to this conspiracy have been reported earlier and will be further discussed in the following paragraphs. Just as financial affairs are kept secret by the Church Authorities, it is thought by several writers, as documented previously, that its plans to dominate the world are also kept secret.

Infallibility of the First Presidency and the Quorum of Twelve Apostles

Preceding chapters provide support for the theory that the last half of the 20th century has seen an increased emphasis by the church in the belief in the infallibility of the First Presidency and the Quorum of Twelve which has diminished the possibility that Utah and surrounding states where Mormonism is strong, will change to a more healthy two-party system. Because Mormons trust their religious leaders in all matters, faithful Mormons are less likely to support positions contrary to their leaders' counsel.

As indicated, the belief in the infallibility of these fifteen men causes them to become a powerful force to use in controlling members. Obedient members are the key ingredients needed for the church hierarchy to succeed in its goal of establishing the Mormon "kingdom of God on earth." In order to keep church members obedient, it is likely that this infallibility will continue to be promoted in the 21st century. It is also likely that the church will continue to oppose such high profile political issues as the Equal Rights Amendment, gay rights and abortion. The church will continue to support the Far Right Christian movement, prayer in schools, anti-flag burning amendments and will try to restrict the power and influence of labor unions.

Influence in National Politics and Governmental Affairs

Examples were presented in preceding chapters of this book that show that the Mormon Church has gained great influence in state and national politics and governmental affairs. Examples of these are:

(1) A larger number of Mormons are found in the FBI, CIA and other influential federal government offices than their proportion to the United States population warrants.

(2) Defeat of the Equal Rights Amendment despite the fact that it had overwhelming political support by Congress and the American people.

(3) Greater influence in the Federal Communications Commission than their numbers deserve.

(4) Larger control of local and national media services such as newspapers, radio and television stations than their numbers warrant.

(5) Much greater influence in foreign affairs than is justified by their numbers.

Brigham Young University a Key to Gaining More Influence and Political Control

Brigham Young University is a key component in what the author believes to be a Mormon conspiracy to control the United States and eventually the world. Students are provided with religious indoctrination courses throughout their four-year undergraduate training that reinforce their obedience to the church hierarchy. The indoctrination is enhanced by the university's practice of providing students with skills necessary to fulfill a lifelong career as well as training for leadership positions in the Mormon Church.

In the previous chapters, information was presented regarding Brigham Young University, which is the largest religious-sponsored university in the United States with over 30,000 students. Students who are admitted and professors who are employed there must adhere to the university policy that requires annual recommendation letters from local Mormon bishops verifying that these persons have continuing temple recommends. Receiving and continuing the temple recommend requires that the member certify that one is loyal to church leaders and is faithful to church teachings. Since nine of the First Presidency and the Quorum of Twelve Apostles are members of the thirteen-member BYU Board of Trustees, the church hierarchy insures that the university professors and students comply with church doctrine.

Brigham Young University Offers Many Foreign Languages and Cultural Studies

Brigham Young University is well-positioned and set up to deliver the education and training necessary to provide leadership for the domination of the governments throughout the world since it offers a wide range of courses in world cultures and foreign languages. Since the church itself is monarchical in organization, it is prepared to take over authoritarian as well as democratic governments. As mentioned before and to emphasize, as one apostle put it during a visit with a People's Republic of China government administrator, Tung Chee Hwa in Hong Kong: Mormon Church members accept the rule of kings, presidents and magistrates, regardless of where they live. (*Ensign*, July 1997, Volume 27 Number 7, page 78) That Brigham Young University is preparing students to work with cultures and languages throughout the world is demonstrated by the offering of 37 languages and 21 separate cultural studies. The major languages of Chinese (Mandarin), French, German, Italian, Japanese, Russian and Spanish are offered with other such minority languages, as Afrikaans, Icelandic and Lithuanian. Cultures included in the university's curriculum include: Asian, Italian, French, German, Japanese, Russian and Chinese studies. (Brigham Young University 2000-2001 catalogue)

This comprehensive offering of languages and cultures at BYU underscores the importance that the church places upon training students to serve in leadership positions in missionary centers throughout the world. This training puts the Mormon Church in a favorable position in establishing its identity all over the world, which the author believes that they hope will eventually lead to drenching the world with Mormonism. An example of the worldwide effort exerted by the Mormon Church, is the 600-megabyte compact disc that was sent to 20,000 media sources throughout the world in 1997. This disc contained information about the movement of over 10,000 Mormon Church members from Nauvoo, Illinois to Salt Lake City, Utah in the late 1840s and early 1850s. It also contained information about the church's beliefs. (*Ensign*, July 1997, Vol. 27 No. 7, p. 78)

Mormon Church Pressures the Federal Administration to Open Doors to Proselytizing in Foreign Countries

The Mormon Church benefits from the prevailing American belief in religious tolerance as well as from the governmental protection that the United States diplomatic services provide to American citizens abroad. If a foreign government has policies or laws that restrict proselytizing in that country, the Mormon Church, through its representatives, lobbies and pressures the United States State Department to use the lever of foreign aid and other diplomatic means to persuade foreign governments to liberalize restrictive laws. Many foreign governments and their citizens need foreign aid and the revenue that trade generates with the United States. Therefore, if they feel that the "American" Mormon Church is being offended and the United States government might cut off financial and trade advantages because of this, they are likely to let Mormon missionary centers be established in their countries. Little do they know that the short-term advantages may result in the long-range domination of their country by the Mormon Church.

Few foreign citizens are aware that the Mormon Church is not predominantly "The American church," but only a minority church. It is not a mainstream American church, nor does the Mormon "American" church uphold the American democratic ideals that many foreigners admire. Instead of American democratic ideals, the Mormon Church is governed by a monarchical style of administration, in which the head of the church, the "President," assisted by apostles and other General Authorities, makes all appointments and decisions of the church. The President of the church is not elected by church members, but assumes power strictly by seniority as the oldest apostle (in seniority as an apostle).

Unfortunately many foreigners are unaware of the governmental structure of the Mormon Church. They are also unaware that the church is based upon doctrine and practices that are unbiblical and not of divine nature. In the canned lessons they receive from the young missionaries, there is no mention of the monarchical style of organization of the church. Few foreigners are exposed to the "unlaundered" history of the Mormon Church, and the many documented accounts that expose the religion as no more than a fanciful story that was created from the imagination of Joseph Smith, and from materials and books he gathered to compose his *Book of*

Mormon, his revelations and other writings. The Mormon Church authorities have no right to allege to citizens of foreign countries that the Mormon Church is an American church which typifies American culture and beliefs.

A possible model for the Mormon Church in gaining domination of the United States is found in the book: *Mormonism, Americanism and Politics*, written by a Mormon writer, Richard Vetterli. This book puts forth a claim that Mormonism and Americanism are designed for one another. The Mormon kingdom of God, according to Vetterli, will be administered with love, gentleness and righteousness. Who is to define love, gentleness and righteousness? Is it the Mormon Church, rather than a combination of churches and religions or a plurality of peoples? According to Vetterli the members of the Mormon Church have been chosen to lead the kingdom of God on earth.

The Nation and the World are Yours, not the Mormon Church's

Uniformity of thinking, as promoted in the Mormon Church, disregards the true nature of people in the United States and the world. The world is composed of many nationalities, religions, non-religious groups, cultures and societies. The author believes that the Mormon Church is conspiring to control the world through one religion, a religion that makes no allowance for free thinking, but preaches that the Mormon apostles alone should interpret religious thought and that members should accept this interpretation without question.

If "one and the same," as championed by the Mormon Church were to come about, the joy of individualism, adventuring and experimenting would be stymied. The author believes that the Mormon Church puts a great burden upon American embassies and consulates in foreign countries to promote and protect its proselytizing activities throughout the world. It is also believed that the liberal taxing policies of the United States provide the church with excessive tax exemptions which are being used by the church to attain its goal of Mormonizing America and the world. It is ironic that the American democracy which promotes free-thinking, individualism, private enterprise, free speech and freedom of the press is also nurturing Mormonism which is bent upon replacing it with an authoritarian religion and government.

AFTERWORD

In the short two years since completion of the first printing of *The Mormon Conspiracy*, I have corresponded with hundreds of Mormons and non-Mormons by e-mail about my book. From this correspondence, and discussions with both critics as well as supporters, it was evident that some aspects of Mormonism needed further elaboration. The internet, with its e-mail and website components, provides ordinary citizens opportunity to investigate the truth and share their opinions about a wide array of topics and events. While powerful organizations, such as the Mormon Church, may gain control of a large share of the public media, the internet is also a powerful organization in itself, since it is easily available and affordable and can counteract self-serving and untruthful public media. It is a tool available world-wide that has the potential to give a greater voice to individuals in controlling and promoting their own interests and welfare, and limits the power of those who attempt to control people by religious or other means. The internet is a freethinker's medium in which one can explore and discover the truth. Public media, on the other hand, can become the mind-controller's medium unless safeguards are made to insure that both minority and majority viewpoints are presented.

Since the first printing of my book, I have read several investigations and reports on Mormonism. With this information, and the e-mails received from almost every state in the United States and many foreign countries, I have compiled the following information to supplement the conclusions that were discussed in the first printing.

Lack of Scientific and Logical Backing For Mormon Beliefs and Doctrine

Many Mormons accept the fact that there is no scientific or logical proof regarding the truthfulness of that which is taught by

church leaders concerning Mormonism. However, many still believe
that the truth is received from an emotional experience that "God
tells me it is true." Countless Mormon believers have told me to
read the *Book of Mormon*, pray about it, and God will tell you it is
true. The good feeling that they receive from praying and reading
Smith's *Book of Mormon* provides them with their testimony "I
know that the *Book of Mormon* is true." However one of their own,
Grant M. Palmer, (*An Insider's View of Mormon Origins*) questions
this emotional response as verification that it is the truth. In his
book, Palmer, who has spent his lifetime working within the
Mormon Church Educational System as a teacher and supervisor of
teachers in CES, questions the value of the emotional experience of
feeling good about the *Book of Mormon,* as a basis for determining
the truth of this book.

A handful of Mormon believers have tried to show the authenticity of Mormonism by offering "scientific and logical" proof that
Joseph Smith's *Book of Mormon* is true by trying to show that it is a
factual history of the ancient Indians of Central and South America.
They have attempted to show that Smith's book is authentic since
studies comparing the *Book of Mormon* with other ancient writings
show that Smith's word usage and writings correlate favorably with
these ancient writings. This, they claim, would show that Smith did
indeed translate from the ancient golden plates when writing his
Book of Mormon.

A few devout Mormons have disputed DNA and archaeological studies that clearly show that Smith's Lamanite (Indian) ancestors emigrated from Eastern Asia. They argue that the DNA of
Joseph Smith's Lamanites has disappeared in the centuries following the time period of Smith's book. These arguments are promi-
nently placed in official Mormon Church internet websites. The
official Mormon Church website focuses primarily on providing
church-sponsored "research" that contradicts factual research that
disproves Mormon beliefs and teaching.

Concerning Mormon Church-sponsored "research," Raymond
Richards writes: "Each field of scholarship has its own pseudo-
scholars. Geography has its flat earthers. Biology has its creation
scientists.   Archeology has it believers in ancient astronauts.
Medicine has homeopaths. Physics has inventors of perpetual
motion machines. Astronomy has astrologers. Historians have
holocaust deniers - and the Mormon church. There are other reli-

gious groups from the United States with false and dangerous ideas—7th-day Adventists, Christian Scientists, and the cult of Jehovah's Witnesses - but none of them has the millions of members or billions of dollars of the Mormon church. We must take the Mormons seriously. ....When a religion claims to be the supreme fount of fact, when it contradicts research and opposes freedom of inquiry, then it should be challenged by academics. Although students are often victims of this church, we should fail students who use unsound methodology to believe in pseudo-scholarship, such as Creationism or the Book of Mormon as history. If we grant degrees to incompetent students, then universities are a joke." (Raymond Richards, paper presented at University of Waikato, Hamilton, New Zealand)

Control of the Public Media

In my book, I reached several conclusions based upon my research into Mormonism, one being that Mormon Church authorities are buying up radio and television stations, newspapers and other media in order to gain control of public media outlets. If total control of such media could be achieved, this would be very dangerous to our American democracy since it would hinder the free flow of information. I had thought that all people, including Mormons, would be opposed to allowing one group or one organization to be in control of the public media. But much to my surprise, Mormons enthusiastically and almost gleefully supported their church leaders gaining control. "We trust our church leaders to promote high morals and wouldn't it be nice to remove the immoral literature that we are now receiving through the media."

Mind Control

In his book: *Combatting Cult Mind Control*, Steven Hassan list four components of Mind Control, *control of behavior, control of thoughts, control of emotions* and *control of information.* This is accomplished, according to Hassan, by *unfreezing, changing* and *refreezing.* The control of members by the use of these four components is accomplished in many ways, including the large number of social activities promoted by the church, the testimonials at church meetings, the teaching visits in the homes, satellite programs beamed into local ward houses by higher authorities of the church, periodicals such as the *Ensign,* faith-promoting books from the Church's publishing house and television programs from church-owned stations.

What is it that causes people to believe in magical and mystical organizations such as the Mormon Church, an organization basing its beliefs on a fairy-like story of Joseph Smith's golden plates and his translation of these plates (with God's help) in writing the *Book of Mormon*? How is it that an organization is able to attract and keep members whose donations allow it to build a 50 billion dollar empire? I believe that Larry and Tammy Braithwaite, former members of the church, have put forth a credible answer to this question in their book, *Journey to the Center of My Soul.*   This is the concept of *The Pattern,* (a method of fear and control that the Mormon Church uses to keep members) *The Binder,* (Church leadership binds "us heart and soul to the perpetual requirements of being a good Mormon") and *The Bound* ("We gradually give up questioning the doctrine and history of the Church that seemed vague and troublesome and try to concentrate on doing all we could to be worthy of the larger, eternal blessings.")

The *Double-Bind* is then employed that confuses and denies the *Bound* the ability to "think or feel rationally." For example, whereas church doctrine (D&C 93:36) teaches *The glory of God is intelligence, or, in other words, light and truth,* church leaders say *You will remain silent on those* [doctrines] *where differences exist between you and the Brethren.* (Bruce McConkie's Letter, Feb. 19, 1981)

"What *The Pattern* does, in effect, is turn the independent rational mind around so that the *Bound* reflects only the mind of the *Binder*, as a mirror. It creates a whole new orientation of the world, a conversion from the logical to the illogical— the real to the unreal — the truth to lies."

This concept is explained further: "In the real world, nature provides us with an open system of trial and error, awareness and learning. Exercising our own bodies, senses, minds and self-direction allows us to reach for the stars, to see a greater range of possibilities and fulfill ourselves by being true to ourselves. In contrast, *The Pattern*, or upside-down world of Mormonism, took away our individuality. We became part of the mass known as the Latter-day Saints. We were instructed several times a week about what to think, what to believe, how to behave, what to read, how to dress and how to spend our money."

Joseph Smith, the founder of the Mormon Church, was a master at using *The Pattern* in sidestepping any questions or problems that he faced in his leadership of the Church.

One example of Smith's use of *The Pattern* is when he told Oliver Cowdery and Hiram Page that he had a revelation from God that they should go to Toronto, Canada and sell the copyright of his *Book of Mormon*. After returning in failure, these men asked Smith why their mission had failed since it was a revelation from God. Smith went into another room for a few minutes and returned saying that the whole thing had merely been a test to see if they would do all things whatsoever the Lord commanded them. (It wasn't God or Joseph who messed up, it was Hiram and Oliver, who needed to be tested, who failed.)

The Reinforcing of Mind Control by Church Leaders

Following are some of the answers to questions given by Church officials in order to reinforce mind control, that transfers faults of the Church, Joseph Smith or church leaders to rank and file members:

1. *Some things haven't been revealed yet and will be revealed to you later or in eternal life.*

2. *Lucifer wins a great victory when he can get members of the Church to speak against their leaders and do their own thinking.*

3. *You are not trying hard enough. Try harder and pray about it.*

4. Or if a member of the Priesthood's blessing does not cure a health problem: *It is not the blessing that didn't help you to overcome your sickness, it was your lack of faith. You need to have faith and pray about it.*

5. Or if you don't believe in the authenticity of the *Book of Mormon, you don't know enough about it to understand it.* Here again, it's not church leaders', God's or Joseph Smith's fault, it is your fault and you should feel guilty to question the word of God, Joseph Smith or church leaders.

6. If a person questions why they aren't receiving the church's promised blessings, *You need to examine your life and see why you aren't righteous enough to deserve these blessings.*

7. If a member questions the church's claim that Joseph Smith is a prophet of God, or a fraud, *You need to kneel down and pray about it and God will tell you that Joseph Smith is a true prophet.*

8. Or a member questions church doctrine or practices, *Pray about it "And ye shall know the truth and the truth shall set you free."*

9. If you question the authorities of the church, *"You must not speak out against the Lord's anointed."*

10. Or if a member violates a church rule, *"Satan has gotten ahold of you; ask a member of the priesthood to remove Satan from your body."*

11. If you have written something critical of the church, *"You are doing Satan's work in attempting to harm the church."*

The Mormon Church teaches: *Nothing is ever God's, church leaders', or the church's fault. It is always the fault of the member's behavior or a misunderstanding of church doctrine, or that Satan has led you in the wrong direction.* This is a carryover from Joseph Smith, the founder of the church, who was very clever in always making the person feel guilty and responsible when he failed or questioned church policy. Bishops and other church leaders generally give the same responses that Smith made to his followers. If you question church doctrine or the *Book of Mormon*, the Bishop or other church officials will tell you to *read it again, be humble, remember you are a child of God, pray about it and he will tell you that it is true.* Doubters of the truth of Mormonism are told that they are risking apostasy and separation from their families for eternity. This line is a powerful mind control tactic.

The following from an e-mail writer also describes ways to reinforce mind control:

"I took 4 years of LDS seminary throughout high school just to realize how brainwashed these people really are. They truly believe in a blind faith that will take 10 percent of their earnings until the time of their death. Kids who receive the priesthood and then abandon the church are taught that they will spend an eternity in Hell, whereas if you murder millions of people, like Hitler did, the most time you can spend in hell is 1000 years." These kids are forced to stick with the church on the belief that if they leave they are worse human beings in God's eye than Hitler was.

Testimonies and Mind Control *I know, I know, I know*

The testimony is an integral part of mind control that church leaders exercise over Mormon Church members. Tammy Braithwaite, a former long time member of the Church, taught her young children a testimony, as soon as they were able to talk. She remembers her son repeating his testimony: *"I know that Joseph Smith was a pwoffut and the Book of Mommun is twoo."* She now knows that she was teaching her son to lie and realizes that "This kind of repetition of meaningless mantras is, of course, one of the techniques in brainwashing."

These testimonies are often repeated in church meetings with such testimonies often beginning with *I know that the Church of Jesus Christ of Latter-day Saints is the only true church on the face of the earth. I know that Gordon B. Hinckley is a Prophet of God, etc.*

Temples and Mind Control

Realizing that they have the keys that control entry into temple ceremonies (such as marriage) church leaders have utilized this tool to further the binding of members to church teaching. Some elements of mind control that are used in temple ceremonies include members repeating vows of loyalty, submitting their bodies to washing and anointing in order to remove sins, wearing of special temple garments and experiencing an imaginary heaven by being pulled through the veil.

A temple ceremony is necessary to achieve the church's promise of eternal family life in heaven, since members must be sealed to their fathers in a special temple ritual. This results in further mind control, by increasing the *binder* to the *bound* members. And since only those members who pay full 10% tithing are allowed in the temple, this also increases the coffers of the church.

Garments and Mind Control

Officially designed undergarments are required to be worn at all times for those who receive temple ordinances and for women who are married in the temple. This is mind control of the highest order since garments signify the church's control over the individ-

ual. Garments are also a phobia (a tactic used in mind control) since
Mormons fear that if they don't wear them, something awful will
happen to them. The garment serves as another *binder* of the *bound*
Mormon to Mormonism.

Missionaries and Mind Control

According to church sources, more than 60,000 missionaries
are serving in missionary centers throughout the United States and
the world, or about one-fourth of this age level(19 and 20 year olds).

Following the few weeks' training session, missionaries are
assigned to a missionary center, manned usually by a husband and
wife team who insures correct behavior and monitors the work of
these young missionaries. However, the greatest element of mind
control by the church is that the two missionaries are expected to
always be together in missionary work, recreational and non-work
activities. In this respect, they are the watch-dog for each other.
This insures that one or the other is unlikely to break any missionary rules such as dating, making unapproved telephone calls, or mis-
representing the approved text of the church. This togetherness is
another example of the *binder* of the church controlling the *bound*
church member.

Infallibility of Church Leaders and Mind Control

Since the fifteen Mormon Apostles (President, his two counselors and the twelve Apostles) are considered to be God's representatives and therefore cannot make a mistake, they are considered
infallible by church members. *When the Prophet speaks, the thinking has been done.* This is a very effective mind control tactic used
by the Mormon Church that reinforces the concept that if *these men
are God's representatives, God will not allow them to make a mistake.* Therefore, if the Apostles teach that Joseph Smith was a
Prophet of God, then Joseph Smith was a representative of God, and
therefore, his doctrine, revelations and his book, the *Book of
Mormon* is the truth, the same as if spoken by God. Again, the
Binder (church leaders) is controlling the *Bound* (church member).

Boy Scouts as a Recruiting Tool

In one of my conclusions, I write that the Boy Scouting program of the Mormon Church is an excellent tool used to bring more converts into the Mormon Church. Many readers have verified the accuracy of this statement. For example, one writes: "I read a preview of the book [*The Mormon Conspiracy*] where it says that Boy Scouts are used to get kids to join the church. Where I live that is the complete truth. In fact I went to a friend's Eagle Scout ceremony to celebrate with him on his accomplishment. It was at the Mormon church, and everybody who stood up and talked, for some reason turned it into a religious speech. Every speaker threw in personal experiences and then proclaimed that the church is true."

Poverty in Mormonism

In one section of my book, I describe the poor living conditions that some students at BYU face and other members face by living in trailer courts. I suggested that instead of the church spending millions of dollars glorifying Mormonism by building temples and "historical" monuments having expensive statues of Joseph Smith and other early church leaders, that this money could be more appropriately spent in assisting those families and students who live in austere circumstances. One e-mail respondent wrote "…wow I have seen with my own eyes how poor and distressed a few of its members are. The friend, who is a member, introduced me to some elders —she pay's tiths (sic) regularly and she is so bad off that I have even bought groceries for her so she won't go hungry…."

The Mormon Kingdom of God on Earth

A major theme of my book is that Church leaders are carrying forward the plans of Joseph Smith and Brigham Young to establish a theocracy of Mormonism throughout the United States and eventually the world. Actually this plan is more successful in some foreign countries than it is in the United States as exemplified by the following e-mail received from New Zealand.

"The Mormons DO have quite a hold on things in the city of Hamilton [New Zealand]. Ever since that sister's threat, I've had a tough go of it. She and her mum know a lot of high-placed people in the church. It seems that Mormons "force" people into high positions and high paying jobs….. (or else?) I do know the highest status lawyer in the Waikato region is a strong Mormon…. Very active

in the Hamilton, NZ church... and he's the head coroner and has a
strong relationship with the police.

"I am here in New Zealand and see that the Mormon church
has literally corrupted and destroyed many of the local Maori people. The church has convinced them that they are [the church] a
very whanau, (pronounced "fawnau" meaning 'family') friendly
church. What the Mormons are doing is, once rooking a Maori
father into the church, they promise him that (through God) his family will (magically) be better off. When the "better life" doesn't
materialize the church tells these (unknowing about the Mormons)
folks that they need to talk the rest of the Whanau into joining the
LDS church or cut themselves off from the non-members, because
that (the non-Mormon family members, e. g. cousins, aunties,
uncles, etc) is the cause of the failing of the coming of the "promised" good life.

"The truth is, the most devastating thing one can do to a Maori
family is to tell them to cut themselves off from their family
(whanau). Knowing this, the Mormon church exploits this to the
max."

The following concerns of an American succinctly illustrate
the Mormon Church's control of politics in the United States: "Our
school district has a very large Mormon base, several of whom are
direct descendants of previous church presidents and original apostles. These individuals tend to use their social status to influence
politics within the area. I am very concerned about some of the
issues that may arise from the growth of the Mormon church, and
the political power that seems to be building in the organization. I
have done quite a bit of research into the origins of this religion and
find it quite baffling that any logical person could believe the
authenticity of what Joseph Smith claimed to have happened. The
fact that so many people are doing so, seemingly blindly, is very
unnerving."

The Belief that a Worthy Mormon Man May Become God of His Own Planet

I was aware that the Mormon Church teaches "What God is, Man
may become." However since this belief is so bizarre, I didn't
include it in the first printing of *The Mormon Conspiracy*. In my e-
mail correspondence with male Mormon Church members, I asked

them if they believe that they may become Gods of their own planets. I was surprised when many said that they did. The following was one member's answers to my questions:

Is it true that you believe that you may become a God of your own planet?

Answer: *Yes*

If you become God of your own planet, how will you get there? How will you find a planet that has the same life-giving environment as Earth?

Answer: *I will have the power to create my own planet just as God had the power to create the earth upon which we live. It will not be necessary for me to find one but to create one of my own.*

How can you be with God when you are away on another planet? How can you be together with your family, if your daughters and sons are married to others and your sons and your daughters' husbands are Gods of other planets?

Answer: *Being with God does not necessarily mean one has to be physically within His presence at all times. It simply means that you are worthy of being in the physical presence of God if you choose to be.*

APPENDIX

Important Dates in the history of the Mormon Church

1805

Joseph Smith, founder of the Mormon Church, born December 23 in Sharon, Vermont.

1820

Joseph Smith at age14 claims to have received a vision from God and Jesus Christ who said to him that he has been appointed to be a prophet to restore the true church on the face of the earth, "for they were all wrong...and all their creeds were abomination..."

1823

Joseph Smith at age 17 claims that the angel Moroni appeared, showed him where the golden plates were hidden, (but he will not receive them for another four years).

(Joseph Smith's History in the *Pearl of Great Price*, 1:53.)

1826

Joseph Smith, on March 20 is brought to trial in the court case *People v. Joseph Smith* The Glass Looker, charged with being "a disorderly person and an impostor" for money digging and using of a peep stone to find buried treasure.

1827

Joseph Smith at age 21 claims that he has the golden plates and by use of Urim and Thummin translated them from a reformed Egyptian language into English for the *Book of Mormon*.

1830

The *Book of Mormon* is published by Joseph Smith and he with other men organized the Mormon Church in Fayette, Seneca County, New York.

1831

The church moves its members and center to Kirtland, Ohio.

1832

Church members begin to move from Kirtland, Ohio to Missouri. They met stiff resistance from non-Mormons for bank fraud committed in Joseph Smith's new bank.

1839

Nauvoo, Illinois becomes the new home for Mormons, after Missourian non-Mormons through intense persecution, force them to move.

1844

Joseph Smith, Mayor of Nauvoo, orders the newspaper *Nauvoo Expositor,* destroyed since it is printing information considered detrimental to Smith.

1844

Joseph Smith and his brother Hyrum are shot and killed in a shootout with a mob (during which Smith mortally wounded two non-Mormons) while they were being held in jail for charges based upon destroying The *Nauvoo Expositor*.

1846

Brigham Young, after gaining control of the church, organizes the migration to Salt Lake City, Utah to escape the harassment of the surrounding non-Mormons of Nauvoo, Illinois.

1847

Settlement of Salt Lake City begins in earnest as migrants arrive from the winter quarters in Council Bluffs, Iowa.

1849

The State of Deseret consisting of parts of the present states of Utah, Idaho, California, Oregon, Nevada, Wyoming and Arizona begins to be organized.

1850

Utah becomes a territory of the United States.

1857

First Federal troops are sent to Utah, which causes the "Mormon War" and precipitates the Mountain Meadows Massacre.

1857

One Hundred and twenty-six men, women, and children are massacred by 50-60 Mormon militia men and some Indians. The Mormon militia and Indians were led by Mormon Church leaders from Cedar City, and Iron County, Utah. The 126 persons of the Fancher train were duped into believing that by giving up their weapons, they would be protected by the Mormons from danger from the Indians. As they walked from their barricades without their weapons, they were murdered by the Mormon militia and Indians. Only one member of the Mormon militia, John D. Lee was convicted and executed for this crime two decades later.

1869
First railroad across the continental United States is finished.

1877
Brigham Young dies in August.

1877
Quorum of Twelve sustains John Taylor as president in September.

1882
Edmunds Act, establishing heavy penalties for practicing polygamy is passed by the United States Congress.

1882
John Taylor, President of the Mormon Church formally announces to general conference that the 1880 U. S. Census report shows Utah territory has 120,283 Mormons, and 14,155 "gentiles" and 6,988 "apostates." Utah is only place in 1880 that U. S. Government includes religion in census. (D. Michael Quinn *Mormon Hierarchy, Extention of Power,* 780.)

1887
Edmunds-Tucker Act disincorporates Mormon Church, provides for confiscation of it assets and properties, dissolves Perpetual Emigrating Fund Company, disfranchises all Utah's women and dissolves Utah militia ("Nauvoo Legion"). (D. Michael Quinn *Mormon Hierarchy, Extention of Power*, 787.)

1887
John Taylor dies in July on "the Underground" while hiding for being a polygamist.

1889
April Conference sustains Wilford Woodruff as church president.

1890
President Wilford Woodruff ends polygamy for the Mormon Church .

1893
In January, soon to leave office, U. S. President Benjamin Harrison issues amnesty for all who lived in polygamous marriage before 1 November,1890., (D. Michael Quinn *Mormon Hierarchy, Extention of Power*, 794.)

1895

August, U. S. President Cleveland issues amnesty for previous violations of anti-polygamy laws and restores civil rights to disenfranchised polygamists. (D. Michael Quinn *Mormon Hierarchy, Extention of Power*, 796.)

1896

Court dismisses longstanding indictment against John M. Higbee. Other participants say privately that he was the most bloodthirsty man at Mountain Meadows Massacre. (D. Michael Quinn *Mormon Hierarchy, Extention of Power*, 797.)

1896

U. S. President Cleveland signs act to return confiscated real estate of LDS church. (D. Michael Quinn *Mormon Hierarchy, Extention of Power*, 797.)

1896

Utah becomes a State.

1898

Wilford Woodruff, President of LDS Church, dies.

1898

Quorum of Twelve Apostles sustains Lorenzo Snow as church president. (D. Michael Quinn *Mormon Hierarchy, Extention of Power*, 800.)

1900

U. S. President William McKinley promises Apostle John Henry Smith to defeat proposed U. S. amendment against polygamy and polygamous cohabitation in exchange for Utah's vote in the November election. (D. Michael Quinn *Mormon Hierarchy, Extention of Power*, 80.)

1901

President Lorenzo Snow dies.

1902

Quorum of Twelve Apostles sustain Joseph F. Smith as church president who ordains his oldest son Hyrum M. Smith, as new member of the Quorum of Twelve Apostles.

1902

First Presidency and Apostles read letter that U. S. President Theodore Roosevelt and Republican Party leader Mark Hanna guarantee they will arrange to defeat proposed constitutional amendment on polygamy and unlawful cohabitation. They expect Mormons to vote Republican in exchange.

1918

Joseph F. Smith dies

1918

Quorum of Twelve Apostles sustains Heber J. Grant as church President.

1922

Brigham H. Roberts presents detailed textual and historical problems in the *Book of Mormon*...He recommends that these problems should be researched and publicly discussed.

1928

The remains of brothers Joseph and Hyrum Smith from coffin-less burial place kept secret since 1844 are reburied in coffins, one on each side of Emma Hale Smith Bidamon next to Mansion House in Nauvoo. (D. Michael Quinn *Mormon hierarchy, Extention of Power*, 820.)

1945

Death of Heber J. Grant., (D. Michael Quinn *Mormon Hierarchy, Extention of Power*, 831.)

1945

Conference sustains George Albert Smith as church President, (D. Michael Quinn *Mormon Hierarchy, Extention of Power*, 831.)

1951

George Albert Smith Dies.

1951

Conference sustains David O. McKay as church president.

1955

Congress defines full-time missionaries as eligible for ministerial deferments from military service.

1967

Joseph Smith's *Book of Abraham* is found not to be a translation of an Egyptian papyrus, supposedly written by Old Testament prophet Abraham, as claimed by Smith. The Egyptian papyri which Smith claimed he used to translate the *Book of Abraham* was found to be an Egyptian funeral text called a *"Book of Breathings."*

1970

David O. McKay's dies at age 96, oldest Mormon President. He served sixty-three years and nine months as a General Authority.

1970

Quorum of Twelve Apostles ordains Joseph Fielding Smith (age 93) as church President.

1972

Joseph Fielding Smith dies.

1972

Quorum of Twelve sustains Harold B. Lee as church President.

1973

Harold B. Lee, LDS church President, dies at age 74.

1973

Quorum of Twelve Apostles sustains Spencer W. Kimball as church President.

1977

Readers Digest publishes first eight page insert of advertisement of the Mormon Church, unprecedented for this media representative of America's conservative, middle-class values. In May 1982, *Book of Mormon* insert reaches 19.2 million subscribers in U. S. and Europe., (D. Michael Quinn *Mormon Hierarchy, Extention of Power*, 870.)

1978

Black men who previously had been allowed to become members of the Mormon Church, but were not allowed to hold the priesthood, were given the right to receive the priesthood.

1979

Mormon Church leadership instrumental in blocking the Equal Rights Amendment.

1983

Second counselor Gordon B. Hinckley pays document dealer Mark Hofmann $15,000 for alleged Joseph Smith letter about his treasure-digging activities. He has Hofmann agree not to mention transaction to anyone else and then he sequesters document in First Presidency's vault. First Presidency does not acknowledge its existence until *Los Angeles Times* is about to release story about document, which Hofmann later admits he had forged.

1985

Spencer W. Kimball dies.

1985

Quorum of Twelve sustains Ezra Taft Benson as church President, with Gordon B. Hinckley and Thomas S. Monson as Counselors. Benson is first LDS church President with a graduate degree (M. S. Iowa State University)

1988

On October 1, reports federal judge's decision that FBI has been guilty of systematic discrimination because "Mormon supervisors made personnel decisions which favored members of their church at the expense of Hispanic" FBI agents. Principal offender named is Richard Bretzing, former FBI chief of Los Angeles and current director of LDS Security Department. In December, federal judge also rules that FBI used illegal methods to discredit Hispanic FBI agent who had accused Bretzing of protecting Richard N. Miller from arrest as Communist spy because Bretzing was Miller's Mormon bishop. (Miller was later convicted of spying in 1991)

1994

Ezra Taft Benson dies on Memorial Day.

1994

Quorum of Twelve sustains Howard W. Hunter as church President with Gordon B. Hinckley and Thomas S. Monson as counselors.

1995

President Howard W. Hunter dies.

1995

Quorum of Twelve sustains Gordon B. Hinckley as church President. Hinckley is first LDS president since Joseph Fielding Smith who has worked his entire adult life in church bureaucracy, church-controlled business, and headquarters administration. (D. Michael Quinn *Mormon Hierarchy, Extention of Power*, 893.)

1998

Mormon Church claims 10,000,000 members, most of whom live in foreign countries. Of these members, 4,890,000 live in the United States, 2,220,000 live in South America, 775,000 live in Mexico, 645,000 live in Asia, 395,000 live in Central America, 390,000 live in Europe, 340,000 live in the South Pacific, 150,000 live in Canada, 110,000 live in Africa, and 95,000 live in Caribbean. (*Ensign,* January 1998, p. 74)

2000

Mormon Church claims 11,000,000 members worldwide.

Endnotes

Chapter One

1. Joseph F. Smith (President of Mormon Church 1902-1918) *Doctrines of Salvation,* Vol. 1, 188-189.

2. B. H. Roberts, *Studies of the Book of Mormon,* (Salt Lake City: Signature Books, 1992), 58.

3. Fawn M. Brodie, *No Man Knows My History,* (New York: Alfred A Knopf Inc, A Division of Random House, Inc.,1945), 82. (Copyright © 1971 by Fawn M. Brodie, Reprinted by Permission of Alfred A. Knopf, Inc)

4. Ibid., 63.

5. Bernard DeVoto, *The Year of Decision, 1846,* (Boston: Houghton Mifflin Company, 1943), 82.

6. Latayne Colvett Scott, *The Mormon Mirage,* (Grand Rapids, Michigan: Zondervan Publishing House, 1979), 29. Used by permission of Zondervan Publishing House.

7. Fawn M. Brodie, *No Man Knows My History,* 62.

8. Ethan Smith, *View of the Hebrews, or The Tribes of Israel in America,* (Poultney, Vermont: Smith and Smith 1825).

9. Fawn M. Brodie, *No Man Knows My History*, 61-62.

10. Ibid., 55.

11. Brian M. Fagan, *The Archaeology of a Continent,* (London: Thames and Hudson Ltd, London, 1995), 67.

12. Ibid., 70-71.

13. Jerald and Sandra Tanner, *Ferguson's Manuscript Unveiled,* (Salt Lake City: Utah Lighthouse Ministry), (Introduction), 3.

14. Ethan Smith, *View of the Hebrews.*

15. B. H. Roberts, Studies of the *Book of Mormon,* 30.

16. Ibid., 149.

17. Ibid., 154-155.

18. Laytayne Colvett Scott, *The Mormon Mirage,* 31.

19. Walter Martin, Web page, Internet, P. O. Box 25220, St. Paul Minnesota 55125.

20. Laytayne Colvett Scott, *The Mormon Mirage*, 85.

21. Ibid., 231-232.

22. John Doyle Lee, *The Mormon Menace*, (New York: Home Protection Publishing Co.) 195.

23. Bernard Devoto, *The Year of Decision, 1846,* 85.

24. Wallace Stegner, *Mormon Country*, (Lincoln: University of Nebraska Press, 1942, 1970), 72.

25. John R. Farkas and David A. Reed, *Mormonism, Changes, Contradictions and Errors*, (Grand Rapids, Michigan: Baker Books, 1995), 239.

26. Jerald and Sandra Tanner, *Confession of John D. Lee*, as reported in *Mormonism, Shadow or Reality*, (Salt Lake City, Utah: Utah Lighthouse Ministry, 1982), 495.

27. Ibid., 501.

28. Ibid., 501.

29. Ibid., 505.

30. Ibid., 507.

31. Juanita Brooks, *The Mountain Meadow Massacre*, (Normon: University of Oklahoma Press, 1950, 1962), vii.

32. *The Baxter Bulletin*, of Baxter County, Arkansas, September 15, 1999 taken from excerpts of Gordon B. Hinckley remarks as reported by Sandy Fox Media Representative for the LDS Church.

33. J. H. Carleton Bvt. Major U. S. A. Captain 1st Dragoons *Special Report of the Mountain Meadows Massacre,* (Spokane, Washington: Arthur H. Clark Company 1995), 26.

34. Ibid., 25-26.

35. D. Michael Quinn, *The Mormon Hierarchy, Extensions of Power*, (Salt Lake City: Signature Books, 1997), 755-756.

36. Ibid., 757.

37. Ibid., 760.

38. Ibid., 767.

39. Juanita Brooks, *Mountain Meadows Massacre*, 195.

40. *Spectrum,* January 2, 1999.

41. John D. Lee, *The Mormon Menace*, 204.

42. Ibid., 204-205.

43. Ibid., 206.

44. Ibid., 206.

45. D. Michael Quinn, *Mormon Hierarchy, Extension of Power*, 750.

46. Ibid., 750.

17. Bill Hickman (Explanatory Notes by J. H. Beadle, Esq.) *Brigham's Destroying Angel: Being the Life, Confession and Startling Disclosure of the Notorious Bill Hickman, the Danite Chief of Utah* (Salt Lake City, Utah: Shephard Publishing Company, Publishers, 1904).

48. D. Michael Quinn, *Mormon Hierarchy, Extension of Power*, 765.

49. Irving Wallace, *The Twenty-Seventh Wife*, (New York: Simon and Schuster, 1961), 168-173.

50. Ibid., 275- 345.

51. Ibid., 334.

52. Ibid., 323- 324.

53. John Doyle Lee, *The Mormon Menace*, 183-187.

54. Laytayne Colvett Scott, *The Mormon Mirage,* 113. (Also Jerald and Sandra Tanner, *Mormonism, Shadow or Reality*, [Salt Lake City: Lighthouse Ministry], p 225.)

55. Ibid., 113. (Also John A. Widtsoe, *Evidences and Reconciliations*, [Salt Lake City: Bookcraft, 1960], 390.)

56. Ibid,. 113 (Taken from John A. Widtsoe, *Evidences and Reconciliations*)

57. D. Michael Quinn, *Mormon Hierarchy, Extension of Power*, 767

58. Ibid., 768.

59. *Deseret News*, Church Section, May 26, 1945, 5.

60. Herbert C. Kimball *Journal of Discourses* 6:32, November 8, 1957.

61. Ernest H. Taves, *This is the Place*, (Amherst, NY: Prometheus Books Copyright 1991), 237. Reprinted by permission of the publisher.

62. Ibid, 239-240 (Quoted from Thomas B. H. Stenhouse, *Rocky Mountain Saints*, [New York, 1893], Flake 8404, 637.)

63. Ibid., 240.

64. Ibid., 240. (Quoted from Hubert Howe Bancroft, *The History of Utah*, [San Francisco, The History Company, 1890], Flake 287, 649.)

65. Ibid., 240. (Quoted from Stephen Naifeh and Gregory White Smith, *The Mormon Murders,* (New York: Weidenfield and Nicholson, 1988, 148.)

66. Sonia Johnson, *From Housewife to Heretic*, (Albuquerque, NM: Wildfire Books, 1989), 297.

67. Ibid., 286.

68. Ibid., 291-292.

Chapter Two
69. Deborah Laake, *Secret Ceremonies*, (New York: William Morrow and Company, 1993), 78. (EXCERPTS TOTALING 3-4 Reprinted by permission)
70. Jerald and Sandra Tanner, *Mormonism, Shadow or Reality*, 454.
71. Latayne Colvett Scott, *The Mormon Mirage*, 193. Used by permission of Zondervan Publishing House.)
72. Ibid., 194.
73. Ibid.,194-195 (Also, *Journal of Discourses*, xix, p 229.)
74. Ibid., 195
75. Robert L. Millet, *The Mormon Faith, A New Look at Christianity*, (Salt Lake City: Deseret Book Company, 1998) 102.
76. Ibid., 67.
77. Ibid., 67-68.
78. Deborah Laake, *Secret Ceremonies*, 17.
79. Ibid., 60.
81. Ibid., 60.
81. Ibid., 61.
82. Ibid., 63.
83. Robert L. Millet, *The Mormon Faith, A New Look at Christianity*, 147-148.
84. Ibid., 54.
85. Ibid., 63.
86. Wallace Turner, *The Mormon Establishment*, (Boston: Houghton Mifflin Company, 1966), 40. (Excerpt reprinted by permission of Houghton Mifflin Company. All rights reserved.)
87. "The Revival of Polygamy," Burton Hendrick, *M'Clure's Magazine*, 1911. Taken from *The Latter-Day Saints*, Ruth Kauffman and Reginald Wright Kauffman, 1912.
88. Deborah Laake, *Secret Ceremonies*, 43-44.
89. *The Salt Lake Tribune*, December 5, 1998.
90. Ibid.,
91. Deborah Laake, *Secret Ceremonies*, 145-148.
92. Ibid., 167.
93. Ibid., 168.
94. Judy Robertson, *No Regrets, How I found My Way Out of Mormonism*, (Light and Life Communications, 1997), 65.
95. Ibid., 66.
96. Laytayne Colvett Scott, *Mormon Mirage*, 193.
97. Ibid., 193.

98. Ibid., 193.

99. James Coates, *In Mormon Circles: Gentiles, Jack Mormons, and Latter-Day Saints*, (New York: Addison-Wesley Publishing Company, Inc., 1991), 85. Reprinted by permission of Perseus Books, L.L.C.)

100. Laytayne Colvett Scott, *The Mormon Mirage*, 217.

101. Deborah Laake, *Secret Ceremonies*, 13.

102. Ibid., 20.

103. James Coates, *In Mormon Circles*, 88, 89.

104. Ibid., 168-169.

105. Laytayne Colvett Scott, *The Mormon Mirage*, 203. (Also Joseph Smith Jr., *Documentary History of the Church*, IV, 552.)

106. Ibid., 203.

107. Deborah Laake, *Secret Ceremonies*, 73, 74.

108. Ibid., 74, 75.

109. Judy Robertson, *No Regrets, How I found My way out of Mormonism*, 61.

110. Deborah Laake, *Secret Ceremonies*, 78,79.

111. Ibid., 81.

112. Ibid., 84.

113. Ibid., 88-89.

114. Ibid., 90.

115. Laytayne Colvett Scott, *The Mormon Mirage*, 222.

116. Ibid., 221.

117. Ibid., 205.

118. Ibid., 205.

119. Robert L. Millet, *The Mormon Faith, A New Look at Christianity*, 95.

120. Ibid., 143.

121. Joseph Smith, Jun, *Book of Mormon*, (Salt Lake City: Corporation of the President of the Church of Jesus Christ of Latter-Day Saints,1830, 1981), Introduction.

Chapter Three

122. Laytayne Colvett Scott, *The Mormon Mirage*, 234. (Also *Improvement Era*, June, 1945, 354). (Used by permission of Zondervan Publishing House.)

123. Ibid., 234.

124. Ernest H. Taves, *This is the Place*, (Buffalo, New York: Prometheus Books, 1991), 239, 240 (Taken from Stenhouse, Thomas

B. H. *The Rocky Mountain Saints*: [New York, Applelton, 1873], Flake 8404, 637.)

125. Sonia Johnson, *From Housewife to Heretic*, (Albuquerque, Wildfire Books, Fourth Edition, 1989), 15.

126. James Coates, *In Mormon Circles, Gentiles, Jack Mormons, and Latter-Day Saints*, 204-205.

127. Ibid., 205.

128. Ibid., 206, 207.

129. Ibid., 207-208, (see also Linda Sillitoe and Allen Roberts, *Salamander*, [Salt Lake City, 1989], 237.)

130. Ibid., 209. (See also Linda Sillitoe and Allen Roberts, *Salamander*, [Salt Lake City, 1989], 237-244.)

131. Anson Shupe, *The Darker Side of Virtue, Corruption, Scandal And The Mormon Empire*, (Buffalo, New York: Prometheus Books, 1991), 97. (With permission of the author.)

Chapter Four

132. Anson Shupe, *Wealth and Power in American Zion,* (Lewiston, New York: The Edwin Mellen Press, 1992), 3. (With permission of the author.)

133. Laytayne Colvett Scott, *The Mormon Mirage*, 219.

134. Ibid., 233.

135. Ibid., 219.

136. Coates, James, *In Mormon Circles, Gentiles, Jack Mormons, and Latter-Day Saints*, Preface xii and xiii.

137. D. Michael Quinn *The Mormon Hierarchy Extensions of Power*, 263.

138. Ibid., 263-264.

139. "The Election," *Salt Lake Daily Herald,* 3 Aug. 1880.

140. D. Michael Quinn, *The Mormon Hierarchy Extensions of Power,* 268.

141. Ibid., 302.

142. Ibid., 355-360.

143. Ibid., 366.

144. Ibid., 369.

145. Anson Shupe, *Wealth and Power in American Zion*, 126.

146. Ibid., 125.

147. *Time*, August 4, 1997.

148. Anson Shupe, *Wealth and Power in American Zion*, 118.

149. Richard N. Ostling and Joan K. Ostling, *The Power and*

Promise of Mormon America, (New York: HarperCollins Publishers, 1999), 118-119. (Submitted excerpts reprinted by permission of HarperCollins Publishers.)

150. Anson Shupe, *Wealth and Power in American Zion,* 235, 236.

151. Ibid., 236-246.

152. Ibid., 242.

153. Ibid., 244-246.

154. *Time,* August 4, 1997.

155. Anson Shupe, *Wealth and Power in American Zion,* 247.

156. Ibid., 51,52.

157. Ibid., 123.

158. Ibid., 88.

159. Ibid., 102.

160. Ibid., 102.

161. Ibid., 103.

162. D. Michael Quinn, *The Mormon Hierarchy, Extensions of Power,* 200.

163. Ibid., 203.

164. *The Arizona Republic* June 30, 1991, Front page A1.

165. Ibid., July 1, 1991 Front page: A1.

166. D. Michael Quinn, *The Mormon Hierarchy, Extensions of Power,* 204.

167. Richard N. Ostling and Joan K. Ostling, *The Power and Promise of Mormon America,* 179.

168. D. Michael Quinn, *The Mormon Hierarchy, Extensions of Power,* 199.

169. Ibid., 207-208.

170. Ibid., 206.

171. Ibid., 210-211.

172. Ibid., 219.

173. Ibid., 220.

174. Ibid., 225.

Chapter 5

175. (1) Richard N. Ostling and Joan K. Ostling, *The Power and The Promise of Mormon America,* 182.

176. D. Michael Quinn, *Mormon Hierarchy, Extensions of Power,* 857.

177. Ibid., 864.

178. *Ensign* July, 1997, 73.

179. Ibid., 78.

180. D. Michael Quinn, *The Mormon Hierarchy, Extensions of Power*, 889.

181. Richard N. Ostling and Joan K. Ostling, *The Power and The Promise, Mormon America,* 221.

182. Deborah Laake, *Secret Ceremonies,* 43-44.

183. Richard N. Ostling and Joan K. Ostling, *The Power and The Promise of Mormon America,* 224.

184. D. Michael Quinn, *The Mormon Hierarchy, Extensions of Power,* 882.

185. Anson Shupe, *Wealth and Power in American Zion,* 205.

186. Ibid., 206. (Blake Ostler, "7EP interview: Sterling McMurrin," *Seventh East Press,* 11 January 1983, 1.)

187. Richard N. Ostling and Joan K. Ostling, *The Power and the Promise of Mormon America,* 234.

188. Ibid., 234-235.

189. D. Michael Quinn, *The Mormon Hierarchy, Extensions of Power,* 897.

190. Anson Shupe, *Wealth And Power In American Zion,* 208.

191. Richard N. Ostling and Joan K. Ostling, *The Power and the Promise of Mormon America,* 224-225.

192. Ibid., 227.

193. Ibid., 228-229.

194. Ibid., 229.

195. St. George, Utah, *Spectrum,* September 1, 1999

196. Richard N. Ostling and Joan K. Ostling, *The Power and Promise Mormon America,* 249.

197. Apostle Dallin H. Oaks. "Reading Church History," Ninth Annual Church Education System Religious Educators' Symposium, August 16, 1985, Brigham Young University.

198. Richard N. Ostling and Joan K. Ostling, *The Power and Promise of Mormon America,* 235-236.

199. D. Michael Quinn, *The Mormon Hierarchy, Extensions of Power,* 846.

200. Richard N. Ostling and Joan K. Ostling, *The Power and Promise of Mormon America,* 237.

201. Ibid., 249.

202. Ibid., 252.

203. Brigham Young University Catalog, 2000-2001 xii.

204. Ibid., xix.

205. Ibid., xix.

206. Ibid., xix.

207. Paul M. Rose, "The Zion University Reverie: A Quanitative and Qualitative Assessment of BYU's Academic Climate," *Dialogue* Volume 32, No. 1, Spring 1999, 36.

208. Ibid., 38-39.

209. Ibid., 48-49.

210. Ibid., 49.

211. Larry N. Jensen, "One Man's Definition of LDS Membership, Dialogue" *Dialogue,* Volume 32, No. 3, Fall 1999, 146.

212. D. Michael Quinn, *Mormon Hierarchy, Extensions of Power*, 831-832.

213. Ibid., 852.

214. Ibid., 854.

215. Ibid., 855.

216. Ibid., 857.

217. Ibid., 873.

Chapter 6

218. Latayne Colvett Scott, *The Mormon Mirage*, 225.

219. *The Arizona Republic*, July 1, 1991, Front Page:A1.

220. D. Michael Quinn, *The Mormon Hierarchy, Extensions of Power*, 897.

221. Latayne Colvett Scott, *The Mormon Mirage*, 228.

222. Jerald and Sandra Tanner, *Mormonism, Shadow or Reality,* 96.

223. D. Michael Quinn, *The Mormon Hierarchy: Extensions of Power,* 890.

224. Richard N. Ostling and Joan K. Ostling, *The Power and the Promise of Mormon America*, 214.

225. Latayne Colvett Scott, *The Mormon Mirage*, 224.

226. Ibid., 224.

227. Richard N. and Joan K. Ostling, *The Power and the Promise of Mormon America*, 210.

228. D. Michael Quinn, *The Mormon Hierarchy, Extensions of Power*, 819, 871.

229. James Coats, *In Mormon Circles, Gentiles, Jack Mormons and Latter-Day Saints*, 142.

230. Latayne Colvett Scott, *The Mormon Mirage*, 225.

231. Ibid., 223.

232. Ibid., 226-228.

233. Janice Hutchinson, *The Mormon Missionaries*, (Grand Rapids, Michigan: Kregel Resources, 1995), 16. (Used by permission.)
234. Ibid., 18-19.
235. Ibid., 33.
236. Ibid., 42.
237. Ibid., 47-48.
238. Ibid., 54.
239. Ibid., 66-67.
240. Ibid., 76.
241. Ibid., 80.
242. Ibid., 84.
243. Ibid., 91.
244. Ibid., 136.
245. Ibid., 136,137,138.
246. Ibid., 171-173.
247. Ibid., 186-187.
248. Richard N. and Joan K. Ostling, *Mormon America, the Power and the Promise*, 216.

Chapter 7
249. Wallace Turner, *The Mormon Establishment*, 51-53.
250. Fawn M. Brodie *No Man Knows My History*, 73.
251. Lucy Smith, *Biographical Sketches of Joseph Smith the Prophet and his Progenitors for many Generations*, (Liverpool, England: Published for Orson Pratt by S. W. Richards, 1853), 85.
252. Jerald and Sandra Tanner, *Introduction to Joseph Smith's History by his Mother* (Salt Lake City: Utah Lighthouse Ministry), 4.
253. Fawn M. Brodie, *No Man Knows My History*, 92.
254. Ibid., 100-101.
255. Ibid., 153-155.
256. Ibid., 156.
257. Ibid., 162.
258. Ibid., 201-203.
259. Ibid., 207.
260. Ibid., 213-218.
261. Ibid., 220.
262. Ibid., 226-240.
263. Ibid, 255.
264. Ibid., 263.
265. Ibid., 264-271.

266. Ibid., 157 188.

267. Beardsley, Harry M., *Joseph Smith and His Mormon Empire*, (Boston and New York: Houghton Mifflin Company, 1931), 320-321.

268. Ibid., 323.

269. Ibid., 325-326.

270. Ibid., 328-329.

271. Ibid., 329.

272. Ibid., 329-330.

273. Ibid., 389-390.

274. Ibid., 390-391.

275. Fawn Brodie, *No Man Knows My History,* 459.

276. Ibid., 298-302

277. Ibid., 302.

278. Ibid., 306-307.

279. Ibid., 307.

280. Ibid., 341.

281. Ibid., 309-322.

282. Ibid., 318.

283. Ibid., 323-324.

284. Ibid., 324.

285. Ibid., 329.

286. Ibid., 331.

287. Ibid. 367-371.

288. *Nauvoo Expositor*, Vol. No. 1, June 7, 1844, 2.

289. Ibid., 2.

290. Ibid., 2.

291. Ibid., 3.

292. Ibid., 4.

293. D. Michael Quinn, *Mormon Hierarchy, Origins of Power*, 191.

294. Harry M. Beardsley, *Joseph Smith and his Mormon Empire,* 335.

295. Ibid., 343.

296. Fawn M. Brodie, *No Man Knows My History*, 380.

297. Harry M. Beardsley, *Joseph Smith and his Mormon Empire,* 347.

298. Ibid., 347.

299. Ibid., 351-352.

300. Ibid., 352.

301. Ibid., 356.

302. Ibid., 358.

303. Ibid., 360-362.

304. Ibid., 362-363.

305. Ibid., 364-367.

306. Fawn M. Brodie, *No Man Knows My History,* 393-394.

307. J. H. Beadle, Esq., *Brigham's Destroying Angel: Being the Life, Confession and Startling Disclosures of the Notorious Bill Hickman, the Danite Chief of Utah,* 11-15.

308. David L. Bigler, *The Forgotten Kingdom, The Mormon Theocracy in the American West, 1847-1896,* (Spokane, Washington: Arthur H. Clark Company, 1998), 44-47.(Reprinted by Permission of the Publisher)

309. Ibid., 51.

310. Ibid., 50.

311. Ibid., 50.

312. Ibid., 53.

313. D. Michael Quinn, *The Mormon Hierarchy, Extensions of Power,* 754.

314. David L. Bigler, *The Forgotten Kingdom, The Mormon Theocracy in the American West, 1847-1896,* 53.

315. Ibid., 87.

316. Ibid., 123. (Taken from Kenney, edl., *Wilford Woodruff's Journal,* 4:451)

317. Ibid., 124 (Taken from Brigham Young, February 25, *Journal of Discourses,* 4:219-20)

318. Ibid., 125.

319. D. Michael Quinn, *The Mormon Hierarchy, Extensions of Power,* 242-244.

320. Ibid., 246.

321. Ibid., 248.

322. Ibid., 248.

323. Ibid., 253.

324. Ibid., 253.

325. Ibid., 255.

326. Ibid., 257.

327. Ibid., 260.

328. David L. Bigler, *The Forgotten Kingdom, The Mormon Theocracy in the American West, 1847-1896,* 126.

329. Ibid., 218-219.

330. Ibid., 218-219.

331. Ibid., 222.

332. Ibid., 240.

333. Ibid., 241.

334. Ibid., 248.

335. Ibid., 261.

336. Ibid., 261.

337. Ibid., 261-262. (Taken from Brigham Young, February 8, 1868, *Journal of Discourses,* 12:159)

338. Ibid., 262. (Taken from Brigham Young, October 8, 1868, *Journal of Discourses*, 12:286)

339. Ibid., 262. (Taken from Brigham Young, November 29, 1868, 314)

340. *Nauvoo Expositor,* June 7, 1844 Vol. 1 No. 1 (This issue and Printing Press was burned, 1844)

341. *Millennial Star*, October 21, 1865, 2. (As reported by Jerald and Sandra Tanner, Introduction *Joseph Smith's History by his Mother*)

342. David L. Bigler, *The Forgotten Kingdom, The Mormon Theocracy in the American West, 1847-1896*, 313.

343. Ibid., 335.

344. Ibid., 349.

345. D. Michael Quinn, *The Mormon Hierarchy, Extensions of Power*, 328.

346. Ibid., 328.

347. David L. Bigler, *The Forgotten Kingdom, The Mormon Theocracy in the American West, 1847-1896*, 355. (Taken from Kenney, ed., *Wilford Woodruff's Journal,* 912:06 9:69)

348. D. Michael Quinn, *The Mormon Hierarchy, Extensions of Power,* 369.

349. Ibid., 369.

350. Ibid., 371.

351. Ibid., 368.

352. Congressional Record: Aug. 6, Vol. 117.

353. Maurine Ward, *From Adam's Rib to Women's Lib*, (Salt Lake City, Bookcraft Inc. 1981), 78.

354. Rex E. Lee, *A Lawyer Looks at the Equal Rights Amendment*, (Provo, Utah: Brigham Young University Press, 1983), 35-37.

355. Marjorie Childs, *Fabric of the ERA, Congressional Intent*, (Smithtown, New York: Exposition Press, 1980), 1-80.

356. Sonia Johnson, *From Housewife to Heretic*, 164-166.

357. Ibid., 165.

358. Ibid., 128.

359. Ibid., 132-134.

360. Ibid., 137.

361. Maurine Ward, *From Adam's Rib, To Women's Lib*, 78.

362. D. Michael Quinn, *The Mormon Hierarchy, Extensions of Power*, 373.

363. Sonia Johnson, *From Housewife to Heretic*, 164-166.

364. Deborah Laake, *Secret Ceremonies*, 357.

365. D. Michael Quinn, *The Mormon Hierarchy, Extensions of Power*, 882.

366. Deborah Laake, *Secret Ceremonies*, 358-360.

367. D. Michael Quinn, *The Mormon Hierarchy, Extensions of Power*, 822.

368. Ibid., 864.

369. Ibid., 893.

370. St. George *Spectrum*, November, 1976.

371. St. George *Spectrum*, November, 1980,1984, 1988.

372. St. George *Spectrum,* November, 1992.

373. St. George, Spectrum, November, 2000.

Bibliography

Beardsley, Harry M. *Joseph Smith and His Mormon Empire*, Boston and New York: Houghton Mifflin Company, 1931.

Beadle, Esq., J. H. *Brigham's Destroying Angel: Being the Life, Confession and Startling Disclosures of the Notorious Bill Hickman*. Shepard Publishing Company, Publishers, 1904.

Bigler, David L. *The Forgotten Kingdom, The Mormon Theocracy in the American West, 1847-1896*. Spokane, Washington: Arthur H. Clark Company, 1998.

Brodie, Fawn M. *No Man Knows My History*. New York: Vintage Books, 1945 (First Vintage Books Edition, August 1995).

Brooks, Juanita. *The Mountain Meadow Massacre*. Normon: University of Oklahoma Press, 1950, 1962.

Carleton, J. H., Bvt. Major U. S. A. Captain 1st Dragoons. *Special Report of the Mountain Meadows Massacre*. Introduced by Robert A. Clark. Spokane, Washington: Arthur H. Clark Company 1995.

Coates, James. *In Mormon Circles, Gentiles, Jack Mormons, and Latter-Day Saints*. New York: Addison-Wesley Publishing Company, Inc., 1991.

DeVoto, Bernard. *The Year of Decision, 1846*. Boston: Houghton Mifflin Company, 1943.

Fagan, Brian M. *The Archaeology of a Continent*. London: Thames and Hudson Ltd, London, 1995.

Farkas John R. and David A. Reed. *Mormonism, Changes, Contradictions and Errors*. Grand Rapids, Michigan: Baker Books, 1995.

Hutchinson, Janice. *The Mormon Missionaries*. Grand Rapids, Michigan: Kregel Resources, 1995; Salt Lake City: Utah Lighthouse Ministry, 1982.

Johnson, Sonia. *From Housewife to Heretic*. Albuquerque, NM: Wildfire Books, 1989.

Kauffman, Reginald Wright and Ruth. *The Latter Day Saints*. London: William and Northgate 1912.

Laake, Deborah. *Secret Ceremonies*. New York:, William Morrow and Company, Inc.,1993.

Ostling, Richard N. and Joan K. *The Power and Promise of Mormon America*. New York: HarperCollins Publishers, 1999.

Quinn, D. Michael. *The Mormon Hierarchy, Extensions of Power*. Salt Lake City: Signature Books, 1997.

Roberts, B. H. *Studies of the Book of Mormon*. Salt Lake City, Signature Books, 1992.

Robertson, Judy. *No Regrets, How I found My Way Out of Mormonism*. Light and Life Communications, 1997.

Scott, Latayne Colvett. *The Mormon Mirage*. Grand Rapids, Michigan: Zondervan Publishing House, 1979.

Shupe, Anson. *The Darker Side of Virtue, Corruption, Scandal And The Mormon Empire*. Buffalo, New York: Prometheus Books, 1991.

Shupe, Anson. *Wealth and Power in American Zion*. Lewiston, New York: The Edwin Mellen Press, 1992.

Smith, Ethan. *View of the Hebrews, or The Tribes of Israel in America*. Poultney, Vermont: Smith and Smith, 1825).

Smith, Lucy. *Biographical Sketches of Joseph Smith the Prophet and his Progenitors for many Generations*. Liverpool, England: Published for Orson Pratt by S. W. Richards, 1853.

Stegner, Wallace. *Mormon Country*. Lincoln: University of Nebraska Press, 1942, 1970.

Tanner, Jerald and Sandra. *Confession of John D. Lee*, as reported in *Mormonism, Shadow or Reality*. Salt Lake City, Utah: Utah Lighthouse Ministry, 1982.

Taves, Ernest H., *This is the Place*, Buffalo. New York: Prometheus Books, 1991.

Turner, Wallace. *The Mormon Establishment*. Boston: Houghton Mifflin Company, 1966.

Wallace, Irving. *The Twenty-Seventh Wife*. New York: Simon and Schuster, 1961.

Journal Articles and Newspapers

The Arizona Republic. June 30, 1991, Front page A1.

Jensen, Larry N. "One Man's Definition of LDS Membership", *Dialogue*. Volume 32, No. 3, Fall 1999.

Millennial Star. October 21, 1865 (As reported by Jerald and Sandra Tanner, Introduction Joseph Smith's History by his Mother).

Nauvoo Expositor. Vol. No. 1, June 7, 1844.

Rose, Paul M. "The Zion University Reverie: A Quanitative and Qualitative Assessment of BYU's Academic Climate", *Dialogue*. Volume 32, No. 1, Spring 1999.

Internet

Recovery From Mormonism. (http://www.exmormon.org) A site for those who are questioning their faith in the organization and those who need support as they transition their lives to normal.

Index

View of the Hebrews, 6, 14, 39, 80, 141, 168
Visiting teachers, 115
Vitterli, Richard, 234

Wahid, President Abdurrahman, 139
Washing and anointing ritual, 57
Wealth of the Church, 98
Whigs, 18
White, Emiline, 181
White Indians, 9
White, O. Kendall, 220
Wilkinson, Ernest L., 134
Woodruff, Wilford, 41, 203, 210
Word of Wisdom, 44, 53, 118

Young, Brigham 21, 26-31, 61, 72, 95, 107-108, 110, 128, 137, 183, 199-212, 228

Zion's Camp, 171, 173